A TIME TO SPEAK

A TIME TO SPEAK

A Psycholinguistic Inquiry into the Critical Period for Human Speech

Thomas Scovel

NEWBURY HOUSE PUBLISHERS

A division of Harper & Row, Publishers, Inc.

Cambridge, New York, Philadelphia, San Francisco, Washington, D.C.
London, Mexico City, São Paulo, Singapore, Sidney

Director: Laurie E. Likoff
Sponsoring Editor: Leslie Berriman
Production Coordinator: Cynthia Funkhouser
Compositor: TCSystems, Inc.
Printer and Binder: Malloy Lithographing Inc.

NEWBURY HOUSE PUBLISHERS
A division of Harper & Row, Publishers, Inc.

Language Science
Language Teaching
Language Learning

A Time to Speak: A Psycholinguistic Inquiry into the Critical Period for Human Speech

Library of Congress Cataloging in Publication Data

Scovel, Thomas, 1939–
    A time to speak : a psycholinguistic inquiry into the critical
period for human speech / Thomas Scovel.
        p. cm. — (Issues in second language research)
    Bibliography: p. 187
    Includes index.
    ISBN 0-06-632532-3
    1. Language acquisition—Age factors. I. Title. II. Series.
P118.S33 1988
401′.9—dc19   88-6924
                                                                          CIP

Printed in the U.S.A.
63-25328   First Printing: April 1988
                        88 89 90 91 9 8 7 6 5 4 3 2 1

For Janene
Sine Qua Non

ACKNOWLEDGEMENTS

When one spends almost two decades mulling over ideas before putting them down in book form, it is obvious that they have been discussed back and forth with a great many people and have been heavily influenced by a wide range of presentations and publications. So extensive is this network of influence, and so deeply has it affected my beliefs and attitudes about second language acquisition, that it is nearly impossible for me to acknowledge everyone to whom I am indebted for most of the ideas that are found on the following pages. When those ideas are sharp and the evidence incisive, then the voices and opinions of my colleagues are probably speaking most clearly through me. And when notions begin to falter, and evidence starts to fade, I alone am most probably to blame.

So many of my students, friends, and professional colleagues have helped me in my quest to complete this book, that it almost seems unfair to single a few names out for special commendation. A general vote of thanks should certainly be expressed to my former students and fellow faculty members at the University of Pittsburgh, Chiengmai University (Thailand), and the Tianijn Foreign Languages Institute (China). My present students and faculty colleagues at San Francisco State University have been more than patient with my frequent expositions about the critical period hypothesis, and to them, I also owe an expression of gratitude.

Several individuals have been particularly helpful to me and deserve mention by name, for they have given me a great deal of time, advice, and attention at various periods when I have been working on this research. John Lamendella has long been a source of valuable counsel. Fred Marshall helped sharpen many of the ideas that are found in these pages. I am extremely indebted to Michael Long and James Flege, who read this manuscript with great care and who provided me with many useful suggestions. The staff at Newbury House has been efficient and supportive at every step of the way, and to Leslie Berriman, who helped me in the writing and the organization of this book, and to Cindy Funkhouser, who supervised the final production, I am especially grateful. Finally, I wish to thank my wife and two children who challenged me constantly, yet gently, to complete this project, and who have been generous enough throughout our life to give me a time to write and a time to speak.

January, 1988
San Francisco

CONTENTS

CONTENTS

INTRODUCTION

Then Jephthah gathered together all the men of Gilead and fought with Ephraim: and the men of Gilead smote Ephraim, because they said, Ye Gileadites are fugitives of Ephraim among the Ephraimites, and among the Manassites.

And the Gileadites took the passages of Jordan before the Ephraimites: and it was so, that when those Ephraimites which were escaped said, Let me go over; that the men of Gilead said unto him, Art thou an Ephraimite? If he said Nay; then said they unto him, Say now Shibboleth: and he said Sibboleth: for he could not frame to pronounce it right. Then they took him, and slew him at the passages of the Jordan: and there fell at that time of the Ephraimites forty and two thousand.

Judges 12:4–6

It is not at all surprising that this minor incident recorded in the book of Judges has lasted some three thousand years, for it contains all the ingredients that characterize any great epic in literature: It has heroes and heroics, violence and victory, cunning and conquest. But most importantly, like all good myth, the shibboleth story relates an eternal truth. Put quite simply, it tells us that there are certain constraints that nature and nurture have woven about us, and even when our very life is on the line, as it was in the case of the defeated Ephraimites who feebly attempted to masquerade as Gileadites, the taut trammels of early learning leave us literally tongue-tied, and we are betrayed by something that is as ubiquitous as the air we breathe—our speech.

1

It is quite irrelevant that the casualty rate of the enemy is obviously grossly exaggerated in this account; whether forty-two thousand fell or only a thousandth of that sum, what is important is that the tiny difference between the two sibilants /š/ and /s/, which even we English speakers transpose when forced to race through a phrase like "She sells seashells by the seashore," helps to distinguish between several dialects of the Semitic languages spoken by the people in that part of the world, even to this present day, and that speakers of a language without a phonemic /š/ find it extremely difficult to produce a consistent contrast between their native /s/ and this more marked /š/ sound. Fortunately, most of us never encounter a pronunciation test as pernicious as the one to which the Ephraimites were subjected, but the point of the story serves as a suitable introduction to any investigation of the hypothesis that there is a critical period for language learning that leaves us in some ways forever constrained in any future attempts to master a foreign tongue. The strong version of such a theory is encapsulated in this story from Judges: Even in a life-or-death situation, we cannot make the minute neuromuscular changes necessary to spare our souls. If this is true, then this period of time for language acquisition is indeed critical!

In brief, the critical period hypothesis is the notion that language is best learned during the early years of childhood, and that after about the first dozen years of life, everyone faces certain constraints in the ability to pick up a new language. When these constraints are manifested, what specifically these constraints are, and why language learning in humans is constrained in this fashion are all questions that have been deliberated, discussed, and debated by scholars for many years, and thus it is the purpose of this book to review the different answers which have been given to these questions, to synthesize often conflicting evidence and perspectives into one cohesive approach to this interesting topic, and to demonstrate why the critical period is an issue of great relevance, not only for language teachers but for anyone interested in the study of behavior.

There are several reasons why I have been fascinated with this hypothesis for many years—many reaons why I have decided to write this book. Some of them are completely personal. Having achieved an almost legendary ability to fail French courses during my college days, I may harbor an unconscious desire to vindicate my poor performance by discovering, through this investigation, that my low grades were due to a biological constraint and not a result of youthful lackadaisicalness! More probably, my interest stems from my early life abroad: I lived the first decade of my life in China and attended high school in northern India. After completing university studies in the United States, I lived for seven years in two different areas of Thailand. Thus, it is only natural that I have become interested in how people speak and why they sound the way they do.

There are several professional reasons for my interest in this topic as well, and these have to do with my linguistics training, my experience as a foreign language teacher, and my current interests in applied psycholinguistics. But it is not I, of course, but you, whose interest must be piqued. Let me try to accomplish this by suggesting why the critical period hypothesis merits our attention.

For those who continually seek some practical benefit from theoretical inquiries, there is at least one direct pedagogical application of this hypothesis, and this concerns the goals of a foreign language curriculum for adult learners. If it is true that nativelike pronunciation in any language is attainable only by children, it stands to reason that when we are teaching second or foreign languages to adults, we should not plan to place undue emphasis on oral production skills. Even though there are probably few, if any, programs that espouse native fluency as an explicit goal, the critical period hypothesis, at least according to the arguments that I will subsequently introduce, suggests that because there are no apparent boundaries to the learning of new words and new rules, most of the energy expended in foreign language programs, especially for intermediate and advanced learners, should be channeled into the acquisition of vocabulary and syntax in the target language. The critical period, if it truly exists, should not in any way detract from the importance of teaching oral production skills, a qualification I would like to make abundantly clear at the outset, but it does suggest an ultimate ranking of priorities because of certain immutable constraints, and I offer this modest advice as an example of one sound and unqualified practical application of the hypothesis.

Another useful insight that can be applied to the "real world" from the theory is in the area of bilingual education. There has been much debate in North America for the past two decades over the exact nature of bilingualism and the precise policies the government should adopt toward it. The arguments have centered around macroissues such as whether American society is, or should be, a "melting pot," a "fruit salad," or a "kaleidoscope" and have swirled about such microissues as how many non-English-speaking students in a school district are necessary to qualify it as a legitimate recipient of federal funding. These questions have frequently generated considerable heat but little light, and part of the reason for this contentiousness lies in the fact that even though these issues are clearly sociolinguistic, they are founded on such fundamental psycholinguistic questions as What is the optimal age for learning another language? Let me be quick to acknowledge that the subsequent pages will not provide a satisfactory answer to this important query; nevertheless, the critical period hypothesis, at least the version that I will try to define and refine for you, does speak directly to the question of optimal age and can, in both a specific and a general manner, help us to devise better bilingual programs and policies for the children of this ever-shrinking and increasingly interdependent planet.

From the time of the great classical philosophers to the immediate present, man has been intrigued by the central concern of all psychology—

how to resolve the mind/body problem. This dichotomy is adroitly addressed in a story that has been passed down to us from the rich tradition of Buddhist philosophy. An Indian sage was asked by his pupil, "Is life matter?" "No matter," replied the wise guru. "Ah, then surely it must be all in the mind" was the student's prompt response. "Never mind" was the laconic reply.

Without becoming enmeshed in the philosophical debate over whether the universe is best represented by a monistic or a dualistic model, there is that provoking problem of where to seat the mind, the spirit, the soul—call it what you will. It is only natural that beginning with the phrenologists of two centuries ago, then continuing with the work of neurologists like Jackson in England, Broca in France, and Wernicke in Austria during the last century, and culminating in the work of modern neuropsychologists like the late Alexander Luria of the USSR or the Nobel laureate Roger Sperry of the United States, we have directed our attention to the few pounds of senseless tissue that sits on top of our spinal cord as the center of consciousness. It is no wonder that brain research has generated enormous excitement in the past few decades, for neuropsychologists are, in small measure, coming tantalizingly close to resolving the mind/body paradox, and we are beginning to discover some fascinating ways in which the brain controls behavior, feeling, and thought. It is surely mind-boggling to contemplate the brain contemplating itself.

With all success come stringent liabilities, however, and the beneficial insights that have been gleaned from contemporary neuropsychology have, unfortunately, been sometimes embezzled or prostituted by those social scientists and educationists who find the human brain a quick fix to all the vexing problems they have heretofore been unable to answer about the mind and behavior: How does the mind learn? Why do some minds not learn very well? And why do some minds turn pathological? Ideas about the critical period have also been influenced by this neuropsychological revolution, and since I, myself, have been guilty in the past of overextrapolating conclusions about the mind on the basis of recent research on the brain, I am especially cognizant of the dangers of looking to the physical world of the brain for all the answers to our metaphysical questions about the mind. Never mind! I do believe that there is strong evidence that neuropsychology can provide some of the answers to our questions about why a critical period for language learning exists, and another important justification for examining this hypothesis is that it can serve to test some of our current theories about how the brain controls behavior, especially language-learning behavior. At the same time, there are clear limitations as to how far we can push this modern model of the mind, and this will become readily apparent, I believe, in subsequent discussions about the possible neurological etiology of foreign accents. And to those materialists who would reduce all questions about the mind to the two cerebral hemispheres, I can only retort, No matter!

There are some metatheoretical benefits to be derived from the critical period hypothesis too. Like most behavioral and social scientists, applied linguists who are interested in theory building and model construction are infatuated with dichotomies, and there is abundant enthusiasm exhibited in the pages of professional journals and on the floors of national and international conferences these days about distinctions between compound and coordinate bilingualism (Ervin & Osgood, 1954), instrumental and integrative motivation (Gardner & Lambert, 1972), acquisition and learning (Krashen, 1985), acculturational and instructional factors (Schumann, 1978), and left and right hemisphere processing (Springer & Deutsch, 1981). To be sure, all of these are important and, at the very least, serve some heuristic value by extricating us from an awkward theoretical dead end and pointing us back to the right direction again, but there is a danger in dichotomies, especially when they become oversimplified, and this risk is illustrated by a discussion I witnessed several years ago at a plenary session of an otherwise excellent conference. The session was entitled "Does L1A = L2A?" That is, the selected panel of about half a dozen experts in language acquisition attempted to address the issue of whether child first language acquisition was similar to adult second language learning. Given such a binary and nebulous title, the kind of "chicken or egg?" riddle which is inherently unanswerable, it was not surprising that the topic quickly got away from the panel and the afternoon ended up devoted to the practical but not completely relevant problem of how to help teachers get jobs in bilingual education.

Providing employment opportunities for language teachers is clearly beyond the province of the critical period hypothesis, and yet there is an important metatheoretical conclusion that can be drawn from this anecdote to which the critical period speaks. The hypothesis is founded on the belief that many, if not all, of the dichotomies in the social sciences are superficially drawn, and that science as a whole is not well served by models that set up binary constructs like two competing tennis players on either side of an imaginary court, but progresses best when these constructs are viewed as integral and complementary parts of a holistic and integrated model. Much of what I read in the language-learning literature is the "divide and conquer" stuff, but to me, nature is ultimately always embracing and encircling, and the great contributions in science have always recognized this fact. As with Einstein's theory of relativity, nature does not distinguish between matter and energy—they are simply different roles performed by the same actor.

So it is with the critical period theory, which holds that it is neither nature or nurture, neither genetic endowment nor environment that serves to shape our linguistic experiences, but it is both together, *through time,* that form the foundation for all human learning. The critical period can make a major contribution, then, to the way in which we ask questions and the manner in which we seek answers. Irrespective of its other, practical and theoretical contributions, I find this metatheoretical insight of import to all of us who are engaged in language-learning research, whether we are sociolinguists, psycholinguists, or applied linguists. And it is this holistic approach that makes this hypothesis so refreshingly wholesome—surely, it warrants our attention on these grounds alone.

I believe that this integrative and holistic approach to language acquisition is so important that I have organized an outline of how the chapters should interrelate. From this three-by-three matrix (Table 1) you can see that the critical period is examined sequentially through the fields of biology (Chapters 1–3), anthropology (Chapters 4–6), and psycholinguistics (Chapters 7–9). Simultaneously, I want us to consider the impact of nature, nurture, and time as we progress through the research and the issues that arise in various chapters. As you might expect, there will be times when the material of a certain chapter might not perfectly match the symmetry of this outline, but I share this overall schema with you so that you will have a rough idea of where we are going in each chapter and where we have been.

Finally, the critical period is not simply a hypothesis about certain aspects of language acquisition: It may have ramifications for other sorts of learning behavior as well, and, more significantly, I firmly believe that it is ultimately a hypothesis about the way in which humans become socialized. There is a touch of irony here when we consider the fact that this theory marshals evidence from the social sciences—from linguistics, psychology, and anthropology, and it even draws from some of the natural sciences too—ethology, biology, and neurology, but it is first and foremost a theory that attempts to grapple with the principal questions of the humanities: What is man? Who are we? How do we learn? When do we make that social commitment that carries us across the cultural Rubicon which separates child from adult? In what ways are our lives shaped by the natural states of being and by the natural processes of becoming? What parts of our behavior hark back to our animal heritage and what parts mark us as uniquely human?

The narrow concerns of this book are dwarfed by such momentous

TABLE 1

	Nature (evolution)	Nurture (environment)	Time (age)
Biological foundations	Chapter 1 Evolutionary Beginnings	Chapter 2 Ethological Foundations	Chapter 3 The Coming of Age
Anthropological considerations	Chapter 4 Genes and Teens	Chapter 5 The Influence of Environment	Chapter 6 The Tide of Time
Psycholinguistic experiments	Chapter 7 Nature's Cruel and Unusual Experiments	Chapter 8 Arguments and Counter-arguments	Chapter 9 Questions, Consequences, and Conclusions

questions, of course, but the hypothesis can still provide a tiny, microscopic laboratory in which we can test certain beliefs and ideas about human behavior, and I hope you will encounter some of the excitement and revelation that I have enjoyed by entering this little arena of psycholinguistic inquiry with me. It has taught me something about the irrevocable constraints of our natural universe, and, at the same moment, something about the miraculous abilities of our human potential. Most of all, I have learned that human behavior, like relativity, is molded and measured by time. But of course, this is nothing new. Even more well known than the shibboleth story are the words from Ecclesiastes:

> To every thing there is a season, and a time to every purpose under the heaven.
> A time to be born, and a time to die;
> A time to plant, and a time to pluck up that which is planted . . .
> A time to keep silence, and a time to speak.
>
> Ecclesiastes 3:1–2,7

1

EVOLUTIONARY BEGINNINGS—THE PHYLOGENESIS OF THE HUMAN PROPENSITY FOR SPEECH

The time was 1967. If not embroiled with the sociopolitical storms that encircled them in college campuses, students of linguistics were turning their attention to Noam Chomsky's first major revision of his revolutionary trans-formational-generative grammar. The publication of *Aspects of the Theory of Syntax* (Chomsky, 1965) just two years previous was a bold attempt to deal with the interface of syntax and semantics, and it caught the interest of almost every linguist because even then, there was a growing split in the transformational-generative ranks between those who adhered to Chomsky's original attempts to posit a syntactic base for language and the increasing number of young generativists who were turning toward seman-tic-based models. Lost in this debate was the publication of a far weightier tome that transcended *Aspects* in both range of subject matter and depth of experimental detail. In addition, it contributed enormously to the burgeoning field of developmental psycholinguistics and almost single-handedly spawned the now fashionable field of neurolinguistics. Ironically enough, as if to give the book greater credence and publicity, it was released with an essay appended to the back, a concluding afterthought as it were, in which the renowned syntactician expressed some not-too-relevant thoughts on the formal nature of language. Buried in the polemics of politics and syntax, then, was a book that would challenge our ideas about the origin and evolution of human speech and language and would carefully document the intertwining of nature, nurture, and time in the processes and products of language acquisition. So meticulously did it compile the evidence for an innate, biological basis for human communication that it demonstrated, beyond a shadow of incredulity, that language is part of our genetic endowment. The title of the book was *Biological Foundations of Language;* the author, Eric Lenneberg (1967).

LENNEBERG'S LEGACY

Any inquiry into the critical period must begin with an examination of biological foundations and hence with Lenneberg's work. He was the first to posit some sort of explicit relationship between second language acquisition and a biologically based critical period, and he too was the first to introduce a wide sweep of evidence on hominid evolution in an attempt to prove that human nature is as important as human nurture. Up until Lenneberg's time, many social scientists held to the behavioral tenet that one of the major ways in which humans differed from animals in the learning of complex behavior was that animals had "instincts," genetically preprogrammed patterns to follow that were not learned through laborious social interaction; humans, however, had no "instincts" and learned almost all behavior through environmental conditioning. Even the acquisition of such a complex human behavior as language was no exception to this nonbiological environmentalist explanation (Skinner, 1957). So it is apparent why we should begin with a biological and an evolutionary perspective, and with Lenneberg's initial explication of this nonbehaviorist approach.

In order to arrive at a lucid understanding of language acquisition, it is necessary to follow Lenneberg's lead and explore the evolutionary and genetic origins of communication in *Homo sapiens,* or *Homo loquens,* to use a more linguistically biased nomenclature. There are two aspects of hominid evolution that are of particular relevance to language, and we will examine both in this chapter: the evolution of the larynx and the evolution of the brain. In reviewing all of this evidence, we are not just underscoring the significance of Lenneberg's work and the research that he has directly or indirectly encouraged, but we acknowledge the profundity of nature's influence upon our lives—an acknowledgment that has been reiterated throughout history—once long ago by Plato, more recently by Descartes, and in this century by biologists like Dubos (1968).

The question of origins stirs strong feelings within us. We are proud of our name and our family tree, and we zealously dig among our roots in order to discover our true lineage. We are equally enthusiastic about passing on the family myths we have heard from others, or that we have conveniently embellished for our offspring. It is no small wonder that the quest for human origins stirs so much controversy, especially among people with ardent religious convictions. Like the issue of abortion, which deals in a very direct manner with the conception of an individual life and which has exacerbated fervent emotions among sometimes well-meaning people, so has the question of evolution, which grapples with the origin of our collective life, provoked controversy in various quarters. Why? Because evolution deals with the very stuff we are made of. We can be dispassionate about the stars, but it is hard to be disinterested about ourselves. All the more reason, then, to scrutinize the data carefully and to establish a biological foundation for the remaining chapters of this book. My inquiry is a scientific one because I am convinced that the evidence for a prolonged and natural emergence of *Homo sapiens* from other primates is overwhelming; therefore, I will proceed with a brief anthropological summary of what we now know about man's origins—especially as it pertains to human language.

HOMINID EVOLUTION

Bishop Usher's date of 4004 B.C. for the appearance of Adam is looking more and more tardy. Although fossil records are admittedly haphazard and incomplete, and the process of speciation still not well understood, we have solid evidence for *Homo sapiens* emerging in the Pleistocene (glacial age) and for hominids of another genus appearing in the Pliocene or possibly the Miocene (Table 1.1). Having made this statement and having introduced only a few fragmentary pieces of information in the table, I must state quite baldly that the evidence is both exceedingly strong and, at the same time, controversial. Let me try to reconcile this apparent contradiction. From the fossil records patiently collected by paleontologists like Raymond Dart in South Africa (Ardrey, 1970), David Pilbeam in South Asia (Pilbeam, 1970), or the Leakeys who worked the Olduvai site in East Africa, we have remains that stretch from contemporary archeological discoveries back through the glacial era to preglacial sites which date to over a million years ago. The evidence accumulated is hard—very hard!—skulls, skeletal bones, jaws, and teeth all fossilized into rock and all dated reasonably accurately from the geological strata in which they were entombed and, in many cases, corroborated through radiocarbon dating techniques.

Complementing this paleontological data is the comparative evidence gleaned from what we have learned about the anatomy, physiology, and behavior of extant species—especially those that are almost as phylogenetically "advanced" as we humans. What has aided physical anthropologists is not simply the degree to which certain structures and behaviors in related species are analogous to those found in *Homo,* but relationships in animal structures and behavior that are *homologous* to man. Homologous similarities between animals like the great apes and man refer to structures that are

10

TABLE 1.1 Summary of Hominoid Evolution

Taxonomic classification	Anatomical features	Geological age	Years before present
Homo sapiens sapiens	Fully modern teeth and jaws with chins, big brains (c. 1000–2000 cc), striding bipedalism and precision grips	Holocene	Contemporary
Homo sapiens neaderthalensis	Brow ridges, receding chin, large brains (c. 1000–1600 cc), good bipedalism, power and perhaps precision grips	Late Pleistocene	400,000
Homo erectus (*Pithecanthropus*)	Heavy brow ridges, no chin, large teeth, smaller brain (c. 750–1200 cc), good bipedalism, grips unknown	Middle Pleistocene	1 million
Homo habilis and Australopithecus	Hominid dentition, small brains (c. 500–700 cc), early bipedalism, grips unknown	Early Pleistocene	2 million
Ramapithecus and Kenyapithecus	Hominid dentition (nothing else known)	Pliocene	2 to 13 million
Split between hominoids and anthropoids	Virtually no evidence	Miocene	13 to 25 million

Source: After Day (1970: 153). Reprinted by permission of Grosset & Dunlap from *Fossil Man* by Michael H. Day, © 1970 by Grosset & Dunlap, Inc., © 1969 by The Hamlyn Group.

genetically and anatomically related and which share behavioral similarities as well: a nimble hand, mobile face, and a pectoral girdle for swinging in the jungle or on a jungle gym, depending on the species. These homologues have been identified by zoologists from comparative studies that antedate Darwin, and they lead to the conclusion that apes are more similar to man phylogenetically than any other mammals. Thus, primatologists place man and the great apes in the same suborder, *Anthropoidea,* but enough differences remain to distinguish at least two major branches of that suborder: a superfamily of pongids and another called hominoids. Chimps, gorillas, and orangutans represent the former: We alone are the surviving species that comprises the group of hominids, the subfamily of the superfamily of hominoids, which were the most humanlike of the apes (Day, 1970). This, then, is the comparative evidence which physical anthropologists have assembled in their quest to discover man's specific anatomical and physiological identity and which leads paleontologists to look for evolutionary continuities—missing links, if you will—between the two major classes of contemporary anthropoids.

Although all of this data is strong, recall that it was also deemed controversial. Part of the discord comes from the paucity of data. As you might suspect, and as implied by Table 1.1, both the quantity and quality of comparative material is inversely proportional to its age. Our closets are filled with skeletons of modern humans, but we are lucky to have even a jawbone of the preglacial species that present the huge number of missing links between man and ape. Part of the controversy also stems from pure and simple taxonomy, for paleontological classification, like Oscar Wilde's remark about truth, is rarely pure and never simple. The evolutionary evidence comes to us as a mosaic, and not as a photograph, and a small fragment of a fossil jaw, to cite a typical problem, can exhibit both pongid and hominoid characteristics. If this fossilized portion of an ancient mandible is prognathous, and yet simultaneously contains a humanlike four-cusp molar, to present a typical example, do we have evidence for an early anthropoid with pongid tendencies, or are we holding part of an apelike animal with distinctly human aspirations? The evidence is real enough; it is beyond dispute. The question is the one that haunts all science: What is the data actually telling us?

Finally, part of the variance we encounter in attempting to assess paleontological information is the value we give to input from a relatively recent method for determining evolutionary history—molecular anthropology. For about two decades now, molecular biologists have been examining the DNA molecules of extant species to see how well they match. By quantifying the degree to which molecular information in the cells of two different species fit together, and by assuming that there is a relatively constant rate of genetic change over time, similar to the constant decay of a Carbon 14 molecule proven so useful in radiocarbon dating, molecular anthropologists have recently come up with a new model of anthropoid evolution. Were the molecular evidence congruent with the traditional paleontological and comparative model of evolution (briefly summarized in Table 1.1), we would have one more reason to feel comfortable with our success in finding some of man's missing links. But as if in intentional defiance of our attempts to understand it, nature seems to have given us conflicting clues. The molecular data, as described by Gribbin and Cherfas (1982), conflict with the traditional data in two ways: it implies a reclassification of the anthropoids that pulls the orangutan out of the great apes and leaves them out on a limb, so to speak, and, more radically, it suggests that the major break between hominids and the other two remaining pongids, chimps and gorillas, occurred as recently as 5 million years ago (Figure 1.1). What is in dispute is not the evolutionary model itself, or the accepted classification of the primates. It is the speciation of some members of the primates and the timing of this specia-

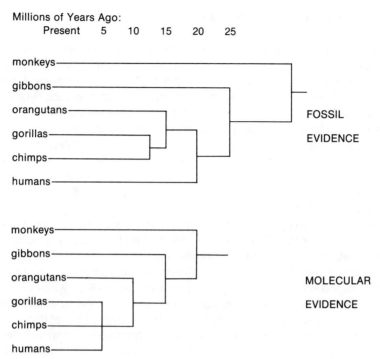

Millions of Years Ago:

Figure 1.1 Comparison of the molecular and paleontological models. (*Source:* After Gribbin & Cherfas, 1982.)

tion that is in question. Gribbin and Cherfas (1982) claim, for example, that the common linkage between humans and apes was as recent as 5 million years ago, and not around 15, as earlier theories imply. It should be noted that even while the dust is still settling from the impact of the molecular evidence, scholars are trying to effect a compromise between the molecular and the paleontological models depicted in Figure 1.1.

Our interests should not, however, be so consumed by the overall evolutionary development of *Homo sapiens,* whatever models end up gaining greatest favor, that we lose sight of those aspects of hominid development that impinge most directly upon speech and language. Again, we must pay tribute to Lenneberg for the enthusiasm he generated for a biologically based interpretation of the saliency of speech in our species, for it was he who first detailed the importance of the phylogenetic evolution of the larynx and of the brain. It was this evidence, along with an ever-increasing amount of data published in subsequent research that will be reviewed and updated here because of its pertinence to the biological foundations of communication in humans.

EVOLUTION FOR HUMAN SPEECH

At this point, let me make a distinction between speech and language, for both tactical and strategic reasons. In the short run, it should be clear that the upper respiratory tract and the brain are of great importance for most human communication, and, as I will attempt to document, the former has phylogenetically evolved into what might be called an "organ of speech," whereas the latter has developed into what could be classified as an "organ of language." But in the longer run, the distinction between speech and language is a subject which sharpens our understanding of the critical period—an issue to be elaborated on in the final chapter. Speech is the linear, oral-aural communication which we employ as members of a community; it is *la parole* or *performance,* to choose the terms that de Saussure (1916) and Chomsky (1965) have used, respectively. Language, on the other hand, is the abstract, hierarchical system of symbols which underlies speech, writing, and other forms of symbolic communication ("la langue" or "competence," to use the corresponding contrasts of the authors just cited). The strategic importance of this distinction is the question of whether or not there is a critical period for *language.* I hope that the evidence mustered in this book for the importance of prepubescent learning for accentless *speech* will convince even the most skeptical reader of limitations on speech performance, but the more intriguing question is whether there is a critical period for language—for linguistic competence—as well. Frankly, I find no evidence for a constraint on competence, although Coppieters (1987) would question this conclusion.

Placing that issue aside for the time being, let us look at the more immediate concern of how *Homo sapiens* has evolved into an animal that has been endowed anatomically for speech and has been programmed neurologically for language. In short, man has emerged historically as "the articulate ape," to use Jean Aitchison's sobriquet (1976).

Our ability to be articulate and to mimic articulate sounds made by other members of our species is almost entirely dependent on the phylogenetic evolution of many species-specific characteristics of the upper respiratory tract. Specifically, they are (1) the ability to control a steady but rhythmic egression of pulmonic air from the lungs, (2) the intrinsic anatomy of the larynx, (3) the unique position of the larynx itself in human beings, and the consequences of that location on the configuration of the vocal tract and the flexibility of the tongue, (4) the musculature of the face, and (5) the innervation of the oral, facial, and laryngeal musculature by the brain. Although we have almost no way of knowing whether these phenomena existed in prehominid forms, from the little paleontological evidence that is available on one of these features alone (the configuration of the oral cavity; Lieberman & Crelin, 1971), and from comparative evidence with other extant mammals, especially the great apes, *Homo sapiens* must have originated from earlier beings that did not possess these speech-making attributes. Let us look at each of these features briefly.

1. Speech is as natural to us as breathing—so natural, in fact, that it seems as if the latter can be suspended indefinitely while the former is in progress. What is happening during speech, of course, is not a state of suspended animation in the speaker (though a telling argument could be made that this state does occur in some listeners, depending on the speaker!), but that a radical compensation of the normal breathing patterns takes place; long periods of controlled, rhythmic egression are only briefly interrupted by imperceptible ingressive gulps. These physiological events are thoroughly reviewed at the end of the third chapter of Lenneberg's treatise, and they are more elaborately examined by speech scientists like Adams (1979) and MacKay (1987). The data indicates that we have a universal and innate ability to control egressive air in rhythmic patterns so that breath becomes speech.

> The hypothesis is advanced that the temporal patterns on which the neuromuscular automatisms are based have at their roots a physiological rhythm consisting of periodic changes of "states" at a rate of 6 + or − 1 cps. Indirect evidence is cited that articulation itself reflects such a basic rhythm. (Lenneberg, 1967:120)

2. These rhythmic exhalations progress through the trachea to a fruit-size organ that is prominent in many men and is colloquially referred to as the "Adam's apple," a sex-exclusive appellation if there ever was one since all Eves possess them too. Wind (1970) has meticulously traced the evolution of the larynx and its homologous precursors in vertebrates, beginning with primitive fish, up through amphibians, reptiles, small mammals, primates, and finally humans, in a highly technical but readable anatomical dissertation, *On the Phylogeny and the Ontogeny of the Human Larynx*. What is painstakingly documented is that the larynx began as (and even in modern man still remains) a valve to trap air in the thorax to facilitate muscular contraction during short bursts of heavy physical exertion. This primitive function is quickly demonstrated if you grab a heavy object, like a chair, and lift it with a jerk. You will notice the glottis in your larynx instantly tightens as you yank upwards. The glottal gasp that exudes can be viewed as a phylogenetic recapitulation of how the larynx has additionally evolved into an organ of speech. Wind summarizes in a few phrases how this remarkable transformation has taken place in human history:

> In conclusion, we may state that the roots of human speech are probably found in a long era of sound production, gradually passing into communication; an even longer era of voice production. The emergence of speech based on this must have resulted from the interaction of a large number of characteristics and circumstances. (Wind, 1970:80)

15

Reviewing several comparative anatomy studies of various pongids and man, Lenneberg has described the manner in which the instrinsic anatomy of the human larynx is optimally streamlined for the production of speech. Compared with the rather complicated larynxes of gibbons, orangutans, and chimpanzees, the human voice box is simpler and more highly specialized for speech sounds; it lacks well-developed double vocal cords (the presence of which tends to diffuse the clarity of voicing); it is not designed to make ingressive sounds as easily as egressive noises (phonemic information in all human languages is based almost exclusively on egressive air, flowing up from the lungs through the vocal tract); and it is not surrounded by supplementary pockets of air sacs which could work like some sort of bagpipe for the apes. When coupled to the fact that the laryngeal muscles of man are highly developed,and that the epiglottis and pharynx above the larynx are designed to allow the voice box to spray air efficiently into the oral and nasal cavities, the streamlined system functions like a Stradivarius—the richness of its sound is a direct consequence of its evolutionary design: It is complex enough to produce the nuances of human speech, but it is simple enough to perform articulately without wasted structure and effort, and despite having developed into an organ of speech, it retains its primitive physiological function of trapping air in the thoracic chamber under certain conditions of physical exertion.

3. Far more dramatic than its anatomical utility is the unique anatomical position of the larynx in the adult *Homo sapiens*. Put succinctly, the ascent of man, if linked closely to the emergence of speech in our species, is directly related to the descent of the larynx. Articulate speech has arisen from the lowering of the voice box in human history. Equally remarkable is the way in which ontogeny recapitulates phylogeny here, because the human neonate, much like the early hominid forms (perhaps Neanderthal), is born with a larynx jammed high in the throat, almost directly behind the tongue. This position allows a human baby to breathe through its nose and suck milk at the same time, and this ability to swallow and breathe simultaneously is something that human infants share with all other mammals. Strange though it may sound, this ability is gradually lost as the larynx descends in the throat to become situated at the base of the pharyngeal tube in the adult. No other animal on earth exhibits this unique anatomical feature that is found in all human children and adults, and thus all tiny infants become "human" after about the first year of life, when the larynx has gradually moved down from the very top of the throat and created a true pharynx, which then becomes a common passageway for the inspiration of air and the ingestion of food (Crelin, 1976). Figure 1.2 portrays this unusual anatomical transformation.

Lieberman (1982) and Lieberman and Crelin (1971) have attempted to reconstruct vocal tracts from Neanderthal skulls, and Lieberman (1984) claims that partly owing to the high laryngeal position of this premodern hominid, the back of the tongue was virtually immobilized, severely con-

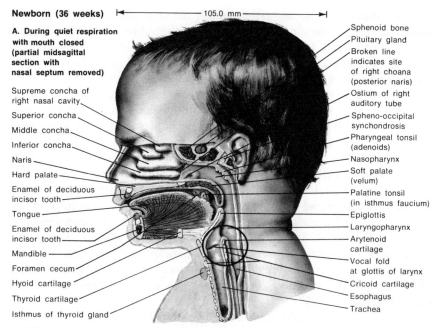

(a) Newborn human infant showing high laryngeal position (circled).

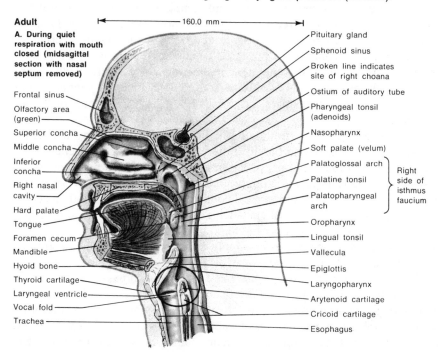

(b) Human adult showing lowered laryngeal position (circled).

Figure 1.2 Contrasting positions of the larynx in infants and adults. (*Source:* After Crelin, 1976:25, 29.) © 1976. CIBA-GEIGY. Reproduced with permission from Clinical Symposia—by Frank H. Netter, MD. All rights reserved.

straining tongue mobility and consequently the production of human speech sounds. There is evidence, for example, that the subtle anatomical changes which are necessary to produce the phonetic contrasts between the high front English vowels in words like *sheep* and *ship* are made at the base of the tongue: The vowel in the first word is pronounced with more of an "advanced tongue root" than the vowel in *ship* (Ladefoged, 1968; MacKay, 1987). Lieberman makes a similar case for human infants, for they also exhibit these vocal limitations in the first year of life. Although Lieberman's thesis is still accepted by some writers of introductory texts in linguistics (e.g., Miller, 1981), his reconstructions and his use of the "La Chapelle skull" as a Neanderthal archetype are a source of considerable controversy in archaeological circles (Carlisle & Siegel, 1974, 1978). Irrespective of the merit of Lieberman and Crelin's claims, I think it is important to point out that we are really talking about phonetic limitations here and not necessarily phonemic constraints. It is a well-established fact in speech science that anatomical changes in the human vocal apparatus often interfere with the sounds of human speech but do not necessarily prevent a speaker from making the phonemic sound contrasts necessary for the speaker's native language (MacKay, 1987).

This having been said, there is still complete agreement that the high position of the larynx in all mammals, except our species (above the age of 1), is a serious impediment to normal and complete human speech. Not only does a lower voice box free the tongue to allow greater flexibility in the production of sounds both in the front and back of the mouth, it creates a third resonating chamber, the pharynx, which along with the oral and nasal chambers creates a multicomponent resonating voice tract. Furthermore, this lowering introduces an additional source for segmental phonemes (the English /h/ sound, for example, originates from this "new" part of the human throat).

However, nature is ruthlessly fair in the way she endows life with a unique blend of ability and liability; there is one awful consequence of the improvements in the organ of speech in adults, a price that no other animal has been willing to pay, and a limitation that human neonates avoid as long as possible. Consider the anatomical comparisons of a child's and an adult's mouth (Figure 1.2). The infant can suckle and breathe at the same time, just as a pet cat can simultaneously lap milk and inhale through its nose, but an adult must swallow with the air supply completely strangled, the trachea securely protected by the epiglottis as food or drink is passed over the windpipe and down the esophagus. The long laryngeal passage and the low position of the voice box, necessary for our ability to be articulate apes, are directly responsible for the fact that we of all animals are most susceptible to death by choking. No wonder that babies are spared this limitation in the first year or two of life, when their primary communicative needs can be met through crying, babbling, and cooing (Reich, 1986) and not through the ability to contrast five vowel phonemes consistently and clearly. But as their vocal apparatus starts to mature, they begin to learn to articulate the segmental contrasts of their mother's tongue, just as they automatically learn to protect their now exposed trachea to liquids and solids. It is a natural blend of form and function maturing in concert.

4. We are not only the most articulate ape, we are also the most "facial" of all living creatures. Even without makeup, there is so much color and information in a human face that it should come as no surprise that our facial musculature is more highly developed than that of any other species, although we, the "thinking" animal, are the least muscularly developed of the mammals. Again, we can turn to Lenneberg for copious documentation of this fact and of its linguistic consequences:

> According to Lightoller (1925) and Huber (1931), the arrangement of muscles around the corner of the mouth in man is most similar to that in chimpanzee and gorilla. Huber emphasizes, however, that the muscles themselves have undergone further differentiation in man, have grown in shape and anatomical distinctiveness, and show more interlacing than in the great apes . . . Clearly, the complexity, size, and number of muscles originating particularly in the corner of the mouth greatly facilitate oral motility in man. The peculiar anatomy of the lips and the shape of the mouth make possible rapid and tight air closure and sudden explosive opening, both being prerequisite for speech articulation. (Lenneberg, 1967:37)

5. Finally, and most important of all in our consideration of factors which en toto transform the upper respiratory system of *Homo sapiens* into an organ of speech, is the neurological wiring to which all of these anatomical structures are attached. It is not the hands of a Rubenstein that make a concert pianist, though his hands were unusually large and allowed him to finger some arpeggios a little more easily than you or I; no, it was his mind and the spirit within it that made him a maestro among mortals. And so it is when we draw a comparison between the vocal tract of humans and that of other species, because none of the anatomical differences reviewed above are individually important if considered in isolation from the entire vocal apparatus and the manner in which this vocal system is innervated by the brain. Wind has speculated that given a human vocal tract and neurological system, it would be theoretically possible to replace a human larynx with one from a chimpanzee so that, to quote Wind directly, "such a person would be able to acquire a speech hardly discernible from the normal" (Wind, 1970:71).

We will look at the brain more closely in a moment, but what we need to focus on here, while we are still preoccupied with the subject of speech production, is the curious way in which the human cortex (basically, the surface of the two large cerebral hemispheres that constitute the great bulk

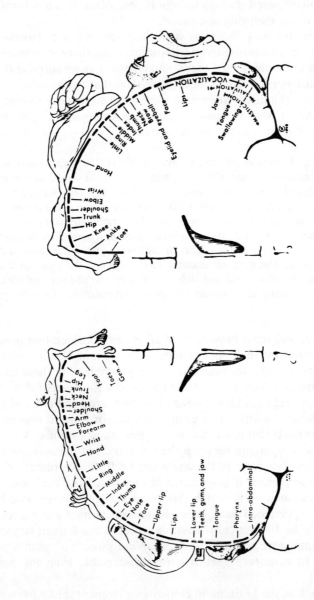

Motor homunculus, drawn overlying a coronal section through the precentral gyrus.

Sensory homunculus, drawn overlying a coronal section through the postcentral gyrus.

Figure 1.3 Coronal section of the motor and sensory cortices showing disproportionate control of body. (*Source:* After Chusid, 1973:6.)

of the brain) allocates space for the control and the perception of various parts of the body. The brain is not at all democratic in this regard; it does not divvy up neurons proportionate to the size and weight of the different organs. If we examine the motor and sensory cortices, the two strips of cerebral cortex that flank both sides of the Rolandic fissure (the main anatomical demarcation between the frontal lobe and the parietal lobe in both hemispheres), we find that these two primary areas for body movement and sensation devote a great deal of space to the hands, throat, and mouth, but are exceedingly parsimonious when it comes to the rest of the body, especially the lower half. When a "homunculus" is drawn proportionate to the allocation of cortical tissue, a grotesque but revealing form emerges (Figure 1.3).

As pictured by this diagram, approximately one-third of the important cortical area is devoted to a comparatively "minor" part of the body, the lower face, the lips, the tongue, and the throat. But is this area really that insignificant? Of course not. What we see is neurological confirmation of the importance of speech in the phylogenetic history of man. Millions of neural connections are wired to the larynx, the pharynx, the oral cavity through the soft tissue and musculature surrounding these areas. The neurological control is much too exquisite for such perfunctory tasks as mastication and swallowing; it is clearly a consequence of the importance of speech production in human life. Attempts to teach human languages to chimps by mimicking the sounds of the human voice (Hayes, 1950) ended in failure because apes are neither constructed nor wired to "speak the speech trippingly on the tongue." Other linguistic modalities were finally resorted to (e.g., plastic symbols, sign language, and computer consoles) to tap the apes' potential for human language (Sebeok & Rosenthal, 1981). Note that apes and other animals are biologically constrained from learning human speech, but they are not necessarily constrained from learning human language. From this we can reach one inescapable conclusion—the central thesis of Lenneberg's 1967 work, and a finding confirmed by abundant recent evidence. We are unique among the species. We are endowed with the organs of speech, and they are as much a part of our biological heritage as eating and breathing.

EVOLUTION OF THE BRAIN FOR LANGUAGE

The evolution of the brain as an organ of language has progressed in step with the development of the upper respiratory tract as an organ of speech. Let me pause to make two prefatory comments before we look at some specific ways in which the brain has evolved into an instrument of language. The first is that just as speech and language cannot be uniformly categorized into two separate forms of behavior, neither can the functions of the respiratory system and the brain be clearly kept apart. You have just read that it is not simply the mechanisms of speech production that account for our evolution into articulate primates, but one must also consider the disproportionate amount of neuromuscular wiring that is directed to the speech apparatus to explain how we humans have evolved into *Homo loquens*. In this chapter, I would like to concentrate on the evolution of the brain and of its importance to the emergence of language, but I do not want to encourage you to adopt what I would call the "neurological imperialism" that has become so popular in education and in the social sciences today. The body functions systematically, and it is essential to maintain a contextual approach when viewing the role of the cerebral cortex in human behavior. Consequently, we should not attribute all human behavior, either normal or pathological, to the brain. Brain and body function in tandem, and both are integrally tied to the influence of heredity and environment.

Equally important, it is instructive to remember that almost every organ plays multiple roles in normal daily activities. Before 1967 it was quite common to view speech as an "overlaid" phenomenon, piggybacking on top of the respiratory functions of the larynx and on top of the mastication function of the mouth (Hockett, 1957), but *Biological Foundations of Language* has dispelled the myth of overlaid functions. Figure 1.2 alone should persuade anyone that the production of speech has played a significant role in the evolution of the human throat. We should also remember though that just as the tongue is not exclusively an instrument of articulation or of mastication, neither is the brain, *nor any particular part of the brain,* solely an organ of language or cognition. This later proviso is especially useful to remember when we confront strong claims about the existence of specific language learning centers in the cortex of humans (Walsh & Diller, 1981). The brain, like the respiratory system, has clearly evolved in ways that have enhanced the use of language in our species, but it has not developed in this manner to the exclusion of other important activities.

The first and most obvious way in which the human brain has evolved is in its size proportionate to body weight. With the possible exception of some cetaceans, we are the animal with the largest brain, a stark contrast to the now extinct stegasaurus, for example, an animal of incredibly disproportionate body-to-weight ratio. Supposedly, this obviously gigantic and possibly gentle behemoth had two "brains," if one can be generous and call a fairly primitive conglomeration of reptilian ganglia a brain—one up front in its skull, and a slightly larger one tucked away back in the pelvic girdle of its freight-car-size body. I remember once reading in a children's book about dinosaurs that the rear "brain" was necessary, because it took so much time for stimuli and responses to get from tail to head and back again that the poor creature would have been constantly out of touch with the further reaches of its ungainly body. In the same passage, I recall a phrase that succinctly captures the primitive nature of the animal's intellect. "It is thought," the book recounted, "that the stegasaurus was so stupid that it was only dimly aware of its own existence!'' This is surely an extreme contrast to the incredible structural and functional complexity of the human cortex, especially because the latter has developed relatively rapidly in its evolutionary history (Lenneberg, 1967:258). An excellent illustration of the quantitative differences between extant species and modern man, and the implied evolutionary growth of *Homo sapiens* is found in Figure 1.4, where we can contrast the relative sizes and shapes of animal brains ranging from fish to humans.

If we direct our attention to archaeological evidence on the cranial capacity of the hominid and prehominid skulls or skull fragments that have been unearthed, we see that there is a relatively predictible pattern between

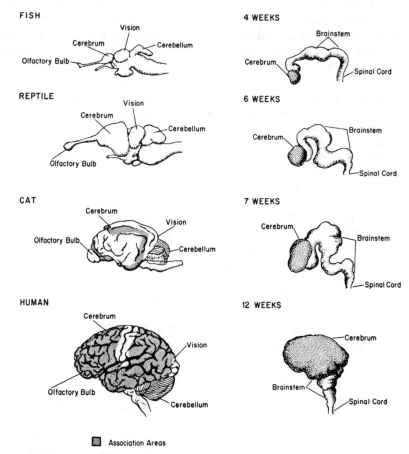

Figure 1.4 Quantitative comparisons of brains in four species. Gray shading indicates association areas. (*Source:* After Teyler, 1976.) From the book *The Human Brain* by M. C. Wittrock and Jackson Beatty, Joseph E. Bogen, Michael S. Gassaniga, Harry J. Jerrison, Stephen D. Krashen, Robert D. Nebes, Timothy J. Teyler, © 1977, used by permission of the publisher, Prentice-Hall, Inc., Englewood Cliffs, N.J.

the size of the cranium (and hence the size of the brain) and the reputed age of the fossil. Paleontologists have studied this relationship carefully; in addition, they have made endocasts from some skulls—latex molds which offer a suggestive model of the size and external topography of fossil brains. Halloway, an anthropologist who has worked diligently in this area of human paleontology, cites the following figures, which illustrate the gradual quantitative growth of hominid brains: the Taung specimen (*Australopithecus:* 2 million years before present) 404 cc; *Homo erectus* (1 million before present) 943 cc; and modern man: c. 1324–1586 cc. One can thus infer a very rough growth rate of about 500 cc per million years (Halloway, 1976:336).

Big is not necessarily better. The importance of the human brain in governing such behaviors as speaking or thinking is not really dependent on its evolutionary increase in size; it is much more a factor of revolutionary *qualitative* changes in neural organization. Lenneberg was certainly aware of this and noted that a large brain, *ceteris paribus,* is not necessarily responsible for complex behavior:

> It is tempting to relate the size of the brain to man's two most outstanding characteristics: his capacity for language and his general cognitive capacities. Intuitively, this relation may be reasonable. But it is important to remember that it rests on no more than just that: intuition. There is no way of demonstrating that cognitive or language capacities either required or resulted from a rapid increase in the number of brain cells. (Lenneberg, 1967:258–259)

Halloway also cautions against the popular but simplistic belief that a big brain correlates neatly with complex behavior, and he presents evidence from cranial endocasts of hominid fossils that there are qualitative changes in the brain that assuredly play a more salient part than cranial capacity itself in determining the emergence of language and intelligence (Halloway, 1976).

The most cogent arguments for the importance of qualitative cerebral evolution over sheer size are presented in Laughlin and d'Aquili in their 1974 work entitled *Biogenetic Structuralism.* Building on previous studies by people like Halloway, they present a strong case for the evolution of major qualitative changes in the human brain after the quantitative growth of the brain had reached a certain optimal stage of evolution:

> Critical to our understanding of the evolution of human cognition is the fact that along with an increase in the absolute size of the brain there also occurred a concomitant increase in the size and dendridic-axonic complexity of the constituent neurons. This in turn led to greater complexity of dendridic-synaptic configurations and neural tracts. A point was reached in the kladogenetic process just outlined when a shift—the *critical shift* in our opinion—in the qualitative buildup of neural complexity created by the time of the australopithecines resulted in an ultimate

qualitative change in the associative capabilities of the hominid brain. (Laughlin & d'Aquili, 1974:35)

What are these qualitative changes? One is the increase in neural complexity alluded to by Laughlin and d'Aquili, and which is illustrated, in part, by Figure 1.4. It is commonly known that the central nervous system of any animal is wired to the rest of the animal's body by two sets of neural connections: afferent pathways that bring sensory stimuli to the brain, and efferent pathways that carry motor responses back to all areas of the body. The human brain is unremarkable from the brains of other animals in this regard, for it functions as a clearinghouse for the processing of sensory input and as an executor for motor output. What is distinctive, though, is the proliferation of *association* pathways in the human cerebrum in the course of evolution—a growth in networks that do not run vertically but run horizontally, so to speak; these pathways link different areas of the brain with other areas so that *Homo sapiens* has ended up with a brain filled with these intracranial connections. This major qualitative change in cerebral organization is depicted by the huge amount of shaded area in Figure 1.4 for the human brain compared with the relative lack of shading in the other species. As you can imagine, this system of interconnection has important implications for our ability to initiate and participate in such complex behavior as language: Association pathways allow us to instantly link sound to sense and sound to sight. In fact, it is impossible for the human brain *not* to seek these immediate linkages, except in those unfortunate cases where neural pathology has impaired certain association pathways, as in the case of certain types of aphasia (Geschwind, 1965).

The human brain has developed such a profuse lattice of interconnecting pathways that even trivial little daily acts, such as pressing the floor number on an elevator panel, immediately engage a system of associative connections for both the sensory and the motor systems of the cerebral cortex (Figure 1.5).

The behavioral consequences stemming from this proliferation of transcortical pathways are obvious, especially when we contemplate the importance of "associations" in linguistic behavior. What, after all, are "symbols," for example? The cerebral ability to link sensory stimuli in an infinite series of relationships is the primary explanation for the unique status of symbolic behavior in communication and cognition in our species. At the motor level, this network of interconnecting systems also gives immense versatility in performing complex muscular tasks, especially those that demand the use of fine motor control of the hands, the voice, and the face, all of which are served by the aforementioned disproportionately large number of neuromuscular pathways which interconnect. Thanks largely to the association systems, we are programmed to process very subtle nuances in sound and sight, and we are programmed to produce an immense range of

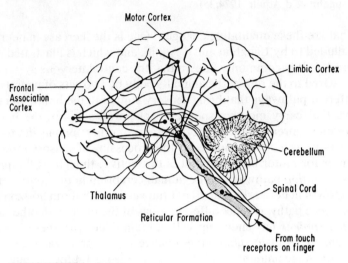

SENSORY CORTEX: Input

Motor Cortex

Limbic Cortex

Frontal
Association
Cortex

Cerebellum

Thalamus

Spinal Cord

Reticular Formation

From touch
receptors on finger

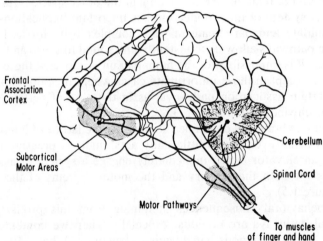

MOTOR CORTEX: Output

Frontal
Association
Cortex

Cerebellum

Subcortical
Motor Areas

Spinal Cord

Motor Pathways

To muscles
of finger and hand

Figure 1.5 Sensory and motor interconnections in the human body for
a simple finger-touching task. (*Source:* After Teyler, 1976.)

vocal and other physical behaviors of almost limitless diversity. The complexity of these associative interconnections are only dimly suggested by the simple two-dimensional diagrams in Figure 1.5.

Other than these qualitative changes in the internal morphology of the brain, there have been important changes in external morphology and cortical structure. Some of these are obvious in the interspecies comparison in

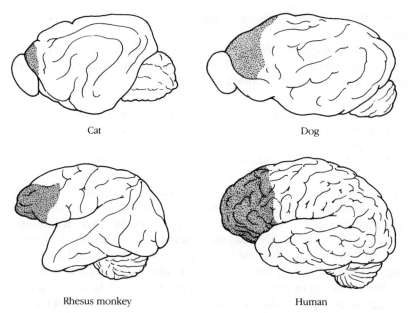

Cat

Dog

Rhesus monkey

Human

Figure 1.6 Lateral view of four mammalian brains highlighting disproportionate growth of human frontal lobe (animal brains enlarged to human scale). (*Source:* After Walsh, 1977.)

Figure 1.4, but even fairly closely related species show differences from the external morphology of the human brain. Figure 1.6 depicts lateral views of the cerebral surfaces of a cat, a dog, a monkey, and a human—the first three being enlarged to human size in order to highlight differences in shape and surface morphology.

Many differences are apparent, even to the eye of a neuroanatomical novice: The surface of the human brain is much more crenulated, allowing for more cortical surface to be squeezed into the cranial vault; the comparative size of the frontal lobes (the left-hand side of each brain) is greatest in man; and the cytoarchitecture—the types of neurons and their structural arrangements, differs for humans too (represented here only in the frontal areas by shading). We do not have extant specimens of prehominid and hominid brains, unfortunately, but if one draws historical inferences from these contemporary comparisons, it is clear that there are many changes in brain morphology that have taken place in human evolution. We still lack adequate understanding of the relationships between histology (the comparative microscopic study of tissue), cytoarchitecture, and neuromorphology, on the one hand, and cognitive and linguistic behavior on the other, but it is reasonable to assume that some of the reasons that the brain has developed into an organ of language in *Homo sapiens* are these distinct qualitative

27

differences which are manifest in the human brain but not in the brains of other species.

Just by looking at the disproportionate growth of the frontal lobes illustrated in Figure 1.6, we can see how language has been phylogenetically predestined in the cerebral cortex of humans:

> Numerous experiments in animals and evidence from pathological lesions in man have demonstrated that the frontal lobes control sequential ordering of elements as well as attention to relevant elements and disattention to irrelevant ones. (Laughlin & d'Aquili, 1974:51)

There are many aspects of cognition in which ordering and selective attention are important, but these two processes certainly play a primary role in all human languages. "Attention to relevant elements" and "disattention to irrelevant ones" is precisely what the noted American linguist Kenneth Pike has called "emic" behavior (Pike, 1967). The ability to attend and disattend selectively allows us to hone in on relevant phonological clues in oral–aural communication. Here is just one example of the way in which qualitative neurological changes in *Homo sapiens* can directly account for linguistic complexity in human communication.

Finally, we come to a truly dramatic qualitative development, a change that has literally doubled the productivity of the brain without imposing any quantitative increase in cerebral tissue. The lateralization of cerebral processes to either the left or the right hemisphere in humans was primarily a discovery of the nineteenth century, but our understanding of the pervasiveness and complexity of lateralization in cognition, perception, and language is only fairly recent, initiated largely through the study of "split brain" patients by the Nobel Prize-winning neurosurgeon, Roger Sperry, and his colleagues Joseph Bogen and Michael Gazzaniga (Gazzaniga, Bogen, & Sperry, 1963). There are a variety of measures which have been used in the last couple of decades to tap the differential lateralization of certain abilities to the left or right hemispheres of most adults: electrical stimulation of the cerebral cortex (Penfield & Roberts, 1959), dichotic listening experiments (Kimura, 1961), visual field preference tasks (Bryden, 1965), temporary anesthetization of one hemisphere—the "Wada test" (Gordon & Bogen, 1974), auditorily evoked potentials (Molfese, Freeman, & Palermo, 1975), computerized axial tomography (Kety, 1979), finger-tapping tasks in rhythm to dichotic listening (Tsunoda, 1985), and others. However, the most voluminous data come from the clinical evidence amassed from literally tens of thousands of neurological cases of aphasia and other neuropsychological pathologies studied for over a century by many different neuropsychologists around the world (for a readable summary of this fascinating evidence for lateralization of functions from clinical cases, see Gardner, 1975).

THE NEUROLINGUISTIC UNIQUENESS OF MAN

All of these studies show that there is a tendency for the human brain to allocate certain cognitive duties and activities to the left cerebral hemisphere and others to the right. The most copious evidence is for language-related activities being handled by the left hemisphere, but there is also strong support for the conclusion that activities involving the recognition of music, patterns, pictures, faces, and emotions tend to be organized by the right hemisphere. These findings have been so intriguing that there has been a prolific vulgarization of laterality evidence in the popular press, and it is important for you to realize that there are many problems in methodology and interpretation of these lateralization phenomena (Segalowitz & Gruber, 1977). Furthermore, you should remember that it is not the behavior itself that is being lateralized (e.g., all "language" is not automatically shunted to the left hemisphere), but the manner in which the particular activity is approached by the individual, especially if the individual is a subject of a neuropsychological experiment. Thus, when language is looked at as a pattern recognition task, it is sometimes processed by the *right* hemisphere; conversely, when facial recognition is viewed as a sequential operation, there are frequently signs that the *left* hemisphere is at work (summarized in Scovel, 1982). The point to be made is that there is an ample improvement in efficiency in the processing and production of various cerebral tasks if the hemispheres can differentially specialize in the supervision of these tasks. By allowing the left hemisphere to focus on "analytic" processing and the right to concentrate on "synthetic," there is an exponential increase in the mental speed and versatility of the human brain. Lateralization of function is by far the most important development in the evolutionary history of our neurological system, and, quite remarkably, it seems to have evolved to a substantial extent only in our species.

Lateralization studies in man have encouraged zoologists to look for homologous continuities in animals, but their search has met with mixed success. An early finding by Nottobohm (1970) was that the singing ability of some birds appeared to be lateralized to either the left or the right hemisphere. In the same year, Dewson, Cowley, and Weiskrantz (1970) published their early work on the unilateral effects of cortical surgery upon auditory processing in monkeys. Dewson has explored this experimentation most fully and contends that we have failed to confront animals, such as monkeys, with tasks that are difficult enough to force lateralization of functions—skills as difficult as language is for the human species (Dewson & Burlingame, 1975). These studies collectively suggest that lateralization might have homologues in animal neurology and may have been a very gradual evolutionary development in man. I would like to cite other evidence that leads to the opposite conclusion, however. I believe that laterali-

29

zation of cognitive functions is an important qualitative difference between humans and animals and that its origin in the former has been rather abrupt and discontinuous in the evolution of our species. Although there was not enough evidence when Lenneberg wrote to address the evolution of lateralization confidently, he also believed in the unique and discontinuous evolution of language in *Homo sapiens* (Lenneberg, 1967:237).

The lateralization of birdsong, unlike lateralization of human language, is not consistently to the same side of the brain; in the great majority of cases (left-handers being a "sinister" exception!), language and languagelike activities are localized to the left hemisphere in man. Given this fact and considering other data that has been gathered from comparative neuroanatomy, it is possible that the cerebral asymmetry of vocalization in birds is not at all homologous with lateralization for speech and language in humans (Springer & Deutsch, 1981:156). As for the experimental examination of cerebral asymmetry in primates, Warren and Nonneman (1976), in a series of experiments, found no consistent patterns of lateralization for complicated cognitive tasks in rhesus monkeys:

> The results of this and four other experiments indicate that there is no cerebral dominance for problem-solving in monkeys. Recent research indicates that handedness in rhesus monkey is only superficially similar to handedness in humans; thus, monkeys appear to lack cerebral dominance for handedness as well as for cognitive behavior. (Warren & Nonneman, 1976:743–744)

Another piece of evidence supporting neurofunctional discontinuity between humans and other primates is work done by Myers (1976), which suggests that monkeys, and quite possibly chimpanzees, have almost no cortical control over vocalization; rather, their calls are innervated by the subcortical areas of the brain, located inferior and medial to the large cerebral hemispheres. Myers claims that there is little support for homologues to lateralization in primates, our most closely related relatives, because the control of vocalization in these animals is located beneath and between the two major hemispheres and thus cannot be lateralized to either side of the cerebral cortex:

> If the present interpretations are valid, it is apparent that the speech of man has evolved not from the vocal responses of lower primates, but rather speech has developed *de novo* in man during his evolutionary development beyond the level of monkeys or, indeed, apparently, of the apes. (Myers, 1976:755)

If lateralization of language and cognition is unique to contemporary *Homo sapiens,* where, when, how, and why did it evolve? These challenging questions are open to any scientists with nimble minds and reasonable imaginations, and there have been few takers (cf. Corballis & Morgan, 1978). Suffice it to say that lateralization remains a salient example of some of the qualitative changes in the human brain which, along with the quantitative increases in size, have predisposed our species to emerge as thinking and speaking animals. Just as the upper respiratory system has evolved into an organ of speech, so, apparently, has the human brain developed, in part and in concert, as an organ of language—an intricate producer and processor of communicative symbols. The evidence for this biological and evolutionary foundation for speech and language is a legacy left to us by Lenneberg, and it is the starting point from which we shall embark in our quest for a critical period.

2

ETHOLOGICAL FOUNDATIONS—
THE ORIGINS OF IMPRINTING

Any inquiry into human behavior that begins with biological foundations—
that is, with nature—sooner or later ends up with a discussion of nurture:
how environment influences natural foundations over time. In like manner,
any investigation that is founded on evolutionary links quickly progresses to
ethology, the study of how evolution and environment work in collaboration
to affect animal behavior. If this chapter had been written 50 years ago, it
might have been entitled "Language Learning as a Human Instinct," but
there has been so much muddled thinking over what is "instinctive" and
what is "learned" that conscious attempts have been made either to redefine
the word or to avoid its use altogether. Hailman (1969), for example, intentionally juxtaposed the two in a *Scientific American* article entitled "How an
instinct is learned," and Edward Wilson, the noted entomologist, flatly
states, "In the history of biology, no distinction has produced a greater
semantic morass than the one between instinct and learning" (Wilson,
1975:26). Even in the study of human behavior, most psychologists take
great pains to address the importance of both innate and experiential factors,
as Streeter (1976) was careful to do in the title of his *Nature* article "Language perception in 2 month old infants shows effects of both innate mechanisms and experience." It is not tautological, then, to examine the interplay
between the species-specific evolutionary foundation that is part of any or-

ganism's nature and the kaleidoscope of stimuli which the environment provides as the substance of nurture. The consequences of this interplay are the central concern of ethology—a relatively new word for the old science of studying animal behavior.

INSTINCTS AND IMPRINTING

If you are an impatient reader, you might feel that this excursion into the ethology of bees, stickleback fish, and greylag geese is so far removed from the enterprise of human language learning that this chapter is a mere diversion from our central concern for the critical period. But it is these very animals, however, that have given us the best evidence for critical periods in learning, and if we are to examine the possibility of a time constraint in the way that humans acquire language, we should consider the evidence for critical periods in less complicated creatures. Because we have both scientific evidence and our own intuitions that human feelings and human behavior are often mirrored in animal life, the field of ethology has captivated many social scientists and humanists.

Another justification for spending some time with these simpler species is that we were preoccupied in the first chapter with humans and their ancestors, so we should redress the imbalance with the worthwhile work on distantly related animals. And besides, for those of us who find it difficult to be objective about ourselves, it is surely easy to be disinterested about animals so far removed from us. Thanks to the magnificent research of a trio of European ethologists, the complex behavior of nonhuman animal life is much more clearly understood, and it is instructive to study the fastidious flight of the bumblebee, the whimsical mating ritual of the stickleback, and the unerring imprinting behavior of tiny goslings. Karl Von Frisch, Nikko Tinbergen, and Konrad Lorenz devoted their lives to these homely animals; they collectively founded the discipline of ethology, and for their efforts, this triumverate triumphantly walked off with the 1973 Nobel Prize in Physiology and Medicine.

Lorenz is certainly the most well known of the three, for he has helped to popularize the study of animal behavior in works like *King Solomon's Ring* (1952) and *On Aggression* (1966); therefore, it is he who provides us with the biological roots of this now popular field: "Just as the *description* of body parts is the foundation for comparative anatomy and morphology, the description of behavioral patterns is the basis for comparative behavioral research, or *ethology*" (Lorenz, 1979:6). But Lorenz's contribution goes beyond definitions and beyond years of observational studies of many animals, most notably geese; his most significant legacy has been a humanistic perception of the field by voicing the hope that the study of animal behavior will help us humans to understand ourselves better. I think it can be claimed without exaggeration that ethology has played a major role in fostering the public interest that has mushroomed over the past few decades in nature and our responsibilities to it, and probably more than any other discipline, the study of animal behavior has helped spawn another new science—ecology. Lorenz concludes one of his more recent books with a plea for this ecological perspective which is based almost entirely on his experiences as an ethologist:

> Far too much of civilized mankind today is alienated from nature. Most people seldom encounter anything but lifeless, manmade things in their daily lives and have lost the capacity to understand living things or to interact with them. That loss explains why mankind as a whole exhibits such vandalism toward the living world of nature that surrounds us and makes our way of life possible. It is an important and worthy undertaking to try to restore the lost contact between human beings and the other living organisms of our planet. In the final analysis, the success or failure of such a venture will determine whether or not mankind destroys itself along with all the other living beings on earth. (Lorenz, 1979:191)

BEES AND INNATE RELEASING MECHANISMS

Let us try to restore some of that lost contact by considering one of the smallest animals on our planet. One of the earliest books (Von Frisch, 1950) to popularize bees was an insignificant paperback written by a nineteenth-century-born German zoologist who had begun his lifelong devotion to animal behavior with a doctoral dissertation in 1910 on color changes in fish, but who, a few years after that, developed a fascination for bees and began an intensive investigation that was to last him more than half a century. When Karl Von Frisch first commenced his study of these familiar social insects, they were known to be intelligent and hardworking creatures whose ambrosia was the envy and goal of every animal with a sweet tooth. It is to Von Frisch's discredit that it took him several decades to realize that the complicated dancing patterns of worker bees in the hive was not a random melee of messengers exchanging scents but was actually an intricate system of communication about the precise location of a new source of nectar. In effect, the more Von Frisch studied these little dynamos of energy, the smarter they became. Griffin (1976) speculates that the 20-year delay between Von Frisch's discovery of waggle dancing in bees and his realization of its communicative function was due to the anthropocentric view of nature among biologists at the time. Conversely, it is to his great credit that Von Frisch disentangled this web of communication and was able to isolate, through both natural observation and experimental intervention, the different signals which bees employ to indicate the location of food to their fellow workers. These investigations of apiarian behavior have not stopped, of course, so bees appear to be getting smarter by the year, and ethologists building on the early foundations laid by Von Frisch have discovered that bees have all kinds of backup navigational systems at their disposal, including a complex scent system using pheromones (Wilson, 1975).

Von Frisch's earliest work revealed a simple but effective means of communicating the location of a source of nectar by the hardworking females of the black Austrian honeybee (*Apis mellifera carnica*). After putting colored dots on their backs in order to keep track of them inside and outside of the hive, he rapidly demonstrated that a worker which stumbled upon a sugar source in her daily foraging was able to return to the hive and attract attention by performing a "round dance" (Figure 2.1), circling quickly in a clockwise and then counterclockwise direction. The more prolonged and vigorous the dance, the more prolific the source of food nearby. The workers surrounding the incoming messenger would fly off and attempt to locate the source from the scent of the flower or the foliage picked up by the messenger bee. Because bees forage for food at great distances, up to 6 miles for some species, the round dance is a terribly imprecise system of communication for any substantial journey, and so Von Frisch discovered that a different type of signaling system, the tail-wagging dance, was used for sources farther than about 100 yards (Figure 2.1).

In the tail-wagging dance, the messenger bee wiggles rapidly in two contiguous semicircles, first one way and then the other, during which it shakes its tail excitedly. Though this dance is superficially similar to the

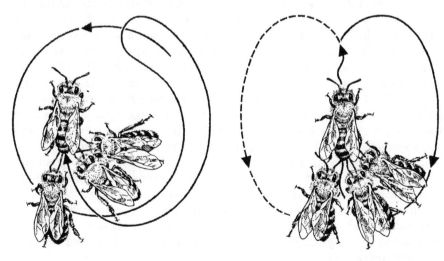

ROUND DANCE, performed by moving in alternating circles to the left and to the right, is used by honeybees to indicate the presence of a nectar source near the hive.

WAGGING DANCE indicates distance and direction of a nectar source farther away. Bee moves in a straight line, wagging her abdomen, then returns to her starting point.

Figure 2.1 Round and tail-wagging dances by bees. (*Source:* From Von Frisch, 1962:4.)

round dance, this second activity is more complex than the former in at least two ways. First, it indicates the direction of the food source through the angle formed by a line drawn from the diameter of the circuit which the bee dances and another line drawn in the direction to the sun. At least this is the system of communication when the scout bee is outside the hive on a horizontal surface. More commonly, however, the scout bee enters the hive and performs the tail-wagging dance inside on the vertical surface of a comb, and here the system is magically transposed to any angle consisting of a line drawn from the diameter of the dance and one drawn straight up and down, as if the sun's light were represented by the pull of gravity (Figure 2.2). This navigational ballet, in either its horizontal or vertical choreography, is carefully employed by other bees as an animated theodolite, and they immediately head for the source of food in a beeline.

The second way in which this tail-wagging dance represents a more elaborate form of behavior from the round dance is that it also signals the approximate distance of the food source. Its location is inversely proportional to the number of revolutions that the signaling bee waltzes per minute. For example, a dance of 30 circumambulations a minute indicates a distance of about 300 yards in the direction of the beeline, but a dance of about 22 circuits a minute suggests almost double that distance.

We have only recently learned that this intricate ritual of communication is expanded to other activities of life in a bee colony besides searching for food. A study by Seeley (1982) shows that scout bees seeking a new home for a migrating hive perform the waggle dance on the surface of the ball formed by the thousands of swarming bees, and that the direction of a suitable new hive is communicated to the swarm in the same way in which the direction of food is danced out on the interior surface of the hive under normal circumstances. The speed of the scouts' dance, however, does not signal distance in this case, since the scouts accompany the swarm and arrest its flight when it reaches the new site, but they do indicate the desirability of the new home site—the faster they dance, the more attractive the home that the scouts have discovered. Because there are several scouts simultaneously reporting on various sites from different directions, the swarming hive miraculously reaches a democratic consensus by gradually selecting the choice of the scout with the most vigorous dance. Although the communicative behavior described here is similar to that observed by Von Frisch many years previous, the work of contemporary entomologists like Seeley shows the importance of Von Frisch's work for present-day observers, and the amazing complexity and variety of behavior exhibited by these busy little insects.

One final point about Von Frisch's classic investigation of bees that is relevant to a book dealing with human language is his discovery of different dialects of dance. Along with his associate, Lindauer, he has classified differences in the way distances to food sources are signaled by various species

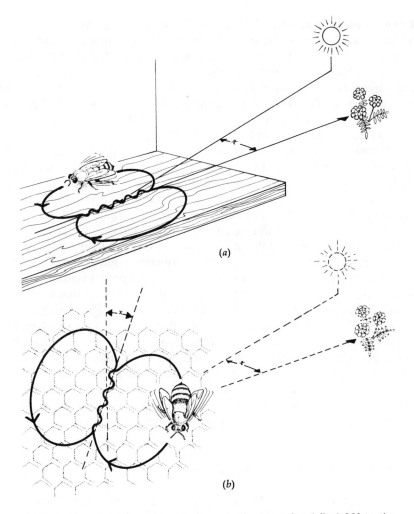

(a)

(b)

In the example shown here the run indicates a food find 20° to the right of the sun as the bee leaves the nest. If the bee performs the dance outside the hive (a), the straight run of the dance points directly toward the food source. If she performs a dance inside the hive (b), she orients herself by gravity, and the point directly overhead takes the place of the sun. The angle x (= 20°) is the same for both dances.

Figure 2.2 How bees indicate direction of nectar. (*Source:* From Wilson, 1975:178.)

of bees (Von Frisch, 1962). Italian and Austrian honeybees, although quite similar in their repertoires, do differ in the exact distance signaled by the revolutions of their respective waggle dances: The Austrian variety dances a bit more rapidly than the Italian species. Recall that distance is inversely proportional to the speed of the dance, so it is easy to divine why an Austrian bee flies too far when following the message of an Italian worker placed in her hive, because for the actual distance that the latter is signaling, the Austrian bee dances in slightly faster circuits.

Certainly, these little communicators are much more intelligent than we have given them credit for in the past, and Von Frisch's contribution to ethology is transparent. The important lesson here is the way that nature and nurture combine in the communicative system of this "primitive" animal: The bee's abilities are largely built from a genetic program, but despite this, bees respond readily to differing environmental changes and can communicate these differences rapidly and accurately. Equally interesting, they exhibit dialectal variation large enough to impede communications between species. Given these behavioral similarities, is bee communication similar to human language? Well, no and yes. Because all of this communicative ability is genetically programmed into bees, because dancing is an "innate releasing mechanism," to use the vocabulary of ethologists, bees cannot learn to communicate about environmental conditions that do not match their genetic repertoire. For example, they cannot learn to communicate about vertical distance; they are essentially two-dimensional animals. Nevertheless, since Lenneberg has shown that human language is at least partially specified genetically, like Von Frisch's bees, we also are probably partly controlled in our communication by an innate releasing mechanism.

STICKLEBACKS AND SIGN STIMULI

The second member of the Nobel trio, Nikko Tinbergen, spent much of his life examining another small creature of a completely separate pedigree and medium. Of the phylum *Chordata,* class *Osteichthyes,* order *Thoracosteida,* and family *Gasterosteidae,* the water-dwelling stickleback looks like an unappetizing cousin of the sardine. But from this fish, Tinbergen (1952) was able to isolate certain "sign stimuli" from the aquatic environment which triggered innate releasing mechanisms in either the female or the male variety. In other words, he was able to specify, for the first time, a particular stimulus in the environment which was necessary and sufficient to elicit a specific "instinctive" response in an animal. Furthermore, by manipulating this sign stimulus, Tinbergen showed that the fish was programmed to respond to only certain *tightly specific features* of the environment. A linguist would say that a stickleback was able to abstract from the maze of "etic" environmental stimuli a particular "emic" stimulus. Let me elaborate.

One of the sign stimuli investigated elicited an attack response from adult males if it was present during the stickleback mating season, and soon, Tinbergen discovered it was not just the presence of another male per se that provoked the attack, but the color associated with the sexually dimorphic markings of a male stickleback:

> Early in our work we noticed that a male patroling its territory would attack a red-colored intruder much more aggressively than a fish of some other color. Even a red mail van passing our windows at a distance of 100 yards could make the males in the tank charge its glass side in that direction. (Tinbergen 1952:2)

The stickleback literally saw the postal vehicle as a "male" van! This modest discovery was buttressed by further evidence for other kinds of sign stimuli in this species: the zigzag courtship dance of the male, the following response of the female, and the fanning of the eggs in the nest by the male to enrich their oxygen supply. The identification of sign stimuli had important implications for the field of ethology, for it demonstrated that the innate, programmed behavior of a species (say, the male attack response in stickleback fish) was triggered not by a vague, general conglomeration of stimuli (e.g., the multitude of features that would identify a sexually mature male stickleback from all other objects in the aquatic environment) but by a few very limited features (e.g., the color *red* plus *movement*). Consequently, Tinbergen's contribution was to prove that the harmony between nature and nurture is a very sophisticated balance between genetically specified behaviors of a highly codified order, and environmental stimuli of an exquisitely precise specification. As far as the attack behavior of these males is concerned, it is not at all necessary to see another male; all they have to do is to see red.

Tinbergen concludes one of his articles on his favorite fish with a whimsical apologia for devoting so much time to this freshwater vertebrate, and his defense captures, I think, part of the enchantment of ethology:

> I am often asked whether it is worthwhile to stick to one animal species for so long a time as we have been studying the stickleback. . . . Because of its relative simplicity, it shows some phenomena more clearly than the behavior of any mammal can. . . . Even those who measure the value of science by its immediate application to human affairs can learn some important lessons from the study of this insignificant little fish. (Tinbergen, 1952:6)

GREYLAGS AND CRITICAL PERIODS

We are well on our way to an important insight about the critical period and its relevance to human affairs when we turn to the third of the Nobel laureates, Konrad Lorenz, and look at the behavior of a much larger and more attractive vertebrate, the greylag goose. It may seem odd to choose the goose because geese, after all, have a reputation for being rather silly fowl, and beyond their value as chopped liver or Christmas fare, their only other domestic attribute is their usefulness as watchdogs. Lorenz himself expresses some disdain for the overbred domesticated variety but waxes eloquent about the behavior of his favorite species, the wild greylag, with almost anthropomorphic subjectivity (Lorenz, 1979). His devoted study of this graceful bird represents an apt synthesis of the study of complex, innately programmed behavior by ethologists like Von Frisch and the investigation of sign stimuli by his one-time colleague, Tinbergen, because Lorenz witnessed both phenomena interacting over brief and specifiable periods of time.

In a contribution to a *festschrift* published in 1935, Lorenz described his now-famous experiment with baby greylag geese which was, in turn, based on earlier observations made by Oskar Heinroth (1910) that goslings raised in incubators often became so attached to their nearby human companions that they would subsequently ignore adult geese which they might meet when they were a bit older. Lorenz observed that greylag goslings, hatched from incubated eggs and kept separate from any other of their own kind or from moving objects, quickly and *permanently* attached themselves to the closest surrogate goose—in this case, the young Lorenz—and would dutifully waddle after him as if he were their Pied Piper. So ardent was this following "instinct" that when other geese were present, in some cases even the actual mother that laid the eggs, the goslings would treat their own species as aliens and continue to trot after their human Mother Goose. Lorenz described this behavior as *Pragung*—German for "coinage," "stamping," or "minting," but the term now used almost universally is *imprinting*. As in Tinbergen's research with sticklebacks, the relevant environmental factors soon became apparent. The goslings were no more genetically programmed to follow the tall, gaunt figure of an Austrian zoologist than they were to trail after an exact replica of their greylag mother. Basically, they were compelled to follow the first moving object that was larger than themselves and that entered their field of vision a certain number of hours after they were hatched:

> For the freshly-hatched Greylag goose, which initially lacks an object for its following instinct, not *every* object can become a guide companion. The relevant object must possess certain characteristics which are necessary for the elicitation of following—above all, it must move. The object need not necessarily be alive, since cases are known where very young Greylag goslings attempted to attach themselves to *boats*. (Lorenz, 1935:135)

The rapidity and permanence of this imprinting response in geese originally led Lorenz to believe that it was a completely different process from learning, but approximately 20 years later, he changed his view and admitted that "imprinting" and "learning" meld with each other (Sluckin, 1964). Lorenz's research in the 1930s and his subsequent popularization of ethology encouraged psychologists interested in alternatives to traditional behavioral models of human learning to test the limits of imprinting in geese and ducks in laboratory-controlled experiments.

EXPERIMENTS WITH OTHER ANIMALS

In the early 1950s, Eckhard Hess and his staff at the University of Chicago attempted to examine the "minting" of following behavior previously observed by Heinroth and Lorenz in natural settings with a series of carefully controlled laboratory experiments with mallard ducklings. Essentially, they were interested in the role of time in the imprinting experience—how long must young ducklings be exposed to an imprinting object in order for the response to be elicited, and what was the critical age of the duckling for the imprinting to occur. In his experiments, Hess gathered wild eggs, incubated them, and reared the newly hatched ducklings in isolated breeding boxes for a certain number of hours. At various specified times, ducklings of different ages were placed on a small lighted runway and exposed to a slowly moving model of an adult mallard. The strength of the duckling's following response was then measured under a set of additional variables (e.g., male decoy vs. female decoy; decoy with taped call vs. silent decoy; etc.), and the most startling result emerged (Hess, 1958). If we define a successful following response as having a baby duck promenade down the runway at least 150 feet after the decoy in the space of about 10 minutes, the critical age for success could be limited quite precisely to a narrow window of time after hatching. That is, it appeared as if baby mallards are born with some sort of biological chronometer that tells them that between 9 and 17 hours after hatching, they must attach themselves to the nearest moving, ducklike object; exposure to such an object triggers no following response if that exposure takes place only a few hours past this period of time (Figure 2.3).

Hess's results have been replicated in other types of experiments with other species of birds. For example, in a study of New Hampshire Red chicks, Jaynes (1977) discovered that following responses could be quickly elicited even several hours after hatching, but if the strength of the following responses by the chicks was taken into consideration and measured along with the number of chicks who were successfully imprinted, a combination of the two scores indicated a critical age of about 20 hours for this domesticated fowl. Remember, then, that genetics can still be seen to play an ex-

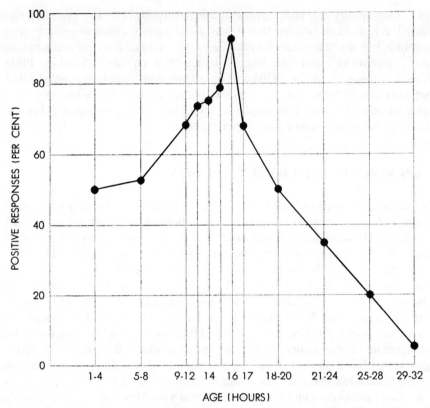

Figure 2.3 Imprinting and the critical period in ducklings. (*Source:* After Hess, 1958.)

tremely significant role in animal behavior, because it is apparent from comparing the average time for mallard ducklings to be imprinted (c. 16 hours) with the slightly longer time required for the New Hampshire Red chicks (c. 20 hours) that the innate releasing mechanism varies with each bird, and so nature sets the hour hands on the imprinting clock individually for each species.

On the other hand, environmental effects are equally significant, as Hess's early experiments demonstrated in several ways. One interesting development that came out of this was the fact that the strength of the following response was closely dependent on the amount of effort the impressionable ducklings expended in trying to pursue their newly perceived surrogate parents: "In other words, the strength of imprinting appeared to be dependent not on the duration of the imprinted period but on the effort exerted by the duckling in following the imprinted object" (Hess, 1958:6).

Another contribution of Hess's investigations was his discovery that the rapid tapering off of the following response in the ducklings that were exposed to a moving object a few hours later than the optimal time was not due to some emotional factor, such as a sudden increase in the fear of strangers. Speculating that the onset of fear responses in the little mallards at the age of about 16 to 20 hours might override the innate following response, Hess gave tranquilizers to 2-day-old ducklings and immediately noticed that although their fear of strangers diminished, these now-relaxed animals, which had not yet been exposed to a moving object, nevertheless imprinted a following response very poorly. This all suggests, of course, that the rapid decline of the following response depicted in Figure 2.3 with ducks was not an artifact of affect, caused by an increasing wariness about strangers, but was an accurate reflection of the power of the critical period. Much more has been written about the interplay of nature and nurture and the timing of this interaction (e.g., Gould & Marler, 1987), but the goundwork laid for us by these three Nobel laureates remains unchanged, and it is because of their laborious work with fairly insignificant animals that we have a standard by which we can measure human performance.

Finally, Hess and other ethologists discovered in subsequent experiments that the effects of these laboratory-manipulated studies were often reversible. This means that after goslings or ducklings had originally been imprinted on decoys or human beings, after only a few hours of contact with "real" mother geese or ducks a few days later, these laboratory-reared animals would frequently fall into line with the other members of the natural brood and waddle after the real mother in lockstep fashion. This finding prompted Hess to abandon laboratory experiments and investigate imprinting in natural or seminatural conditions (Hess, 1972), and these more recent studies of imprinting in more naturalistic conditions have confirmed all of the earlier experimental results, but they have additionally underscored the irrevocable permanence of behavior if it has been imprinted under natural situations. Imprinting research has now been undertaken with cats, dogs, mice, rats, and other rodents (see Colombo, 1982, for a comprehensive review), and there have even been studies looking at such esoteric phenomena as olfactory imprinting and the homing behavior of salmon (Hasler, 1983). Some investigators have even begun to isolate possible changes in protein synthesis in the brain that might indicate the neurological location of a memory for imprinted behavior (Horn, 1986). All of this work on various animals over the past decades has demonstrated how ethological research on imprinting has come full circle; it originated with the naturalistic observations of animals by the Nobel laureates, then it moved into the controlled arena of the laboratory, and now it has progressed to the point where ethologists have tried to combine the precision of experimental manipulation with the naturalness of normal environments where animals can function spontaneously and harmoniously. Sometimes though, things just don't go as planned (Figure 2.4).

Figure 2.4 When imprinting studies go awry. (*Source:* Gary Larson, "The Far Side.") Reprinted by permission of Chronicle Features.

Soon after this imprinting research sifted into public consciousness, developmental psychologists and pediatricians began to extrapolate from these ethological findings to the behavior of human neonates, and there have been suggestions that babies "imprinted" on smiling faces (Gray, 1958) or on the heartbeat of the mother (Salk, 1962). One early speculator (Spitz, 1945) even went so far as to claim that children would gradually wither away if separated from their mothers in the first few months of life! The ideas about neonatal imprinting have been reviewed by Sluckin (1970), who, not denying the possibility of homologous continuities between animals and humans in terms of imprinting behavior, expresses doubts about our ability to muster enough evidence to support claims like the above owing to the complexity and multiplicity of variables involved in the study of human behavior. For example, if it is important for a newborn child to be exposed to smiling from the time of birth in order to ensure that it will grow up into a smiling (though not necessarily happy) adult, what is the length of time necessary for the emergence of this "imprinted" behavior? Surely, we cannot garner sufficient evidence to prove that this gesture is elicited only during exposure to a narrow window of time—say, 16 to 17 hours after birth, like following behavior in mallard ducklings. Without evidence for a time constraint—without a critical period, that is—we are not justified in making strong claims about the smiling response being imprinted in humans; therefore, we are left with the rather vapid and general conclusion that babies who are raised in a smiling atmosphere generally grow up grinning, and those that are not tend to grow up glum.

Evidence for a precise exposure time to the type of behavior under investigation must be thoroughly substantiated before any notions about "imprinting" can be bandied about confidently, and because this evidence is, for the most part, lacking, these popular reports about "bonding" in human babies that have gained currency (e.g., Brewster & Brewster, 1981; Klaus et al., 1972) are not empirical and do not reflect the rigor and prudence of the work that has been carefully transmitted to us by the great ethologists. What we need, then, with this very complex and even more complicated animal called man is evidence for an interplay between an innately specified releasing mechanism and a specific sign stimulus occurring during a fairly precise period of time. If we can gather enough evidence for such behavior, then and only then can we talk about "imprinting" in human beings (Connolly, 1972). Colombo (1982) wisely prescribes several conditions that must be met before the term *critical period* can be applied, and we will address these toward the end of the final chapter.

We have looked at the evolutionary links of nature, and the ethological factors of the environment, but we have yet to carefully examine the question of how these two come together over a precise period of time, so it is now appropriate to see how nature and nurture come together at a certain period of human life to mold the acquisition of language. Because we are dealing with the most complicated and perverse of all creatures, we must realize that from now on, the issues and questions we will address are infinitely more difficult to pinpoint and to answer than the topics we have cursorily reviewed in this chapter, where we were fortunate to be able to focus on the complex but relatively circumscribed factors that affect the behavior of insects, fish, and birds. From now on, we will have to be much more reticent about distinguishing causal variables and more quick to acknowledge the effect of intervening factors. From now on, we will have much more difficulty identifying "innate releasing mechanisms," and "sign stimuli," and because of this, we will find the evidence for the existence of a critical period for any aspect of human learning exceedingly tenuous and elusive.

Only you can judge at the end whether sufficient evidence has been mustered to show that language learning in humans is homologous to the following behavior of greylag geese, to choose just one of the many examples ethology has provided. But if the proof of a time constraint is there, even for an animal so perplexing and exasperating as our species, then we will have evidence for both the continuity and the discontinuity of *Homo sapiens* with other creatures in biological life. Through the way in which language acquisition is somehow naturally constrained, we demonstrate continuity, and yet the existence and use of human language itself seems so far removed from what we know of animal communication (Lenneberg, 1967; Sebeok & Rosenthal, 1981) that we are also clearly unique among all species. Evidence of our contradictory place in nature is seen in the very next chapter when we consider the effect of time on human learning.

3

THE COMING OF AGE—EVIDENCE FOR THE EMERGENCE OF FOREIGN ACCENTS AT PUBERTY

In the famous soliloquy "All the world's a stage, and all the men and women merely players," in Shakespeare's *As You Like It,* the character Jacques describes the seven ages of man, from the "mewling and puking" infant to the pitiful state of second childishness, "sans teeth, sans eyes, sans taste, sans everything." The great bard himself was sharp to observe that life not only is a stage but also can be divided into stages, and this passage shows us how men and women exit from life at a stage which almost exactly recapitulates the first. Ethology has taught us that it is the initial stages of life which are the most crucial to adult behavior, so we must focus on the period of time between the mewling and puking infant and the sighing and singing lover. Somewhere during this remarkable transformation, the young human comes of age, and it is our goal here to learn how this limited span of physical, cognitive, and social maturation has far-reaching consequences for the growth of language. Although evidence will be presented later to defend the choice, at this point we will select the somewhat arbitrary figure of 12 years as an appropriate number to represent this important initial span of time for the "imprinting" of language in humans. Why 12? After all, how many eggs are in a dozen, months in a year; how many tribes of Israel are there, or cranial nerves, for that matter? An even dozen seems a reasonable approximation for the moment, and in later chapters it will become clear that all of the experimental data accumulated thus far points to 12 as a happy medium between 10 and the early teens, the range of ages suggested by the main studies undertaken on the effects of age on first and second language acquisition to date.

STAGES IN HUMAN LIFE

There are several different perspectives one could select when examining the changes which transpire during this period of human childhood, but in keeping with the biological viewpoint of the first three chapters of this book, I would like to confine our attention to two: the conspicuous changes in the body that are precipitated by the onset of puberty, and the dramatic transformations in the brain that are equally prevalent during these first dozen or so years of life. What about the important social changes in the transition from childhood to adolescence? What about the remarkable cognitive progress? Don't these deserve equal billing with biological factors, if they do not, in fact, even supersede them in relevance? Most researchers of second language acquisition would answer in the affirmative, and the adoption of this biological or "natural" perspective is certainly the minority position nowadays in this field, but I hope successive chapters will encourage you to conclude that, at the very least, all of these viewpoints *together* can lead to a more insightful understanding of how language acquisition is natural and is nurtured by the environment. And the very most I could expect to accomplish is to convince you that for some rare and esoteric abilities, such as growing up learning to speak a language sounding exactly like a native speaker, biological factors are not just useful subsidiary variables but are indeed the determinants of success. The coming of age for a language learner depends on the coming of age in body growth and in brain development.

PUBESCENCE

Desmond Morris (1967) is right, of course, in saying we among all primates are the naked apes. This notwithstanding, the term *pubescence,* the process of going through puberty, is taken from the Latin and means "to become hairy." Another Latin derivative, *adolescence,* is generally used to refer to the behavior and social stages through which a child progresses during this period of life, and thus *pubescence* usually refers only to the physiological and anatomical transformations a child experiences (Sommer, 1978). All of these changes are viewed by society as if they collectively represented a single event in the child's life. You were once a child, but now you have put away childish things. However, pubescence is actually a conglomeration of many long, gradual processes that begin at different periods of time in the first decade of life and taper off, in some cases, in the very late teens. Marshall and Tanner (1974:124) classify five of the most predominant processes: (1) acceleration and then deceleration of skeletal growth (the adolescent growth spurt); (2) altered body composition as a result of skeletal and muscular growth, together with changes in the quantity and distribution of fat; (3) development of the circulatory and respiratory systems, leading, particularly in boys, to increased strength and endurance; (4) development of the gonads, reproductive organs, secondary sex characters; (5) combination of factors, not yet fully understood, that modulates the activity of those nervous and endocrine elements that initiate and coordinate all these changes.

The biological alarm clock that precipitates all of these changes is the most intriguing category of all, and, as the authors admit in their enumeration of the fifth factor, the timing mechanism for the release of sex hormones into the blood stream of a pubescent child remains a mystery. The types of hormones and the differential effects on girls and boys have been identified, though, and it is because of their influence that sexual dimorphism becomes so obvious. The most important evolutionary consequence of these changes is that adolescents of both sexes are subsequently capable of copulation. It is one of nature's many ironies that it is only after girls and boys are made to look so very different from one another that they begin to find each other attractive. Similarity breeds contempt! The hormones produced by the adrenal cortex and the gonads are triggered by this mysterious cerebral chronometer, and they are the chemical compounds which regulate all of the changes which lead to sexual maturity in adolescents.

When do these hormonal changes take place? The determining age is not nearly as precise as the time when ducklings imprint on a moving decoy, so puberty comes at different times for different individuals and social groups. There is also the question of what variables you choose to measure the onset, peak, and completion of puberty since, as depicted in Figure 3.1, there are several somatic and physiological changes occurring. Here we can already see the complexity of human development and behavior when compared to bees, sticklebacks, and geese. For children in the United States, several large-scale surveys indicate a range from about 8½ to 13 years for puberty in girls and from about 9½ to 15 in boys (Reynolds & Wines, 1948, 1951). In light of historical records available on the age of menarche (the beginning of menstruation for girls) in several European countries over the past century, it seems that the onset age has steadily declined from an average of roughly 16 years old in about 1880 to about 13 years of age at present (Tanner, 1973). This gradual decline is evidenced in other ways for boys as well and is known in either sex as "the secular trend." This gradually earlier onset of puberty, coupled with documented evidence on increasing average heights among young people, is probably a consequence of improved nutrition in European and American children. Lest anyone worry that pubescence will continue to decline to gradually younger and younger children, it appears that growth rates and age of menarche have stabilized in the West over the past few decades (Zacharias, Rand, & Wurtman, 1976).

We must not forget that the body functions as a system of systems, both in its normal day-to-day performance and in ontological development, and because pubescence is just one set of systems, there are other changes in

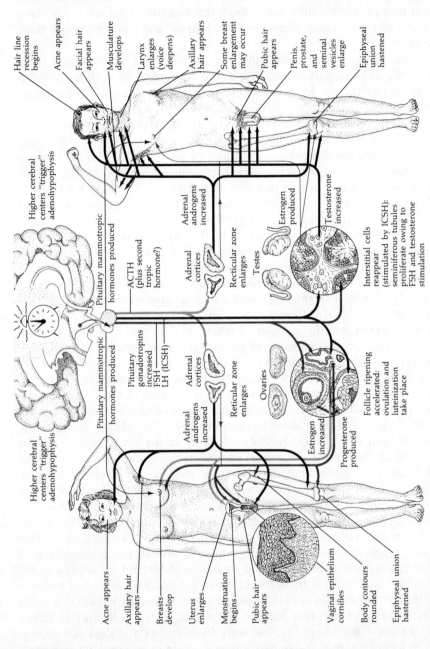

Figure 3.1 Effects of sex hormones on development at puberty. (*Source:* From Katchadourian, 1977:96.)

Hair line recession begins

Acne appears

Facial hair appears

Musculature develops

Larynx enlarges (voice deepens)

Axillary hair appears

Some breast enlargement may occur

Pubic hair appears

Penis, prostate, and seminal vesicles enlarge

Epiphyseal union hastened

Higher cerebral centers "trigger" adenohypophysis

Pituitary mammotropic hormones produced

ACTH (plus second tropic hormone?)

Adrenal cortices

Adrenal androgens increased

Reticular zone enlarges

Testes

Estrogen produced

Testosterone increased

Interstitial cells reappear (stimulated by ICSH): seminiferous tubules proliferate owing to FSH and testosterone stimulation

Pituitary gonadotropins increased FSH LH (ICSH)

Pituitary mammotropic hormones produced

Higher cerebral centers "trigger" adenohypophysis

Adrenal cortices

Adrenal androgens increased

Reticular zone enlarges

Ovaries

Estrogen increased

Progesterone produced

Follicle ripening accelerated; ovulation and luteinization take place

Acne appears

Axillary hair appears

Breasts develop

Uterus enlarges

Menstruation begins

Pubic hair appears

Vaginal epithelium cornifies

Body contours rounded

Epiphyseal union hastened

the body that are taking place prior to, simultaneous with, and subsequent to the transformations that mark puberty. Note, for example, how the curves in Figure 3.2 reveal brain ("neural") growth peaking at early childhood, how lymphoid growth leaps and then diminishes at pubescence, and how the full development of the genital organs is not completed until the very late teens.

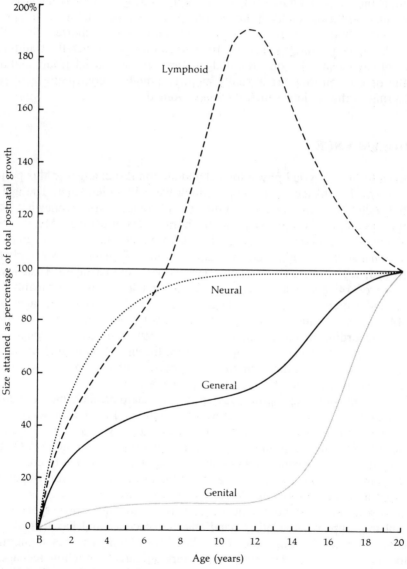

Figure 3.2 Four main human growth curves. (*Source:* From Katchadourian, 1977:25.)

The line titled "general" growth rate indicates that puberty lies roughly in the center of four major changes that demarcate the boundary between infancy and adulthood. Referring back to the statistics on age of onset cited from Tanner, and realizing that his surveys are of American children who represent the slightly younger age rate for the secular trend, we can estimate that a mean age range for both girls (8½ to 13) and boys (9½ to 15) is a combined average of approximately 9 to 14 for pubescence. This, then, is the ballpark figure we will use for measuring the time when girls and boys have put away childish things and become women and men, at least in the United States, where the majority of the research reported on in this book has been pursued. This is the time when they go through the traditional rites of passage and become full-fledged members of a social group, and this is the time when they are sexually mature enough to contribute their own offspring to the society which they have joined.

ADOLESCENCE

Linked to these myriad physiological and anatomical changes at this period of life are the changes in behavior which we call adolescence. The age at which a child becomes an adult in the eyes of society varies somewhat from culture to culture, whether there are elaborate rites of passage (Mead, 1935) or simply the assessment of the adult fare for public transportation. In more traditional societies, adolescence marks the time when a child is eligible for marriage; according to Roman law, a girl was ripe for marriage at 12, a boy at the age of 14, and Shakespeare's star-crossed lovers were probably not much older than that when they began their tragic love affair. The ages of 9 to 14 also serve, then, as an acceptable measure of adolescence, the time when, according to the psychiatrist Redl (1969), children go through two forms of migration: They "emigrate" from the life of their nuclear family and, at the same time, they "immigrate" not so much into an adult world but into the society created by their teenage peers.

Viewing both these processes, the physioanatomical changes of pubescence and the sociopsychological transformations of adolescence, is it not reasonable to assume that the two might be causally related to the emergence of a foreign accent in young members of a speech community? On the one hand, the pubescent child is now sexually mature enough to contribute new members to the community, and, all things being equal, it is important for that individual to be completely recognizable as a member of the group and to recognize potential spouses from the individual's own speech and social in-group. On the other hand, the adolescent child has formally or tacitly emigrated from the confines of the nuclear family and has immigrated into a much less homogeneous group composed largely of fellow teenagers. A foreign accent becomes a symbol of adulthood for the young child; it is a passport which identifies the child's ethnolinguistic heritage as precisely as a photograph or a fingerprint. It is only natural that once the child is old enough to emigrate from the family, old enough to immigrate into a much more diverse community, and old enough to contribute offspring to society, the child's language becomes something more than a vehicle of interpersonal communication—it becomes an emblem of birthright and betrothal.

There is another way the coming of age is marked biologically, however, and this is in the culmination of certain neurological processes in the brain at about the end of the first decade of life which appear to taper off and plateau just about the same time that the physiological and anatomical changes in puberty begin to accelerate; it is as if the brain and the body were dancing a maturational *pas de deux* where first one partner, and then the other, takes a turn at dominating the general development of the child. Again we must remember the proviso that we are dealing with changes that represent an interrelated set of systems. They do not pop out all of sudden out of the blue but have causes and antecedents that begin very early in an individual's life. This qualification has, on occasion, proven to be an unfortunate stumbling block to a proper awareness of how brain changes might account for the emergence of foreign accents in language learning, the central concern of this book, and one of my practical goals is to set the record straight concerning the possibility of a neurological or biological explanation for the appearance of nonnative accents in language acquisition if it takes place after about the first decade of life.

PENFIELD'S THOUGHTS ABOUT EARLY IMMERSION

The first person to publicize the notion that the time constraints identified by ethologists for animals might lead us to consider neurological constraints on language learning in humans was the great Canadian neurologist, Wilder Penfield. Though Penfield was a highly respected neurosurgeon and a widely traveled lecturer on topics ranging from neurophysiology to bilingual education, certain of his beliefs have proven to be erroneous in the light of the prolific data gained over the last two or three decades in neurolinguistics and neuropsychology. In a published address which he gave to the American Academy of Sciences in Boston, he claimed that (1) "when a baby comes into the world, the speech areas of the cerebral cortex are like a clean slate, ready to be written upon" (Penfield, 1963:117), and that (2) "the two cerebral hemispheres of man are homologous; they are mirror images of each other" (Penfield, 1963:119). At about the same time Penfield penned these words, evidence was beginning to mount from anatomical, clinical, and experimental sources that children are not born with a tabula rasa for language but perceive linguistic differences from birth (Morse, 1976), and one of the possible reasons for this is that the two cerebral hemispheres are not equal because, among other things, the left or "linguistic" hemisphere is slightly larger in certain places than the right in the brain of a young infant (Geschwind & Levitsky, 1968).

The discrepancy between Penfield's claims and the weight of ever-mounting evidence is one measure of the enormous growth of knowledge about brain mechanisms and is an example of the ease with which even prominent professionals can present misinformed descriptions of neuropsychological phenomena. Despite all of this, Penfield was an inspiring and generally well-informed writer and lecturer, and it was he who first articulated the belief that neurological mechanisms in the young human brain were primarily responsible for the reputed ease and accuracy displayed by children in acquiring a second tongue. You might be interested in knowing that Penfield was chosen to deliver the annual Vanuxem Lecture at Princeton University in 1956, a year after another scholar of international repute, Konrad Lorenz.

Throughout the 1950s, Penfield gave talks to various educational and civic groups with variations of the same theme: "The time to begin what might be called general schooling in secondary languages in accordance with the demands of brain capacity and normal psychology is between four and ten. The child sets off for school then, and he can still learn new languages without imposing the speech units of his mother tongue" (Penfield, 1963:132). "Speaking, and the understanding of speech, also reading and writing, depend upon the employment of certain specialized areas of the cerebrum. There is an optimal age when these special areas are plastic and receptive" (Penfield, 1963:118).

So zealously did he adhere to these beliefs that Penfield plunged his four children into a German-speaking and then a French-speaking milieu for several years of their early life to give them a chance to develop increased second language fluency. His public pronouncements on the efficacy of early schooling in second languages in addition to his personal example of immersing his own children into bilingual education at a tender age were a major impetus for the emergence of bilingual "immersion" programs in Montreal and other Canadian cities. From his collective work, I think there are three important observations we can make concerning Penfield's claims about possible neurological influences on language learning during early life: (1) The "optimal" or "critical" age was never specifically defined but is apparently accepted as coincident with the first decade of life; (2) the neurological processes reputedly influencing early success in language acquisition (and quite possibly in other skills too) are subsumed under a general rubric, "plasticity," and are never described in greater detail; and finally, (3) Penfield does not limit this critical time of learning to one or two aspects of the language; he tends to see this period as being beneficial to the acquisition of *any* part of the language—from phonetics to semantics. It is therefore evident that Penfield's insights about the role of the brain and an early age in second language learning, though popular and provocative, need to be much more tightly defined and scrutinized if they are to be accepted by the scientific community as readily as the work on animal behavior by the Nobel Prize-winning ethologists.

LENNEBERG'S NOTIONS ABOUT NEUROPLASTICITY

We return to Lenneberg for an explication of the first two observations above, and we will postpone, for the moment, a discussion of which, if any, specific linguistic skills are affected by early versus late learning. Lenneberg (1967) devoted an entire chapter of his major work to the topic of "Language in the context of growth and maturation," and in this chapter he reviews, in copious detail, information which Penfield depicted in only the broadest of strokes. These include (1) the approximate age at which neurological "plasticity" was lost, and (2) the neurological mechanisms in the maturing brain which seemed to account for the gradual loss of neurolinguistic plasticity.

Concerning the age at which plasticity might be lost, Lenneberg cites two sources of evidence from his chapter—case histories of children who have recovered from aphasic symptoms induced by brain damage at early ages, and case histories of children who because of serious cases of brain pathology (e.g., severe epilepsy or infiltrating brain tumors) have had an entire cerebral hemisphere removed. For the first set of data, Lenneberg reviews 25 cases of childhood aphasia he either culled from the clinical literature or personally collected at the Children's Hospital Medical Center of Boston, and an additional 92 childhood cases compiled from the aphasiological literature by Basser (1962). Lenneberg summarizes all of this data by making the following generalization about the ages at which the brain somehow has the ability to rebound from traumatic injury so that a child can recover even such highly complex intellectual skills as speech, which was initially adversely affected by the injury:

> Between the age of three and four, language learning and language interference may compete for a few weeks, but within a short period of time, the aphasic handicap is overcome. In patients older than four and younger than ten, the clinical picture is that of typical aphasia which gradually subsides. At the same time, the child appears to have no difficulty expanding his vocabulary and learning new and complex grammatical constructions. (Lenneberg, 1967:150)

The second set of data is truly astonishing. Owing to severe neurological conditions, like those just cited, in extreme situations neurosurgeons will perform a hemispherectomy, an operation in which they remove almost the entire hemisphere from the patient—most usually a child (Hoffman, Hen-

55

drick, Dennis, & Armstrong, 1979). For a young patient, even if the left hemisphere is the one removed, speech functions readily return, suggesting somehow that the right hemisphere has also coded information, and that the brain of a child is in some way functionally flexible (Gott, 1973). If we liken the two hemispheres to the two disk drives of a computer, for the young brain, whatever program is in disk drive A is automatically copied into disk drive B and vice versa. For the adult brain, however, to pursue the analogy, this "copying" procedure does not seem to be a natural or spontaneous phenomenon, and therefore, a hemispherectomy is rarely performed. In the rare instances where this drastic step is taken, removal of the left hemisphere portends permanent and global aphasic deficit. The hemispherectomy data, also taken from Basser, is depicted by Lenneberg in Table 3.1.

If we look at the incidence of permanent aphasia occurring from a left hemispherectomy and remember that this is the side most typically responsible for linguistic processing, we can see that only 3 out of 49 children appeared to have permanent aphasic disability, whereas all 6 of the adults with left hemispherectomies suffered complete and permanent aphasia. Lenneberg gives us strong evidence, then, that the plasticity Penfield alluded to could be linked to the ability of the brain to recuperate from injury without lasting aphasic disability. It would be just as hard to pinpoint the age when neuroplasticity is lost as it would to delimit the precise age when puberty is completed, and obviously, like all other developmental processes, we are talking about a gradual change occurring over several years and not an abrupt transformation that takes place on a certain birthday. But it seems from Lenneberg's collective evidence that the approximate age for this general loss of plasticity is around 10. We will return to this issue of plasticity and the neurological arguments both for and against it in Chapter 8, because it is an important piece of evidence for my contention that part of language learning is biologically constrained and because there are new findings and

TABLE 3.1 Speech in Children and Adults After Hemispherectomy

Lesions acquired	Hemisphere operated on	Speech not affected or improved postoperatively	Permanent aphasia
Before teens[a]	Left	49	3 (had aphasia before operation)
	Right	38	5 (had aphasia before operation)
Adult[a]	Left	None	6 (1 had aphasia before operation)
	Right	25	None

[a] Based on Basser (1962).
Source: From Lenneberg (1967: 152).

contentions about plasticity that have been published in the 20 years since Lenneberg's work. For now, however, it is enough to conclude that we have a good case for a neurological explanation of Penfield's observations that children are biologically predisposed to be better language learners than adults.

We look now at the second general area that Penfield first brought to public attention but which Lenneberg examined with care and scrutiny—the actual neurological processes which might account for the plasticity of the young brain. The rigor with which Lenneberg approaches this topic in his book might be too distracting for those of us unenamored with neurophysiology; however, in sum, in approximately 18 pages and some dozen figures, he is able to indicate how the proliferation of neurons in the cerebral cortex, the increase in neurotransmitters, the variation of amplitudes of certain brain waves, and the proportionately rapid growth of the brain relative to body weight, all taken together, suggest an early exponential increase in brain development during the first few years of life, with a definite plateauing effect for all of these neurological growth rates by puberty (refer back to the "neural" growth curve in Figure 3.2). Lenneberg did not attempt to define plasticity in terms of any combination of these neurological changes, but he did leave the impression that they, along with lateralization of functions, collectively represent the neurological substrates of language in *Homo sapiens*. His concluding paragraph for this section of his work reads like a terse telegram—summarizing the biological perspective which he so assiduously propounded: "The development of language, also a species-specific phenomenon, is related physiologically, structurally, and developmentally to the other two typically human characteristics, cerebral dominance and maturational history" (Lenneberg, 1967:175).

Concerning the third observation we made about Penfield's neurological perspective for language pedagogy, curiously, Lenneberg was really not any more precise about what aspects of foreign language acquisition might be affected than Penfield was. Although Lenneberg has been cited frequently as being the first to document a biological or neurological basis for a critical period for language learning, there are only two instances in his 1967 text where he talks about a critical period for a "foreign accent," and in both cases, his remarks are more suggestive than explicit. In a brief section entitled "Further comments on the critical period for language acquisition," he makes the following statement about postpubescent language learners:

> Most individuals of average intelligence are able to learn a second language after the beginning of their second decade, although the incidence of "language-learning-blocks" rapidly increases after puberty. Also automatic acquisition from mere exposure to a given language seems to disappear after this age, and foreign languages have to be taught and learned through a labored effort. *Foreign accents cannot be overcome easily after puberty*. However, a person *can* learn to communicate in a

foreign language at the age of forty. (Lenneberg, 1967:176; emphasis added)

The only other citation of his dealing with foreign accents is in a table concluding his chapter on the maturation of language, and again, we find that a possible relationship between the emergence of a nonnative pronunciation and certain chronological and neurological milestones is only hinted at indirectly. The potential interaction between these phenomena is once again not made explicit. In his table summarizing the data he had compiled for the fourth chapter of his book, Lenneberg simply lists, among the behaviors cited for the ages 11 to 14, the emergence of foreign accents, the irreversibility of some aphasic symptoms, and the marked lateralization of language to the left hemisphere (Lenneberg, 1967:181). His list is suggestive but not precise, much like the quotation just cited. Given that these are the only two references to the potential linkage between constraints on language learning and neurological changes, Lenneberg was not at all clear about the link.

In some ways, then, we must view Lenneberg's final statements about a critical period for second language learning as being inconclusive. He was more concerned with the development of the mother tongue in the maturation of the normal or abnormal child than he was with the acquisition of a second or foreign language by children and adults; nonetheless, his major contribution has been the exacting substantiation of a neurological basis for language acquisition in children and the documentation of evidence for the role of age as a predictor of ultimate success in this most important of all childhood enterprises. Because of this, his study of language learning in humans fits comfortably into the tradition of ethological research on complex behavior in animals left to us by Von Frisch, Tinbergen, and Lorenz:

> Thus we may speak of a critical period for language acquisition. At the beginning it is limited by lack of maturation. Its termination seems to be related to a loss of adaptability and in ability for reorganization in the brain, particularly with respect to the topographical extent of neurophysiological processes. (Lenneberg, 1967:179)

Let us look back again at the third observation made about Penfield's ideas on language-learning success and cerebral plasticity. This is the issue of what aspects of language are actually affected by neurological changes at a certain age in life. Is there an optimal period for learning sounds? words? syntax? semantic systems? all of these together? This question of what component (or components) of language are constrained by a critical period, granting the existence of such a phenomenon, is of crucial import to language teachers, and in the fields of foreign/second language pedagogy and bilingual education, this question is of primary concern whenever the ideas of Penfield and Lenneberg are considered.

SCOVEL'S IDEAS ABOUT FOREIGN ACCENTS

Ten years after the publication of Penfield and Robert's influential book on speech and brain mechanisms, and two years subsequent to the appearance of Lenneberg's classic, I wrote a short article for *Language Learning* (Scovel, 1969) that tried to address this question directly as well as to examine, however briefly, the problems of age and of what neurological process might be involved in a critical period for language acquisition. "Foreign accents, language acquisition, and cerebral dominance" was published in the fall of 1969, and though limited in length and speculative in content, it prompted several subsequent responses in the same journal—articles which we shall look at in another chapter. Essentially, I tried to argue the validity of three claims: (1) that even relatively unsophisticated native speakers can immediately identify nonnative speakers by their foreign accent, despite hearing only a brief segment of speech; (2) that the inability to sound like a native speaker might stem from the acquisition of a second language after neuroplasticity is lost and lateralization is completed (that is, complex activities like language processing or pattern recognition are lateralized to the left and right hemispheres, respectively); and (3) that a critical period is defensible only for phonological learning and cannot be expanded to include the learning of other linguistic skills, such as the acquisition of new words or new grammatical patterns. Obviously, these three claims are based heavily on the work of Penfield and Lenneberg just reviewed, and I want to emphasize the impact which the significant work of these and other scholars has had on my own thinking in this area, but I also believe that the 1969 article helped to sharpen the focus of the critical period debate by zeroing in on a specific age (before puberty), a specific neurological change (lateralization), and, above all, a specific linguistic skill (the ability to *sound* like a native speaker). Without this narrow focus, discussions concerning the existence of and the reasons for a critical or optimal period for language acquisition remain vapid and unconstructive.

Prompted by abundant anecdotal evidence that postpubescent learners never seem to be able to sound like native speakers of a target language, and that all native speakers seem to possess the ability to spot a nonnative user, even after only a few seconds of listening, for that 1969 paper, I decided to perform an informal experiment with linguistically unsophisticated speakers of American English to confirm the legitimacy of my personal observations. I made a tape of 10 speakers, each repeating the following greeting twice: "Hello Mr. Smith. How are you today?" Five of the taped subjects were native speakers of Standard American English and five were not (one of these latter was actually a native speaker of English but was born and raised in England and thus did not speak American English). All of the nonnative group knew English very well and wrote so competently that it would be impossible to ascertain whether they were "native writers" of American English given their written work alone.

After making this tape of the 10 subjects and randomly mixing the order of their voices, I then played it to 117 students at a junior high school in Ann Arbor, Michigan. All of the students were native speakers of American English, although some were speakers of nonstandard English (e.g., black English). They were asked to listen carefully to each subject and then to respond on a 20-item answer sheet with a "yes" or a "no" to the question "Is this person a native-born American?"

Despite the fact that the judgments were based on only a brief snatch of phonological information, and that this information did not come close to containing all of the segmental and suprasegmental or prosodic information about the English sound system, the accuracy rate for these young judges was about 85%, well above the 50% score one would obtain if the students randomly guessed the identity of each subject. Granted, this was a rudimentary survey and it was not statistically validated. Also, the Englishman, who was a native speaker of English but not of *American* English, and his wife, who had lived in England and in Boston for many years, who was a native speaker of American English but not of the dialect most of the students at this midwestern junior high school were used to hearing, tended to confuse the students. Thus, the former was the "non-American" most misidentified as "American," whereas the latter was the reverse, the "American" subject most frequently misidentified as being "non-American." Given this limitation in two of the subjects I chose, if we assume that most of the students were guessing on the identity of these two subjects, causing a 50% chance of error on the binary Yes/No task of the question, it is possible that these junior high judges were actually closer to an accuracy rate of about 95% on this simple recognition task.

$$85\% \text{ (original score)} + \frac{20\% \text{ (2 out of 10 subjects with indeterminate accents}}{2 \text{ (chances of guessing correctly or incorrectly on a binary question)}} = 95\%$$

From this study, it seemed reasonable to speculate that the anecdotal information was supportive of the belief that people who learn a language (or possibly even a dialect) after childhood (e.g., the five non-American English speakers in this survey) can be easily and accurately identified as nonnative speakers, even by such relatively unsophisticated native speakers as junior high school students, simply on the basis of a brief greeting heard twice. That this ability is not restricted only to linguistically knowledgeable, well-traveled, and phonetically trained native-speaking adult judges is resoundingly demonstrated by the ease with which over a hundred of these teenagers performed the task. We will see in subsequent experiments that even younger children can be just as perspicacious.

The 1969 article also made more explicit the relationship implicity expressed by Lenneberg in the fourth chapter of his book—that the emergence of foreign accents arises at the same time that lateralization of cognitive, linguistic, and perceptual functions appears to be completed in the human brain, the same time that neuroplasticity appears to terminate. I briefly reviewed the evidence given by Lenneberg (1967) and also by Basser (1962) and came up with this conclusion:

> The simultaneous occurrence of brain lateralization and the advent of foreign accents is too great a coincidence to be left neglected. It seems to me that the ability to master a language without a foreign accent before the age of twelve is directly related to the fact that lateralization has not yet become permanent; similarly, it seems apparent that the inability of adults to master a language without a foreign accent after the age of twelve is directly related to the fact that lateralization has become permanent. (Scovel, 1969:252)

The point that should be underscored here is that I did not claim that lateralization of language functions to the so-called dominant left hemisphere caused a subsequent loss of ability to speak a second or foreign language with nativelike phonology; rather, I was speculating that the loss of neuroplasticity, which in some ways is signaled by the completion of lateralization, was directly responsible for the foreign accent phenomenon.

> I mean that the same plasticity that accounts for the ability of the child's brain to relocate speech to the non-dominant hemisphere accounts for the plasticity that must be evident in the neurophysiological mechanisms underlying the production of the sound patterns of a second language. (Scovel, 1969:252)

Here, it might be helpful to pause for a moment and define some terms. Neurologists and neuropsychologists, like specialists in any field, find it useful to employ certain terms with general meanings, avoiding tightly specified definitions. Therefore, *plasticity* or *neuroplasticity* to a neurologist is a term that functions somewhat like the term *sentence* does for a syntactician—in both cases there is general agreement about the scope of meaning without any precise definition of the term being commonly accepted. In fact, too narrow a meaning for terms like this might prevent mutual agreement or understanding about neurological or linguistic behavior among the professionals in the respective fields. The danger, of course, is that definitions and behavior become circular, and we might complain that attempting to explain the existence of a critical period for phonological learning on the existence of neuroplasticity does not explain what plasticity is or how it might account for speech learning.

In Chapter 8 we will look more carefully at how we measure neuroplasticity, but in brief, this term refers to the overall ability of the young brain to program and process new patterns of behavior quickly and efficiently, and to relocate this programming and processing to different areas of the brain if there is congenital damage or injury incurred after birth. This flexibility is most pronounced in the brains of young children up to about the onset of puberty, though it continues on to a diminished degree in adults. Many neurophysiological changes appear to account for its existence, but six that will be reviewed in Chapter 8 are hemispheric specialization, the proportionately rapid growth of the brain compared to body growth, increased production of neurotransmitters, the process of myelinization, the proliferation of nerve pathways in the cerebral cortex, and the speeding up of synaptic transmission. Why is it logical to link neuroplasticity to phonological learning, but not necessarily to the learning of other linguistic skills like morphology, syntax, and pragmatics? It is obvious that pronunciation is the only part of language which is directly "physical" and which demands neuromuscular programming. Only pronunciation requires an incredible talent for sensory feedback of where the articulators are and what they are doing. And only pronunciation forces us to time and sequence motor movement. All other aspects of language are entirely "cognitive" or "perceptual" in that they have no physical reality, or they are only superficially involved with neuromuscular movement (e.g., the use of gestures or handwriting involve very rudimentary neuromuscular programming compared with the production of speech sounds). It seems logical, therefore, to link the gradual loss of neuroplasticity, which is measured by actual physical changes in the brain, to a certain decline of, or constraint on, the ability to produce the most physical aspect of human language—the production of an extremely precise phonetic repertoire. Note that the quotations from the 1969 article above focused on just one measure of plasticity, the lateralization of various behavioral functions to either the left or right hemisphere.

Our understanding of this most transparent form of cerebral specialization is much clearer now than it was in the 1950s and 1960s, when Penfield and Lenenberg were speculating about the possible effect of loss of neuroplasticity on a critical period for language learning. In particular, the view that I expressed about these effects in the 1969 article has been seriously questioned in the light of new information about the onset of lateralization. Specifically, Krashen (1973) has suggested that it is completed long before puberty, the time when accents seem to emerge, and if we accept this reanalysis, it would invalidate my claim that loss of neuroplasticity, *as evidenced by the completion of lateralization at about puberty,* accounts for the emergence of foreign accents at about this stage in life. Because this opposing viewpoint will be given due deliberation in Chapter 8, I want to postpone any discussion of the age when lateralization takes place, but you should be alerted to the controversy that this early claim of mine has engendered.

It might also be appropriate here to mention that there are many other objections and alternative explanations to the position that I adopted in the 1969 article and am presenting to you in this book. You have already been warned that the stance I am taking is the minority position, and when we detail counterarguments to my viewpoint in other chapters, you will begin to understand just how unpopular is the belief in biological constraints on language acquisition among scholars in this line of research. Along with the objection that lateralization is completed at a very early age and cannot be linked to the emergence of accents are other proposals counter to the views that I am presenting to you: (1) that adult learners *can* pass themselves off as native speakers of a target language with intense practice (Neufeld, 1980); (2) that accents arise not from a biological constraint due to loss of neuroplasticity but from a psychological constraint based on the use of incorrect acoustic models of the target phonology by adult speakers (Flege, 1981); (3) that accents are based on affective factors which interfere with the successful acquisition of a second language (Taylor, 1974); (4) that they stem from a different way of language learning owing to the natural cognitive maturation of adults (Dulay, Burt, & Krashen, 1982); or (5) that their very existence depends on the sociocultural expectations about language learning of a given speech community (Hill, 1970). But before we examine the antithesis, we must establish a thesis, and thus we turn back to my 1969 article.

The third contribution that I believe this article made to a keener understanding of the ideas first propounded by Penfield and Lenneberg is the one most directly germane to language pedagogy, for it deals with claims about what specific linguistic skills might be affected by this neurological timetable. What part of foreign language acquisition is subject to maturational constraints for postpubescent learners? How long can we afford to wait in introducing pupils to a second language in our curricula if we are interested in transmitting these skills as efficiently and accurately as possible? Lenneberg was too ardent in his adherence to a biologically based explanation for the evolution of human language and for the acquisition of a first language to deal with these very practical questions, and Penfield probably went overboard at the other end of the continuum—his public lectures and essays encouraged an ''earlier the better'' approach to foreign language teaching, always with the assumption that early immersion would almost invariably accrue benefits for the child in all language skills.

It might be wise to append a historical note here, for I do not want to give the impression that Penfield was the first person to commend the benefits of early foreign language instruction. The notion has been popular a long time, of course, and other scholars interested in language teaching have written or lectured on the apparent advantages children enjoy in picking up another tongue. The father of phonetics, Henry Sweet, who was George Bernard Shaw's "Henry Higgins" in *Pygmalion* and was also caricatured in the musical *My Fair Lady,* believed that children should start foreign languages no later than age 10 (Titone, 1968).

But returning to Penfield, it seems only proper that a theory developed in Canada, Penfield's earlier the better hypothesis, be tested in that bilingual country, and thanks to mounds of research conducted on bilingual education, centered largely at McGill University in Montreal and at the Ontario Institute for Studies in Education in Toronto, there is a large body of evidence that demonstrates that, all things being equal, young children are not at any particular advantage in learning a second language than adolescents or adults, and that Penfield was too zealous in proselytizing this early immersion approach. David Stern sums up the bilingual education evidence in an article entitled "Optimal age: Myth or reality?" and claims that really no single stage of life is more "optimal" than another: "Neither early or late second language learning are of themselves likely to be effective. . . . Each age of language learning has its own particular advantages and disadvantages" (Stern, 1976:291).

More recently, Stern (1982) painstakingly reviews a multitude of studies dealing with the relationship between measures of second language proficiency and the age of learners when they began their bilingual programs, and he concluded again that age alone was not a crucial variable in determining success.

"*Question:* Is there an optimal or critical stage for L2 learning? *Answer:* No. *Comment:* The critical age theory which was widely held 20 years ago has become increasingly eroded" (Stern, 1982:13).

In the face of Stern's august scholarship, buttressed as it is by annotated references to 13 prominent studies on child second language acquisition, what justification is there to hold that there is a critical period for *any* linguistic skill? If the critical age theory which Penfield and Lenneberg introduced and which I am so staunchly advocating has become "increasingly eroded," why should there be any interest in possible age constraints in second language acquisition by older learners? The problem here is that Stern is examining the issue in the same manner as Penfield, and this global perspective on the critical or optimal age question unfortunately obscures the evidence, because all of the language skills are lumped together. In my 1969 article, I tried to lay the groundwork for a much narrower understanding of how language might be age-related by pointing out that many postpubescent learners can master the vocabulary and syntax of a second language but never the phonology—at least not to the degree where they would be mistaken for native speakers:

Although most adults have great difficulty fully learning the syntactic patterns of a second language, there are many instances of adults learning the syntax of a second language completely and yet not being able to lose a foreign accent when speaking. Joseph Conrad, who learned English when he was eighteen, was able to write fluently and creatively in English after a few year's practice. His prose demanded almost no grammatical editing, and yet his strong foreign accent prevented him from lecturing publicly in English. (Scovel, 1969:247)

Incidentally, in one of his lectures on language learning, Penfield implied that even Conrad's pronunciation was perfect: "I have been told by one who knew Conrad after Conrad had become a famous author in England, that he spoke English beautifully. He recalls no obvious accent in the author's speech" (Penfield, 1963:131). This anecdote does not match the accounts given by Gerard (1967), one of Conrad's biographers, who claims that so thick was Conrad's Polish accent that he was too embarrassed to follow the tradition of some other famous authors in England, like Dickens, and go to America on a lucrative lecture circuit.

I have called this mismatch between the potential for perfect lexical and syntactic performance and the impossibility of perfect phonological learning in a second language, if acquired after puberty, the "Joseph Conrad phenomenon" in honor of this brilliant Polish-born English novelist (Scovel, 1981), but it is so common that we could name it after almost any educated adult language learner from almost any culture. To give a personal example, at the time when Henry Kissinger rose to national prominence in the United States, I was living abroad, and though I had read some of his addresses and interviews in the foreign press, I had never heard him speak. Imagine my surprise when I came to America and found out that the stranger I had heard, quite by chance, on a radio interview one evening was not a visiting German diplomat but the American Henry Kissinger! In a bit of diplomatic deference, Brown (1987:46) calls what I term the Joseph Conrad phenomenon "the Henry Kissinger effect."

In an address at the Washington Association of Foreign Language Teachers, Randy Marshall (1985) recounted an incident that took place during President Ford's era during a debate about the five-point proficiency scales used by the Foreign Service Institute of the State Department to assess the foreign language fluency of U.S. government personnel. Given the definition of a 5 to mean the exact equivalent of an "educated native speaker," the question arose how to rank President Ford and Henry Kissinger. It was concluded, according to Marshall, that Ford was a 5 but that Kissinger was a rank lower, at a level of 4, solely on the basis of the latter's accent and not on his degree of education or intelligence.

There are, of course, many other examples of the Joseph Conrad phenomenon, especially in American academia, where nonnative speakers comfortably communicate in English in highly technical fields, but despite their remarkable ability to publish persuasively and prolifically at or beyond the ability of most native users of English, their spoken language instantly betrays the fact that they were not raised in an English-speaking home. And so the third major observation that I made in the 1969 paper was that biological constraints on language learning do not impede ultimate achievement in any linguistic skill *except* nativelike phonological fluency. Other than this relatively insignificant aspect of language acquisition, I would concur completely with Stern and other experts on bilingualism: Age is really not that important a factor. Therefore, the critical period hypothesis, at least as I delineate it, does not support the earlier the better notion of foreign language teaching; it simply states that early exposure is a necessary but insufficient condition for achieving nativelike pronunciation. Sounding like a native is certainly a trivial and unimportant skill for the average language learner compared to the acquisition of a rich vocabulary, a versatile syntactic system, and highly fluent and facile communicative competence. This mismatch between phonological learning and the acquiring of all other language skills when seen chronologically is depicted simply in Figure 3.3.

The coming of age linguistically may not be too relevant to language teaching, but this stage of life possesses significant theoretical implications.

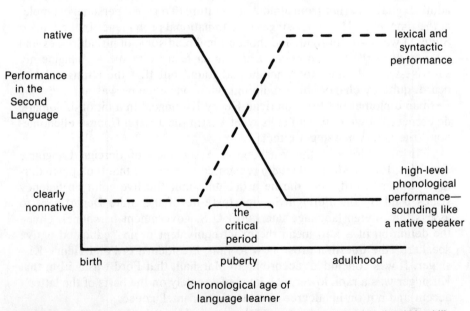

Figure 3.3 Contrasts in success between phonological learning and other linguistic skills viewed chronologically.

Is it analogous to the phenomenon of imprinting in animals? What neurological factors help shape it? What environmental factors? How long does this stage actually last: Does it end at puberty or much earlier? Most intriguing of all, why are we afflicted with this biological constraint: What possible evolutionary benefits might we reap from being marked by accented speech as adults? These questions take us back to the effects of nature and, at the same time, move us from biology to anthropology and to the new and controversial subfield of the latter called sociobiology. According to this view of human behavior, if all the world is a stage, the script has already been written by our genes, and for some reason, coded deep in the genetic theatre of our past, a critical period for language acquisition figures prominently in the opening act of the drama of human evolution.

4

GENES AND TEENS—SOCIOBIOLOGICAL EXPLANATIONS FOR THE PRESENCE OF ACCENTS AFTER PUBERTY

Many years ago, an American wife and husband team of anthropologists embarked on an intriguing experiment concerning the impact of environment on behavior (Hayes, 1950). They devoted several years to raising a baby chimp as if she were their newborn human child, and because it was during the heyday of behaviorism in the social sciences, perhaps we can forgive their zealous expectation that a Pygmalion transformation might have ensued. Vicki (aka *Pan troglodytes*) certainly learned a great deal more about American households than the average chimpanzee, but she did not become particularly human. (By the way, we will eventually turn to look at the other side of the coin in Chapter 7 and consider if children raised by animals lose their humanity.) But Vicki never did learn to form even the most rudimentary form of speech, an achievement all human children acquire, albeit over the span of a few years. Apparently, she was able to pick up one or two words (e.g., *cup, momma*), but that was about the extent of her linguistic prowess.

THE GENES OF CHIMPS—CONSTRAINTS ON SPEECH

Ironically, it was the limited achievement of this privileged primate which set the stage for a wide variety of creative experiments on other chimps by subsequent researchers. Largely through Vicki's failures, people interested in attempting to teach language to chimps have realized the anatomical limitations for human speech production in this species and have designed quite elaborate communicative systems using sign language (Gardner & Gardner, 1971), plastic symbols (Premack & Premack, 1972), and computer-operated electronic consoles (Rumbaugh & Gill, 1976). These studies have led some to suggest that although the production of human speech is not possible, as the Hayeses inadvertently demonstrated with Vicki, symbolic language, previously thought to be only the domain of humans, can be acquired by chimps (Linden, 1976). Personally, I would side with the many linguists (e.g., Katz, 1976) and psychologists (Terrance, 1979) who claim that these elaborate experiments provide no convincing proof that chimps or gorillas have come close to learning human language. Getting back to Vicki, I begin this chapter with her restricted linguistic performance because her behavior so neatly contrasts with that of her human counterparts. As anyone would expect, the behaviors of two infants, chimp and human, if they were raised together in the same house, would invariably differ because we are dealing with two disparate gene pools. Put tersely, it is hard to conceal the DNA molecules of a *Pan troglodytes,* even in a *Homo sapiens* household. (Although some human parents might sometimes suspect genes of the former are scattered among those of their own overactive offspring!) So the genetic script is exceedingly important, and we must learn something of its composition if we are to understand the critical period for language and to appreciate its role in determining foreign accents.

THE SOCIOBIOLOGICAL PERSPECTIVE

Just as Lorenz and Lenneberg were important scholars to review in our respective reflections on ethology and the biological foundation for language, it is necessary to consider the research of Edward Wilson in our deliberations about a sociobiological explanation for a critical period for language in humans, especially as detailed in his magnus opus, *Sociobiology: The New Synthesis* (Wilson, 1975). Unlike the other scholars we have considered, however, Wilson and his fellow sociobiologists are sometimes viewed controversially as scientists who have tried to rationalize or justify the ancient and universal oppression of women by men, for example. Because this misperception creates antipathy toward both the topic and its proponents, sociobiology has frequently become the whipping boy of academic conclaves for political but not scientific reasons (Gaulin, 1978). Part of this misunderstanding can be eliminated if we recognize, right off the bat, that sociobiology is not an academic field or discipline (like psycholinguistics or neurolinguistics) but a viewpoint or perspective (like rationalism or behaviorism). Thus, Wilson's tome is not an introductory textbook, but an encyclopedia of research on various phenomena in animals ranging from ants to zebras, all carefully scrutinized within "the systematic study of biological basis of all social behavior" (Wilson, 1975:4).

Once we accept this prefatory qualification, it is useful to realize that the Nobel laureates and Lenneberg were sociobiologists even before this brand-new term gained currency, and several years before the publication of Wilson's treatise, Lenneberg was clearly advocating a sociobiological stance in the ninth chapter of his major work, titled, "Toward a biological theory of language development":

> The role of language is so important for social integration that such abnormality (language deficits) reduces the opportunity for finding a partner, and if the deviation is marked enough, the individual will become virtually incommunicado with great probability of exclusion from the gene-pool. Furthermore, genetically based alterations of a given trait are likely to be accompanied by other deviations, and thus there is a greater proportion of multiply abnormal individuals among the group of people with latent structure alterations than among a random sample of the population. This is corroborated by the fact that children seen in clinics with complaints of severely defective language abilities have a greater incidence of associated abnormalities than children admitted with infectious diseases. Such confluence of abnormalities in the latent structure deficient group raises barriers to mixing in the general gene-pool and reduces the chances for perpetration of the trait. (Lenneberg, 1967:384)

Given the transparent sociobiological tone of this statement from Lenneberg, and reflecting back on what we have already covered in the first three chapters, is there any difference between the traditional Darwinian view of natural selection that has been the basis of our discussions of evolution, ethology, and imprinting and this "new synthesis" which Wilson propounds? Yes, Wilson and others of like mind are eager to point out. Biologists and ethologists of the Darwinian tradition assume that natural selection is for the group or the species, whereas proponents of sociobiology argue that natural selection is confined to the single gene:

> Natural selection is the process whereby certain genes gain representation in the following generations superior to that of other genes located at the same chromosome positions. . . . Samuel Butler's famous aphorism, that the chicken is only an egg's way of making another egg, has been modernized: the organism is only DNA's way of making more DNA. (Wilson, 1975:3)

Like any approach, sociobiology carries with it the baggage of new terms or of new meanings for familiar terminology, and we witness both lexical types in a couple of ideas that are fundamental to the understanding of what the process of genetic natural selection portends for human language acquisition. Wilson distinguishes between "proximate" causes, those that are found internal or external to the organism within its lifetime, and "ultimate" causes, which are the collective conditions in the environmental history of the genetic evolution of the organism which have ultimately caused certain kinds of adaptive behaviors in that organism. If I understand Wilson correctly, when we focus on the presence or absence of a sign stimulus (e.g., a moving red object for a male stickleback fish in heat), we are talking about proximate causation, but if we look at the propensity for the male stickleback to attack moving red objects (and the failure of other species, like the greylag geese, to act in this manner), then we are talking about ultimate causation. Somewhere in the chromosomal memory of each male stickleback fish is a gene that reflects this "ultimate" sociobiological behavior.

Wilson and other sociobiologists also use traditional terms in new ways, and perhaps this is one reason why they are occasionally misunderstood by the public. The words *altruism, selfishness,* and *spite* are examples of this terminological revisionism, and they are best defined in Figure 4.1, taken from Wilson but based on the earlier work of Hamilton (1972).

Another pair of characteristics that Wilson uses divides animals into two groups, based on the rate of population density plotted against the rate of population growth. "r strategists" are the fugitives of the animal kingdom, recolonizing rapidly in a new location when wiped out from a previous haunt. These animals are asocial, mature rapidly, have a short life-span, and exhibit little intra- or interspecies competition. The bane of the household pet, the common flea, is a typical "r strategist." By contrast, the "K strategist" is highly social, matures slowly, lives long, and displays keen intra- and interspecies competitiveness (Wilson, 1975:101). Among the animals on earth, none is a better exemplar of the mark of "K" than our species. The consequences of our being a "K strategist" in terms of the way we populate the earth and the way we aggressively compete with ourselves and with other species will be considered later in this chapter, because there are implications here for why a human gene might want to carry with it information about a critical period for human language acquisition.

THE GENES OF A SPARROW—A GENIUS FOR SONG

We have delved adequately enough into sociobiology to begin to apply it to the central concern of this book, but you should be forewarned, if you need any words of caution whatsoever, that at this point I am taking the liberty of applying this oversimplified glimpse of sociobiology as a fruitful perspective

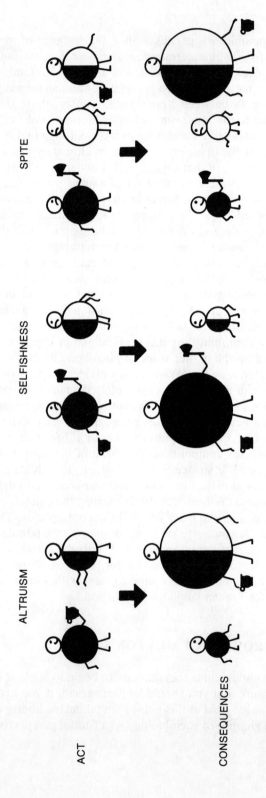

The basic conditions required for the evolution of altruism, selfishness, and spite by means of kin selection. The family has been reduced to an individual and a brother, the fraction of genes in the brother shared by common descent ($r = \frac{1}{2}$) is indicated by the shaded half of the body. A requisite of the environment (food, shelter, access to mate, and so on) is indicated by a vessel, and harmful behavior to another by an axe. *Altruism:* The altruist diminishes his/her own genetic fitness but raises the brother's fitness to the extent that the shared genes are actually increased in the next generation. *Selfishness:* The selfish individual reduces the brother's fitness but enlarges his/her own to an extent that more than compensates. *Spite:* The spiteful individual lowers the fitness of an unrelated competitor (the unshaded figure) while reducing that of his/her own or at least not improving it, however, the act increases the fitness of the brother to a degree that more than compensates.

Figure 4.1 Altruism, selfishness, and spite in genetic evolution. (*Source:* From Wilson, 1975:119.)

for looking at how natural evolution in hominid and human groups has selectively reinforced both the emergence and the recognition of foreign accents in human beings by puberty. In short, I want to claim that the critical period for language acquisition, as it was narrowly defined in Chapter 3, is part of our biological endowment because it is the result of ultimate causation and enhances our status as a K strategist.

An excellent way in which to introduce this sociobiological perspective for human language learning is to look at the fine research that has been performed on the singing of another, though less complicated, K strategist, the white-crowned sparrow. Gould and Marler (1987) review the extensive research done on the acquisition of species-specific songs in these common birds (much of the work undertaken by Marler himself), and they prove that there is an innate releasing mechanism (the bird's inherent ability to sing in its own "accent"), the necessary presence of a sign stimulus (the presence of the songs of mature white-crowned sparrows), and the meeting of both within a critical or sensitive period of time (before 50 days after hatching). Obviously, the transmission of all this information genetically has been important to the maintenance of the white-crowned gene pool, and it is evident from Figure 4.2 that the genes have orchestrated natural, nurtural, and time-related components into one harmonious blend to compose the songs of this species.

Before we examine possible analogies between birdsongs and human speech from a sociobiological perspective, I want to distinguish between those *songs,* which are generally used only by males during mating season, and bird *calls,* which, like other animal calls, tend to be used by all members of the species at any time for signaling danger or distress, maintaining contact, and similar purposes. Because calls are rudimentary forms of communication, they are not subject to the complex imprinting pattern depicted in Figure 4.2, and they are almost entirely innately specified; they are nearly identical to the knee-jerk reflex in humans. But the melodic bursts of singing by white-crowned sparrows and many other species of birds are positively operatic compared with the cacophony of the common calls, and the very complexity of the score demands the interplay of the several and often competing factors shown in the figure. If white-crowned sparrows and a vast number of other species can communicate about food and fancy, fight and flight so effectively with simple calls, why have their genes carried with them the cumbersome and complicated legacy of singing? Surely it is not solely a gift from nature to soothe the troubled heart of man. Wilson goes into some depth in answering this sociobiological question:

> Why are bird songs so complex? It has long been recognized that the vocalizations of males are important premating isolating mechanisms. This means that they collaborate with other kinds of genetically based differences to prevent species from interbreeding. In fact, as W. H.

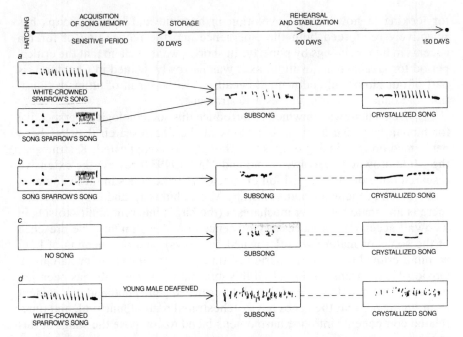

SONG LEARNING in the white-crowned sparrow exhibits great specificity: Young male birds can instinctively identify and preferentially learn the song of their own species. If a young male white-crown is played tape recordings of adult white-crown song and adult song-sparrow song (a), it first begins a period of experimentation, known as subsong, and then produces a crystallized song very similar to the white-crown song it has heard. If it is played only a tape recording of song-sparrow song (b), it will not learn the song: it still goes through subsong, but its final, crystallized song does not resemble either the song-sparrow song or the white-crown song. A bird that is played no song (c) also learns nothing. If the young bird hears a white-crown song but is deafened before subsong begins (d), it is unable to learn how to produce the song it heard; it produces an amorphous song with no melodic structure.

Figure 4.2 White-crowned sparrow song learning. (*Source:* From Gould & Marler, 1987:80.)

Thorpe has said, "it is virtually impossible to think of two closely related species of birds which, possessing full song, are not thereby specifically distinguishable." Bird watchers know that many complexes of similar species, such as the Empidonax flycatchers of North America, are best identified in the field by their songs, the same cues the birds themselves use during the breeding season. According to current speciation theory, most or all bird species begin the multiplication process when a single, ancestral species is broken into two or more geographically isolate populations. . . . As these daughter populations subsequently evolve, they inevitably diverge from one another in many genetically determined traits, representing multiple differences in the environment they inhabit. . . . The theoretically expected result, which can take place in as little

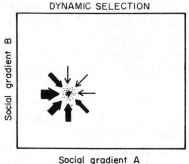

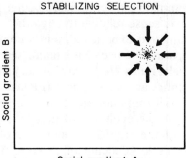

Evolution in two social traits is viewed here as the movement of an entire population of organisms on a plane of phenotypes. The rate and direction of movement is determined by the force field of opposing selection pressures (left figure). The stable states of social traits are reached when the selection pressures balance, the condition called stabilizing selection (right figure).

Figure 4.3 Dynamic and stabilizing selection. (*Source:* From Wilson, 1975:131.)

> as ten generations, is character displacement, in this case the reinforcement of premating isolating mechanisms. (Wilson, 1975:237)

The identification of birdsong is consequently crucial for mating identification and for the ultimate survival of the genes.

Another way of looking at this evolution of species-identifying song is to recognize that this process is a compromise between constantly competing pressures, and that selection moves from a situation of imbalance (or what Wilson calls "dynamic selection") among social and environmental forces to a balanced or "stabilizing" situation. The further a species moves to the right of the graphs in Figure 4.3, the more "advanced" it becomes phylogenetically, and I would surmise that the possession of speech and language is a trait that would account for a great deal of "stabilization" in our species, and since a critical period for acquisition seems to be a significant component of this human trait, it too contributes to the "stabilizing selection" of the gene pool of *Homo sapiens*.

THE PRIMACY OF SOUND IN HUMAN SOCIAL INTERACTION

We need one more piece of the puzzle before we can see the possible role of genetics in the existence of a critical period for human speech. We need evidence that even more than birds, who rely so heavily on calls and songs, humans are a highly auditory animal and rely more heavily on the oral/aural channel than on any other sense for social organization. When we generalize about the five senses that most animals possess, it is impossible to specify in a quantifiable or empirical manner how much a certain species relies on a specific sense relative to any other species, but Wilson, an entomologist by training and experience, and a comparative biologist of high repute, when comparing the use of the major senses for social organization among all the animals, ranks *Homo sapiens* as just about the most "acoustical" species in the entire animal kingdom (Figure 4.4).

Wilson is not alone, of course, in emphasizing the role of sound and voice in the evolution of human social organization. In the famous conference on the origins and evolution of language and speech, convened by the New York Academy of Sciences (Harnad, Stecklis, & Lancaster, 1976), many presenters and discussants argued for the "oralist" interpretation of the emergence of language in man, and though it is neither prudent nor necessary to fully discount the import of a "gesturalist" interpretation for language origins, it is clear from the sum total of all the 93 formal presentations made that speech and language evolved much more definitely from

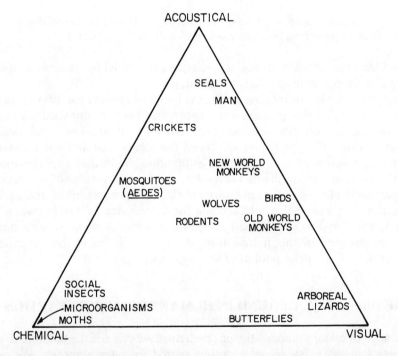

The relative importance of sensory channels in selected groups of organisms. The nearness of the group to each apex indicates, by wholly subjective and intuitive criteria, the proportionate usage of the channel in the species signal repertory. Tactile, surface-wave, and electrical channels are not included.

Figure 4.4 Comparative use of senses among the animals. (*Source:* From Wilson, 1975:240.)

hearing the sounds of the human voice than from seeing the gestures made by the face and body. At this conclave, Andrew (1976), speculated that one of the many advantages of vocalic communication is for affectionate group cohesion, especially in the open vegetation where hominids foraged. Sladen (1981) goes as far as to suggest that dyslexia, the inability to learn how to read, is a contemporary social consequence of our sociobiologically programmed propensity to communicate most efficiently via the auditory rather than the visual channel.

Strong evidence for the primacy of sound in the evolution of human social organization is found in the existence of feature detectors, groups of neurons in the brain that are organized for the perception of a very narrowly defined type of sensory activity. For example, Lettvin, Maturana, McCullock, and Pitts (1959) showed that a frog's brain has feature detectors for specific types of visual movement—for example, one for horizontal left-to-right motion and another for vertical top-to-bottom movement. Although research on the human brain is naturally more restricted and complicated, some, but certainly not all, speech researchers speculate that the identification of the segmental and suprasegmental phonemes of human speech are ultimately dependent on the presence of auditory feature detectors in the human temporal lobe (Abbs & Sussman, 1971; Stevens, 1975; Tartter & Eimas, 1975).

Tartter (1986) presents a useful analysis of how the human ear and brain are wired to perceive exquisitely minute changes in auditory information, and how the existence of feature detectors for speech plays a role in this processing, in the chapter of her text called "Speech perception and production." Studies of neonates, only a couple of months old, give us further corroboration of the presence of genetically specified feature detectors in humans which can develop to play a crucial role in the identification of human voices and language. In studies showing correlations to exposures to voiced/voicing contrasts, human infants have demonstrated a change in sucking rhythm (Morse, 1972), a change in heartbeat (Morse, 1974), and changing brain wave patterns on the left side of the skull measured by an electroencephalograph (Molfese et al., 1975). A detailed review of these and other studies is presented by Reich (1986) in the first chapter of his superb book on language development in children. These neonatal studies all imply that because little babies attend to very discrete kinds of vocalic information, such as changes in voice onset timing that are less than 35 milliseconds (that is, about a third of a hundredth of a second!), it is almost certain that the human brain is evolutionarily programmed with feature detectors (or some other perceptual system that specializes in acoustic processing) that are tuned to the kinds of acoustic information that are relevant to the processing of human speech and to the recognition of the human voice. Strange and Jenkins (1978) summarize the import of all of these findings on the relationship of innate natural abilities and early nurturing:

Infant studies suggest that prior to any extended linguistic experience, several "natural" phonetic boundaries are observed. Such boundaries have been found in linguistic environments where such distinctions are not utilized by adult speakers. Yet, adult studies across languages show marked insensitivity to acoustic dimensions that do not have phonetic significance in the adult's language. Thus, it appears that appreciable modification of innate sensitivities takes place over the formative years while one acquires his native language. (Strange & Jenkins, 1978:161)

What adaptive or selective advantage would there be for having acoustic feature detectors programmed into human DNA chains? First and foremost, they allow for the rapid acquisition of the richly detailed and complicated phonetic and phonological information that underlies all mother tongues. Human speech would not exist if nature compelled us to learn everything about it after birth, and did not provide us with a genetic head start. This is true for every level of human language, not just at the level of phonology, and Chomsky (1976) has been most vocal in arguing for the existence of prepackaged, innate abilities for a universal grammar. But my contention is that there is at least one other reason why the infant *Homo sapiens* comes already assembled with linguistic feature detectors, and this is because they are instrumental in vocal identification. I am not talking about the amazing ability of all people to recognize hundreds and hundreds of individuals simply on the basis of a phrase or two, although this skill is surely based on this same network of acoustic detection. Nor am I considering the equally astounding ability to recognize a stranger's sex (Coleman, 1971), age (Ptacek & Sander, 1966), or whether or not someone is smiling when speaking (Tartter, 1980), though these skills again are based in part not on environmental learning but on inborn propensities. Marvelous and beneficial as these acoustic abilities are for social interaction, it is the talent to identify groups and not individuals that should be our focus here, and so the question naturally arises, what adaptive advantage is there for human beings to possess the innately programmed ability to distinguish *groups* of human voices from each other?

THE COSTS AND BENEFITS OF A CRITICAL PERIOD FOR SPEECH

A sociobiologist looks at a question like this in the same way an accountant examines a new acquisition—what are the costs and benefits of such a trait? That is, a genetically encoded behavior can be seen as an *adaptation,* a trait determined by ultimate causation to have survival value for the gene. Human language behavior, at least the part of it that is biologically specified, is an example of adaptation, though my specific point is that the emergence and recognition of foreign accents in man is also adaptive. In contrast, a trait can also be viewed as a *susceptibility*. Here, the characteristic is viewed as a negative consequence of evolution—part of the cost inherent in a greater benefit. Looking at a critical period for foreign accents in this light, we could consider them a susceptibility, part of the price we must pay for being an articulate ape. Notice that, either way, we would accept a critical period for phonological acquisition as an inherent trait of our species, but its presence in our genes could be either a benefit or a liability.

Gaulin (personal communication, July 23, 1980) explains the situation like this. When we look at the evolution of the hemoglobin molecule in animal circulatory systems, its ability to carry oxygen is distinctly an adaptive trait; however, a consequence of this is that hemoglobin is also "susceptible" to carrying carbon monoxide, since the latter has the same molecular appearance as oxygen. The possibility of CO poisoning has no real selective advantage for any species, and thus it is the kind of susceptibility that must be paid to nature as tribute for the adaptive value of efficient oxygen intake into the bloodstream. Too little is known about the evolution of human speech and language to determine whether the emergence of accents is an adaptation or a susceptibility, but let me try to make a case for its possible evolutionary benefits.

Wilson devotes an entire chapter of his major work to animal aggression, a behavior that is all too apparent in the human animal, though he differs with writers like Robert Ardrey and says that man is not necessarily the most aggressive creature on this planet (Wilson, 1975:247). Regardless of our fame or infamy as a belligerent species, if we fit the biological mold described by Wilson for all other living beings, it is the presence of a stranger that incites the greatest amount of belligerence within us:

> The strongest evoker of aggressive response in animals is the sight of a stranger, especially a territorial intruder. This xenophobic principle has been documented in virtually every group of animals displaying higher forms of social organization. Male lions, normally the more lethargic adults of the prides, are jerked to attention and commence savage rounds of roaring when strange males come into view. Nothing in the day-to-day social life of an ant colony, no matter how stressful, activates the group like the introduction of a few alien workers. The principle extends to the primates. (Wilson, 1975:249)

Recall that K strategist animals, of which we humans are the paragon, are marked by their competitiveness, both within and outside the species, and then consider the statements just made by Wilson. Now reflect, if you will, on the evolution of the hominids and their predecessors, the Hominoids. How were these competing groups of roving and foraging prehumans able to tell each other apart? They did not possess the distinctive scents of insect pheromones, the remarkable plumage of birds, or the melodies of white-crowned sparrows, but they did have their voices, already evolved as a sensitive system of communication. Is it not logical to assume, then, that their voices also served as a means of identification? Through them, individuals could recognize their own groups and distinguish themselves from others; with them, they could identify strangers, even at a great distance. And so, if competitiveness and aggression are part and parcel of biological behavior, the sound of a voice was sufficient to keep friend and foe apart. Remember that among the hominids, racial differences between contiguous groups were minimal, if present at all. Remember too that poor visibility at night limited visual recognition, and once small bands grew into larger groups, it was necessary to cue in on broad, phonemic features of speech for social recognition and not just on the paralinguistic features that identify individual voices. The recognition of strangers and intimates by voice alone seems to me to be the very kind of trait that is adaptive, and this argument appears to fit the "new synthesis" of Wilson, as summarized here, as well as the overall sociobiological perspective apparently presented by Lenneberg in the quote that was cited early in this chapter.

And even if you are unwilling to accept my premise that accent emergence and recognition is an adaptive feature of hominid evolution, you could still accept its presence as a susceptible trait, a costly consequence of our biological endowment for language. In other words, an accent emerging after puberty is the price we have to pay for our preordained ability to be articulate apes: Accents are the carbon monoxide that get picked up in the natural flow of communication. Biologists like Williams (1966) have cautioned that adaptation should not be used as an explanatory factor unless absolutely necessary, so to view the emergence of accents in human language learning as a chance susceptibility is a conservative interpretation of the data. But even this nonadaptive explanation remains firmly grounded in sociobiology.

ADAPTIVE VALUE OF ACCENTS FOR TEENS IN THE GENES

The evolutionary question to answer is why has nature left us with a time constraint of about a dozen years for accentless language acquisition? It seems plausible to assume that both the emergence and the recognition of accents should develop around puberty because, as with all other animal learning, typified by the white-crowned sparrows discussed earlier in this chapter, the imprinting takes place only after an early period of social exposure. But as with all other imprinting behaviors we know of, there is a cutoff time limit for this learning, and for language acquisition in hominid evolution, imprinting wanes at puberty. Why? This is the time that hominids—and humans too, of course—are sexually prepared to contribute to the gene pool, and so it is imperative that by this point the individual is capable of distinguishing mates who might enhance the chances of future genetic success from those who might inhibit those chances.

A speculation very similar to this comes from a rather surprising source. A year after the publication of my 1969 article rearguing the Penfield and Lenneberg claims about a biologically based critical period for language, Jane Hill, an anthropologist and linguist wrote a rejoinder to my paper in the same journal (Hill, 1970). We will look more closely at her reply in Chapter 5, but in sum, although she expressed interest in many of the ideas I had propounded, she questioned the validity of my version of the critical period hypothesis from the perspective of anthropological linguistics. I found it rather surprising, then, that a few years later, she came out with a fascinating article in *American Anthropologist* entitled "On the evolutionary foundations of language" (Hill, 1972), for in this second publication, she makes an articulate and convincing case for an evolutionary explanation for the very phenomenon that was introduced in the 1969 article:

> Scovel (1969) has noted a particularly interesting aspect of this development: the presence in adult language learners (but generally not in children after the early stages) of "foreign accents." Scovel suggests, based on experimental and general observational grounds, that all normal adults beyond early adolescence can recognize a foreign accent in their native language, and are incapable of learning any new language without a foreign accent with which they can, in turn, be recognized. Scovel relates these properties to the completion of cerebral lateralization. I have suggested elsewhere (Hill 1970) that the data are not all in on this proposed universal, but let us suppose for the moment that it is genuine (and the evidence for it is very strong). What could be the adaptive significance of such a trait? The foreign accent seems, if anything, maladaptive in the present world context. However, this feature may have had considerable importance in ancient times. (Hill, 1972:312–313)

In the quotation above, Hill apparently recants her original objections to the ideas I had originally advocated about the critical period, but much more importantly, Hill herself considers the existence of foreign accents from a sociobiological perspective and sets the stage for her explanation of the emergence of accents at puberty:

> Neel (1970:816) has emphasized that a population structure involving small, relatively endogamous, highly competitive demes between which only occasional cross-breeding takes place in a structure which favors extremely rapid evolution, giving great adaptive flexibility to populations displaying this type of organization. The inability of humans to ever blend imperceptibly into new social groups after puberty would surely

foster such a population structure, and make populations in which an upper limit on language acquisition was established perhaps better off evolutionarily than one where language and dialect variation was easily overcome. I do not wish to suggest that gene flow across dialect lines is at all unusual, but we may assume in discussing long-term evolutionary trends that very minor variations in population structure might be of great significance. This hypothesis about the adaptive relevance of the foreign accent phenomenon links it, and cerebral lateralization in general, to the age at which breeding becomes possible; in evolutionary terms, this is a much more significant correlation than simply the two terms of foreign accent and cerebral dominance. (Hill, 1972:313)

A completely independent source of information that tends to substantiate Hill's ideas about the linking of foreign accents, cerebral dominance, and evolutionary success comes from very recent research done on the way hormonal changes in the body appear to affect the destiny of brain maturation. Although the experimental work on this topic is so far mainly confined to laboratory animals, the findings are suggestive. Nordeen and Yahr (1982) surgically placed pellets of estrogen on either the left or the right sides of the lower part of the brains of newborn female rats and discovered that the degree of "feminized" behavior of the rats, when they grew to maturity, appeared to be affected by whether estrogen was placed on the left or on the right side of the brain. The authors were thus able to demonstrate a link between postpubescent behavior, the presence of a sex hormone, and laterality differences in the brain. Though differing greatly in focus and content from this experiment on rats, more recent studies of humans suggest that there is a natural link between certain changes in the brain (e.g., the loss of plasticity), hormonal transformations during puberty, and the presence (or absence) of certain language abilities in adults (Geshwind & Behan, 1982; Sundet, 1986).

However tentative they might be, I find these various ideas from different scholars and different fields all sympathetic to a sociobiological explanation for the presence of a critical period for language in our species. Further, they also appear supportive of the reason why our genes are programmed to complete the acquisition of accentless speech by the time we are in our teens. Whether this phenomenon came about because it was adaptive, as Hill, for example, seems to argue, or whether it arose as a consequence of susceptibility, either way, from the sociobiological way of looking at human history, they are part of our genetic heritage, and thus, to paraphrase both Samuel Butler and Edward Wilson, accents are nature's way of keeping the language of the genes separate!

Because we have dealt with evolution and prehistoric time in this chapter, our evidence has been indirect and our logic has been necessarily inferential. I hope this excursion back to our genetic roots, like the recapitulation we also made in Chapter 1, has not been without insight, and having laid a strong foundation in the natural reasons why time has constrained our ability to learn language, I believe we are now prepared to look at the effects of nurture. And by looking at the possible effects the environment might play on our ability to acquire a new tongue, we will be able to approach these factors much more empirically, but, I trust, with just as much relevance and fascination.

5

THE INFLUENCE OF
ENVIRONMENT—NONBIOLOGICAL EXPLANATIONS
FOR A CRITICAL PERIOD

Principally in response to the demands for teaching an increasingly large number of "guest workers" the national language of the country to which they immigrate in Europe, the need to develop better programs for the instruction of French and English in bilingual Canada, and the ascension of English as the *lingua "anglica"* of today's world, necessitating its instruction as a second language in countries like Great Britain or the United States, or as a foreign language in nations like Japan or the People's Republic of China, the field of second language acquisition has grown into an autonomous and comprehensive discipline (for informative and detailed introductions, see Brown, 1987; Ellis, 1985; Klein, 1986). As a consequence, the notion that there might be a critical period for language has been bandied about extensively and is now widely known; nevertheless, it is my contention that it has not been described intensively, nor has it now become any better understood. Added to the goal of trying to emphasize the biological and evolutionary foundations for this phenomenon, one of the chief purposes I have in writing this book is to review this large body of second language acquisition literature, distilling and synthesizing the data, and going so far in some cases as to actually set the record straight. With these purposes in mind, in this chapter in particular, you will see that my firm belief in the existence of a critical period, my concentration on foreign accents, and my adherence to a biologically based explanation place me distinctly in the minority camp in second language acquisition research, and thus this is written not to belabor the obvious but to advocate the unpopular.

A NIGHT OF BLACK COWS?

There are two popular views that represent the majority of writing and thinking about maturational constraints on learning a second or foreign language today, and you will have an opportunity to become acquainted with both in this chapter. One view holds that after all the data is scrutinized thoroughly, the evidence for child–adult differences in language acquisition is either slim or nonexistent. The second view is more sanguine, at least from the perspective that I have adopted, and this is that there is indeed a critical or sensitive period for language learning, but it is not determined by biological and neurological factors—that is, it is shaped not by nature but by nurture, by environmental forces such as the emotional attitudes of the learner or the context in which the learning took place. This second view is probably the most widely held, and that is why it is the substance of this chapter, but before we reflect on the ideas and experiments that demonstrate the possible effect of environmental forces on the acquisition of a new tongue, let us hear the voices of those who would have us believe that the evidence for a critical period is either slim or simply not in. McLaughlin (1978), a researcher for whom I have great respect, sounds the first note of caution about basing any language-learning constraints on changes in neuro-plasticity:

> In conclusion, it seems that the critical period hypothesis remains very much a hypothesis at the present time. The evidence for functional local-ization based on recent research seems to rule out a strict lateralization model. There appears to be more flexibility with regard to language functions than was believed possible a decade ago. Possibly there is a critical period for the neuromuscular patterns in speech, after which time it becomes more difficult to acquire a new language without an accent. But whether this is the case, whether there are critical periods for other language skills, what the length of the critical period is in each case, and how this relates to the process of lateralization cannot be answered with any certainty. As Hegel said of Schelling's philosophy, this is a night where all cows are black. Fortunately, there is currently a great deal of research on these topics, and some answers may be available in the near future. (McLaughlin, 1978:59)

More recently, McLaughlin (1987:96) repeats his doubts about the critical period hypothesis.

A quick perusal of a variety of texts on psycholinguistics, child language acquisition, and second language learning research written by authors on both sides of the Atlantic demonstrates that McLaughlin's doubts about the possibility of a critical period for language acquisition have been well supported by other researchers. One of the earliest articles to disclaim the notion that children were better than adults in second language learning, even in the acquisition of pronunciation skills, was an experimental study of young and older students of German by Olson and Samuels (1973):

> The general assumption is that younger children learn to produce foreign words with a more native-like accent than older people. Not only is this assumption not supported by the test results but the trend is in a reverse direction favoring older students. (Olson & Samuels, 1973:267)

A few years later, Clark and Clark (1977) wrote the following in their authoritative textbook on psycholinguistics:

> The arguments about the critical period, however, have problems. Many investigators have argued that lateralization occurs long before puberty, and may be complete by age two (Kinsbourne and Smith, 1974). Whether or not there is really a critical period hasn't been established with any certainty yet either. Even if there were a critical period, it may be for the capacity for "propositional, analytic, and serial processing" and not for language alone. These arguments, then, do not necessarily suggest that humans have a capacity that is uniquely associated with language. (Clark & Clark, 1977:520)

In an experimental study published in the *TESOL Quarterly* on 325 Japanese students who had come to America in their childhood, Walberg, Hase, and Rasher (1978) concluded from their assessment of *global* language skills that there was no support for an earlier the better expectation for the learning of English:

> There is no evidence for early-age sensitivity language in the present data. The children in the sample acquire English as a function of time in the United States; the function does not appear to depend on the age of their arrival. In children of all ages in the sample, acquisition proceeds at a fast rate initially, but the amounts of gain diminish with time. (Walberg et al., 1978:436)

In a better-known study published the same year (Snow & Hoefnagel-Hohle, 1978), the authors explored a variety of second language skills in a group of young and teenage children who were learning Dutch and came to the conclusion that the critical period hypothesis (CPH) was untenable:

The results of this study fail to support the CPH. The fastest second language acquisition occurred in subjects aged 12–15 years, and the slowest occurred in subjects aged 3–5 years. Furthermore, subjects of all ages were very similar in the aspects of Dutch they found difficult and those they found easy. At least as far as second language acquisition is concerned, then, the conclusion must be drawn that a critical period extending from age 2 to age 12 does not exist. (Snow & Hoefnagel-Hohle, 1978:1125)

To balance some of these darker comments, it might be noted that a few researchers see gray cows instead of black, though authors as conciliatory as Elliot (1981) are few:

Acquisition of a second language after the critical period may be quite efficient and acquisition of a first language may still be possible. The pattern of development during childhood and adolescence may depend critically on the information-processing skills available to the child. However, we should conclude from these studies, not that biological factors are irrelevant to language-learning ability, but rather that the relation between language acquisition and its biological basis is more elusive and tantalising than earlier accounts indicated. (Elliot, 1981:27–28)

In a copiously documented review of foreign language pedagogy and second language acquisition research, especially rich in its assessment of work done in Europe, van Els, Bongaerts, Extra, van Os, and Janssen-Dieten (1984) conclude their examination of all the writing on the critical period hypothesis (CPH) with this sober summary:

To conclude, the empirical evidence does not support the CPH. Those studies which showed children to be better learners of—some aspects of—an L2, have usually been directed at L2 learning in an L2 environment. This would suggest that not age as such, but the learning situation in combination with age-related affective and cognitive factors . . . could account for some of the variation in success between child and adult L2 learning. (van Els et al., 1984:109)

Ellis (1985) addresses the critical period theory twice in his text on second language acquisition (SLA) research: At first, he is agonistic about its existence, but later on, he adopts a more pessimistic tone:

The process of the lateralization and localization of language functions is a gradual one, carrying on over many years. Different aspects of language are affected at different stages in this process. This explains why adolescents outperform adults in grammar acquisition—around sixteen a critical period affecting grammar may be reached. This explanation is, however, speculative. In general the evidence linking cerebral dominance and age differences in learners is not clear. (Ellis, 1985:108)

The available evidence suggests that the Critical Period Hypothesis is not tenable. . . . Adults seem to do well, if not better, than children, and, more important, they manifest a similar route in SLA. (p. 201)

Reich (1986) concludes his book on the acquisition of a first language by children with a chapter titled "How do they do it?" where he reviews several arguments for the universal ability of children to pick up their mother tongue. He rejects the critical period explanation, which he lists as his third argument:

We shall review the evidence for a critical period later in this chapter. Suffice it to say here that the evidence currently available does not support the existence of a critical period, and thus argument III is rendered invalid. (Reich, 1986:289)

Added to the criticisms raised by Stern (1982) in Canada (discussed in Chapter 3), other international researchers like Holmstrand (1982) in Sweden, and Klein (1986) in Germany have expressed similar doubts about biological constraints:

Arguments in favour of the theory are far from sufficient to outweigh the many critical opinions which have been put forward. Thus the survey of the theoretical arguments clearly indicates that the theory of an early optimal age for learning foreign languages is beset by serious weaknesses and should therefore be abandoned. (Holmstrand, 1982:52)

There can be no question that the critical period theory is of considerable relevance for second language teaching. If it holds true, we are obliged to employ largely different methods of teaching before and after the age of puberty. But there are serious doubts as to whether it is true. (Klein, 1986:10)

Kenji Hakuta, in his readable book on child language acquisition, expresses his own misgivings about a biologically based cause for a critical period for language acquisition, but he simultaneously voices support for nonbiological reasons why children might be more proficient language learners than adults, and because there are many who share this view that the critical period, if it does exist, is shaped by nurture and not by nature, the remainder of this chapter will focus on social, affective, and cognitive explanations. These factors Hakuta calls "malleable," as contrasted with what he terms "hardened" variables, such as the biological constraints he finds unprovable:

> I believe the weight of the evidence moves us away from attributing the pattern of lower attainment to the hardened individual. A biological explanation, at least one formulated in terms of a critical period like that found in Marler's birds, is simply not compatible with the data. (Hakuta, 1986:152)

Steinberg seems to be leaning toward the same "malleable" causes for child–adult language-learning differences when he suggests that the existence of a critical period is defensible, but due to cognitive or situational influences and not because of biology. "Lenneberg could be right but for the wrong reasons" (Steinberg, 1982:179).

Finally, Genesee seems to be discussing a similar dichotomy in his excellent review of the relevance of neuropsychological to second language learning and teaching:

> Although these findings do not support the CPH, it does not follow that they constitute sufficient evidence to reject it either. The CPH identifies two constraints on second language learning: (1) second language learning becomes more difficult and "labored" with age; and (2) native-like proficiency, especially in phonology, becomes difficult to achieve with age. These are conceptually distinct issues, although in reality they may co-occur. (Genesee, 1988:81–112)

THE INFLUENCE OF CULTURE AND SOCIETY

It is no secret that speech and language are among the most communal of all our human behaviors, and one testament of this is that in all cultures and communities, it is considered bizarre to talk to oneself. After all, you do not open your mouth to speak unless there is someone to talk to. Even in the few instances when it is "natural" to talk to yourself, when you utter a brief ejaculation of pain or disgust, this kind of "automatic" language is processed in a different part of the brain and is a completely different sociolinguistic phenomenon from normal "propositional" language (VanLancker, 1975). Therefore, it is logical for scholars of language learning to turn to sociocultural factors as a probable cause of the relative success of children in acquiring a second language if we are to accept the almost universal rejection of a biologically based critical period for language just reviewed.

Let us begin by returning to Hill (1970), who was the first to write a rejoinder to my 1969 *Language Learning* article. We are not at least surprised that Hill, an anthropologist, would opt for a sociocultural explanation for language behavior, and she provides some interesting evidence countering two of the claims that I proposed in my paper. She, like many others, questions the idea that adults can never rid themselves of a foreign accent, and second, she challenges my contention that all native speakers can instantly recognize nonnative speakers by their accent. The bulk of her counterevidence rests on a survey, carried out by Sorensen (1967), of tribal languages spoken in the northwest Amazon region, straddling the border of Colombia and Brazil. Although Tukano serves as the *lingua franca* of the area, as in many remote jungle regions multilingualism abounds, and according to Sorensen, it is so endemic in this area of the world that not only are all adults at least bi- or trilingual but, because marriage is exogamous, husbands and wives invariably speak two different languages. Additionally, since different tribes frequently live together in the same tribal dwelling, children appear to grow up in a literal longhouse of Babel. For monolingual Americans, it must be particularly astonishing to learn that the Indians in this area are almost blasé about their polyglot skills: "The Indians are quite unselfconscious about their multilingualism. They take it for granted" (Sorensen, 1967:678).

Hill rightly assumes from the Sorensen data that in a polylingual sociocultural situation like the northwest Amazon, the construct "foreign accent" would not be as viable and empirically testable as in strongly monolingual communities, such as the almost completely Anglophone society of the United States. Summarizing her review of this region of South America and a few other somewhat similar communities in other continents, she asks, "There must be many people like this in this type of multilingual society; would this type of individual know a 'foreign accent' when he heard one?" (Hill, 1970:243).

Hill's acceptance of the possible influence of sociocultural factors on the ability to sound like a native speaker does not force her, however, to overtly reject my version of the critical period hypothesis; recall that she appears to tacitly accept my ideas in her speculations about the evolutionary etiology of foreign accents, which we covered in Chapter 4 (Hill, 1972). Therefore, I read Hill's 1970 paper not as a rejection of the critical period hypothesis but as a reassessment of it, and her suggestion that certain sociocultural factors, such as the degree of multilingualism in a speech community, should be considered when we discuss "accent" is a point well taken:

> Sorensen's material offers us an example of a society where the acquisition of new languages in adulthood is commonplace and apparently expected of all members of the group. He does not answer some crucial questions posed by Scovel: are all adults in this society equally skilled in second language acquisition, and are they as good at this task as are the children? Sorensen does, however, give enough information to suggest that this group is ripe for investigation with these questions in mind. (Hill, 1970:241)

One of the first researchers in second language acquisition to focus specifically on the sociocultural factors which might impinge on language-learning success was Schumann (1978), whose "acculturation model" acknowledges the role of many nonsocial factors (e.g., "personality," "cognitive," and even "biological" variables), but at least according to his model, sociocultural and affective factors were among the most salient of the dependent variables that affected achievement. Schumann believes that the degree of success is often inversely proportional to the amount of social distance that exists between the learner's mother tongue and the target language itself. For example, one of the important causes for a Hispanic American's not learning English well in California might very well be the social distance between Spanish, clearly a second language in the United States, and English, the prestige target language. According to this model, therefore, the apparently large sociocultural distance between English and Spanish prevents speakers of the latter from successfully learning the former in the United States, but probably because there are really no "prestige" languages in the area of the Amazon described by Sorensen, successful language learning is the norm because there is little social distance among the languages, and the sociocultural and affective motivation is high. Schumann does not go into any detail about what exact linguistic skills are more directly affected in his acculturation model, but I wish to raise a criticism of this explanation that will be voiced continually throughout this review of non-biological explanations for the differential learning of second or foreign languages by adults. Why is it that the social distance model can be used to explain the lack of complete phonological learning by adults, but it apparently does not interfere with the possibility of their eventually attaining perfect lexical, morphological, syntactic, and even communicative skills? In other words, how does the acculturation model account for the Joseph Conrad phenomenon? Why is it that social distance, either real or perceived (Acton, 1979), is strong enough to prevent an adult learner of a target language from ever sounding like a native speaker, but that same social distance does not seem to be powerful enough to prevent that same learner from writing like a native writer? The objection that is being made here is not just addressed to Schumann's otherwise plausible hypothesis, of course, but it is one that applies to virtually every sociocultural, affective, and cognitive explanation for the lack of complete success in second language acquisition by adults. At the end of this chapter, I promise to resolve the apparent contradiction that you are already anticipating: If there is a biological or neurological basis for at least some parts of language acquisition, and if all the investigators reviewed in this chapter are correct in arguing the importance of nonbiological factors, who is right? And if both sides are telling the truth, whose viewpoint is the more veracious? Postponing this question for a moment, let us examine other sociocultural explanations.

In the only introduction to psycholinguistics which has a strong bias toward the acquisition of a second language as an informative way of looking at the functioning of the human mind, Hatch (1983) expresses an openness toward a biological explanation for phonological learning by adults:

If there is to be an optimal age hypothesis at all, I think it must be based, not on age or aging, but on age-related variables. Let me hedge a bit on this statement. Pronunciation and inflectional morphology are areas where we may continue to find differences with age. I am puzzled as to how to explain it. Intuitively, I buy the physiological explanations rather than age-related factors, for this phenomenon. (Hatch, 1983:197)

Despite this caveat, Hatch does speculate about one possible nonbiological reason for the apparent ultimate discrepancy between the performance of children and that of adults, and her reasoning is intriguing although, as she is quick to admit, unsubstantiated by any empirical evidence:

It may be that children are highly successful because of the small range of types of communication they require, while adults may appear highly unsuccessful because of the large range necessary for interaction at the adult level. I suggest it is because adults must read, write, speak, and understand the language in a very wide range of topics, and must participate in interactions that require understanding personal interactions and communication rules, that they fail to acquire the same phonological and morphological accuracy as children. (Hatch, 1983:192)

This discrepancy between a limited and a wide range of sociocultural situations (and expectations, we might add) may account for some of the advantages younger learners enjoy, but on deeper reflection, there does not appear to be too much substance to this idea. Following the logic of this notion, adults who learned a second language in a highly restricted curriculum would tend to be the most successful: That is, one would expect adult EFL students in a curriculum that was designed solely for handling conversational exchanges at an airline ticket counter to be more successful language learners than adults who are forced to engage in a wider range of discourse skills and linguistic activities. We know that, generally speaking, adult learners seem more successful and better motivated in curricula that are more wide-ranging (Montgomery & Eisenstein, 1986). This is one of the reasons that Hatch herself dismisses her own interesting speculation as nothing more than that.

One researcher who has written so much on nonbiological explanations for child–adult differences in language learning that his name and his work will be repeated continuously in the next few chapters is Stephen Krashen. In his model of second language acquisition (aptly described in Dulay et al., 1982), he posits both affective and cognitive causes for the relative lack of success of adult learners, but before we look at these two categories, we might consider an affective explanation which actually is based on sociocultural influences and not so much on straight emotions. Krashen's sociocultural explanation stems from his analysis of Elkind (1970), a Piagetian psychologist who believes that once children pass puberty and pass into the final stage of Piagetian development, formal operational thought, they necessarily become excessively concerned with the belief that others, probably both peers and adults, are preoccupied with their appearance and behavior. As I have noted elsewhere, the adolescent is both an emigrant and an immigrant: emigrating from childhood and immigrating into a community of young adults. And like most immigrants, a teenager naturaly feels conspicuous and self-conscious. It is this socioculturally based feeling that Krashen selects as a potential negative influence on language acquisition which, in part, accounts for the comparative success of younger learners:

> The adolescent's resulting self-consciousness, his reluctance to reveal himself, his feeling of vulnerability, may have a great effect on language learning. As in other forms of behavior involving other people, he may become very unwilling to make what *he* perceives to be an "error." . . .
> In the domain of phonology, this gives rise to the foreign accent. (Krashen, 1975*b*:221)

If you have not already realized it, the boundaries between "social," "affective," and "cognitive" variables is distinctly blurry, as the Krashen reference just cited serves to illustrate, and so the concluding examples of sociocultural variables I want to review could just as well serve as introductory samples of affective factors. I include them under this former category rather than the latter simply because I believe that they represent ways in which sociocultural conditions tend to enhance certain emotional attitudes toward language learning and not the other way around. One of the most appealing reasons I have heard for the existence of foreign accents in adults is that they are intentionally preserved as a charming emblem of international appeal. We all know the import of imports. A French appellation for a piece of dead cow increases the food's price and palatibility, at least in the United States. Bley-Vroman (personal communication, November 8, 1985) calls this perhaps intentional linguistic ostentation the "Charles Boyer phenomenon," but it could just as well be termed the Zsa Zsa Gabor effect. Unfortunately, as social psychologists have amply demonstrated, sounding different can be a liability, and thus the same speaker, completely bilingual in French and English, is subjectively judged by French or English monolinguals with fully different values depending on whether the person is speaking French or speaking English (Lambert, Hodgson, Gardner, & Fillenbaum, 1960). More recent research has simply served to underscore the immediate and not always positive impression that native speakers have about nonstandard or nonnative speakers (Eisenstein, 1982; Shuy & Fasold, 1973).

Looking at the lack of complete success among ESL-learning adult immigrants, Cook (1978) hints at a slightly different kind of social motivation for accents—a reluctance to surrender one's identity:

While one does not wish to deny the strong impression that many people have that some adult immigrants speak their new language poorly. This may be ascribed not so much to an intrinsic deficit in the adult's mind as to differences in situation, in motivation, in willingness to surrender part of one's identity, and so on, that separate children from adults. (Cook, 1978:82)

THE EFFECT OF AFFECT

Surprisingly enough, not much has been written about the possible effect of emotions on the advent of foreign accents around puberty. Although almost anyone interested in the teaching or learning of performance skills such as music, athletics, or language is aware of the import of emotional variables, surely outweighing the influence of sociocultural or cognitive factors, affect tends to be subsumed by categories like "motivation" or "personality." And when people do try to study emotions and their beneficial or detrimental effects on language learning, they often confuse affect with other psychological phenomena or oversimplify the role that emotions play in language acquisition (Scovel, 1978). You have just read some ways in which social and cultural factors interplay with affective variables in the way foreign accents are either produced or perceived. Knowing all of this, we may not be quite so mystified by the relative lack of studies focusing exclusively on the potential relationship between emotions and accents.

Taylor (1974) was one of the few and certainly one of the earliest second language acquisition researchers to write explicitly about the possible affective etiology of foreign accents. After a thorough literature review, he makes several conclusions: that the evidence for a biologically based critical period is weak, that the cognitive strategies employed by children and adults appear to be similar, and, therefore, that only affective factors can legitimately count as a probable cause for the acknowledged differences between child and adult language-learning success:

In view of these affective differences between children and adults and between successful and unsuccessful adult language learners, it seems likely that affective psychological variables may constitute the major reason why adults are not always as successful as children in language acquisition. If we further assume that the psychological learning strategies involved in language acquisition are basically the same for children and adults, differing essentially in the degree of cognitive maturity of the learner, affective variables take on special significance. What may be necessary, then, for the adult to acquire real native proficiency in a second language is a persevering motivation, the desire to identify with another cultural group integratively, and the ability to overcome the empathetic barriers set up by ego-boundaries. (Taylor, 1974:33–34)

94

Certainly, we do not want to deny the benefit that many of the attributes Taylor has listed provide for the good language learner, and again, it should be made clear that I am in no way downplaying the importance of sociocultural, affective, or cognitive forces in the shaping of successful acquisition. But remembering that our attention in this book is directed to the unique ability of children to acquire a native tongue perfectly, our ultimate concern lies not with what helps make language learners good but with what helps make them *perfect*. Therefore, like other nonbiological factors nominated as probable causes of foreign accents, the affective factors that Taylor advocates in his review of the research fail as adequate explanations. Even granting the assumption that children and adults do not vary greatly in cognition (an assumption that will be challenged in the next section), there are several shortcomings in attributing foreign accents, in particular, to emotional causes. For one thing, it is not at all appropriate to assume that when it comes to picking up a language, children are laid-back and adults are uptight. One need not be a parent or an elementary teacher to realize that affective factors play a powerful facilitating and debilitating role in the life and the learning of young children, and it is naive to assume that emotions work to the benefit of the young and to the detriment of the old.

The most telling criticism of the affective cause of accents, however, lies once again in the existence of the Joseph Conrad phenomenon. Why is it that emotional factors interfere with the learning of the phonology of a foreign language after puberty but do not ultimately impede the acquisition of any other linguistic skill? Why is it that the same negative emotions that somehow make an adult sound slightly different from a native speaker do not prevent that very same adult from writing like a native speaker? Why is it that the anxiety that prevents adults from speaking without an accent does not constrain them in any apparent way from acquiring extremely complex syntactic patterns or a vast vocabulary? Here, I am really more interested in challenging Krashen's belief that there is an "affective filter" through which all language input must pass (cf. Dulay et al., 1982) than I am in critiquing Taylor's reliance on an affective explanation. It simply does not seem logical to me that emotions work for good or for ill at the highest degrees of one level of language learning (phonology) but do not seem to influence the very highest reaches of any other levels. There is a reason why a biological explanation for the emergence of accents does affect acquisition differentially, but I would like to finish reviewing all of the nonbiological explanations before revealing this reason to you.

A few years before Taylor's article was published, and mentioned in his review, an almost notorious experiment was undertaken at the University of Michigan which implicates the importance of emotions in picking up a new tongue and in which I had the pleasure of participating. Guiora, Beit-Hallami, Brannon, Dull, and Scovel (1972) conducted an experiment which tried to prove that empathy, experimentally introduced in this study through the ingestion of differing amounts of alcohol, was related to the ability to accurately pronounce the sounds of a foreign tongue. The idea, conceptualized by Guiora, was that empathy, or "permeability of ego boundaries," to be a bit more precise, was directly related to success in sounding more like a native speaker in a new language. Intuitively, I think you will agree that the notion is attractive, and I for one still find it appealing—that the more capable you are of entering into someone else's personality, the more successful you are in sounding like that person.

Despite the intuitive attractiveness of this notion, and despite the clever experimental design, the collaborative industry of the researchers, and the publicity received (*Psychology Today,* in one of its early issues, wrote up this study of drinking and success in learning Thai under the caption "Thai-ing one on"!), the results are not as satisfactory as they are often perceived to be. The published report of the experiment (Guiora et al., 1972) leads one to the conclusion that enough alcohol to lower inhibitions (and raise empathy) will help improve the learning of a foreign phonology— as scrupulously measured in our analysis of the subjects' attempts to pronounce Thai syllables which they heard on a tape recording. But, as you might expect, too much alcohol will eventually lead to a decline in pronunciation ability, simply because there comes a point when all neuromuscular coordination is so adversely affected that the subjects' speech becomes slurred. Unfortunately, if you read the article carefully, you will find that only about half of the subjects performed in the reported manner; the other half were not significantly and favorably influenced through the ingestion of alcohol. In sum, even this well-known attempt to empiricize the importance of emotions in learning to speak a foreign language accurately is inconclusive, and we are therefore forced to conclude that affective variables cannot account for the imperfect second language acquisition of adults.

If the existence of accents in adult speech is not an affair of the heart, then perhaps it is an artifact of the mind, and this is why we will turn now to cognitive influences.

COGNITIVE CAUSES

No one in second language acquisition research has thought more carefully or written more prolifically about the role of cognitive factors in language learning than Krashen; what is not common knowledge, however, but becomes clear after examining the evolution of Krashen's "monitor" model, is that the impetus for his model of second language acquisition and its explicit distinction between conscious "learning" and spontaneous "acquisition" (1981) came from one of his first publications in the field, an article written largely as a rejoinder to my 1969 article and published in the same journal (Krashen, 1973). We will review Krashen's criticisms of a neurological basis for child–adult differences in language acquisition in Chapter 8, so I will not take time to address the contents of the 1973 article here, but by rejecting a biological explanation for certain language-learning phenomena, Krashen naturally introduced the question of what variables did indeed play an intervening role. It did not take long for him to implicate affective and cognitive factors, and 2 years later, he published "The critical period for language acquisition and its possible bases," a reiteration and expansion of his earlier article, and it was in this article that we get the first hints of the learning-acquisition dichotomy that was to be the cornerstone of Krashen's monitor model:

> What I have said here implies the ability to "acquire" a language disappears completely with the onset of formal operations for everyone. Certainly the presence of rule isolation and feedback in all teaching systems presumes this is the case. (Krashen, 1975b:221)

Remembering, of course, that his model does not focus exclusively on cognitive factors, and recognizing that the already-discussed affective filter is also considerably important, our concern here is with the nature of the "monitor" component and its role in regulating language-learning output (Figure 5.1).

Briefly, the model claims that all input from the second language first goes through the affective filter, the sine qua non of language acquisition, for if the filter is not "open," there will ultimately be insufficient intake for the person to process the new language adequately. Assuming that affective conditions are favorable, however, the intake is processed by the innate "organizer," something similar, I believe, to Chomsky's Language Acquisi-

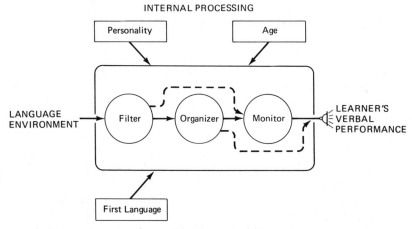

Figure 5.1 Krashen's model of second language acquisition. (*Source:* From Dulay, Burt, & Krashen, 1982:6.)

tion Device (Chomsky, 1965), and then the person is ready to produce spontaneous, natural, and relatively error-free speech. The only overtly active cognitive component of this framework is the monitor, which functions largely in a negative way. If the person picking up a new tongue begins to do so in a conscious manner, then the monitor is activated, and performance in the second language becomes labored and unnatural—in short, the language becomes learned and not acquired: "A fundamental claim of the Monitor Model is that conscious learning may not initiate performance: learning may only be used as a Monitor." (Krashen, 1981:156).

Irrespective of the accuracy and utility of this model and methodologies that have been constructed from it (e.g., *The Natural Approach* by Krashen and Terrell, 1983), the last two points are probably the most controversial—that learning activities are inefficient for successful, communicative language performance, and that these activities cannot be internalized into more spontaneous and efficacious "acquisition." Of chief concern to us, though, is whether or not monitoring accounts for the indelibility of foreign accents in adults. Krashen has never made this claim, but it is interesting to me that even though his rejection of neurological causes for accents initially propelled him into a model for language learning that incorporated only nonbiological influences for second language performance, he has not faced the question of whether the affective filter, the cognitive monitor, or some combination of both is the cause of accented speech in postpubescent foreign language learners *or* acquirers. Be that as it may, if we were to suggest that the culprit in this case is the monitor—that once children have crossed the Piagetian threshold of operational thinking after puberty and start to think about how they are going to articulate a new tongue—we still have to explain away the Joseph Conrad phenomenon. How is it that for highly advanced acquirers of a second language, the monitor somehow always impedes phonological production enough to identify the person as a nonnative, but that the monitor is never powerful enough to affect a nonnative use of vocabulary or of grammatical structures? Popular as Krashen's views may be, and despite the fact they stem historically from his own interest in the possibility of biological constraints on language acquisition, they do not help us understand why there should be a cognitive (or an affective) barrier keeping adults from sounding like native speakers in a second language.

An equally prominent researcher, Jim Cummins, has also written a great deal about language acquisition and has been concerned about the relationship between linguistic and cognitive factors in bilingual children as they progress through the acquisition of two languages simultaneously. It is hard to single out from his ample publications one representative article, but especially germane to our discussion here is his article "Age on arrival and immigrant second language learning in Canada: A reassessment" (Cummins, 1981). The Cummins study is a reanalysis of an earlier Canadian study on bilingualism by Ramsey and Wright (1972) involving 5386 ESL schoolchildren in Toronto and using multiple measures of language proficiency. In his careful scrutiny of this voluminous data, Cummins looked at which factor seemed to play the most salient role in increasing proficiency scores—the age of arrival of the children (the earlier the better) or the length of residence of the children (the longer the better)—and he concluded that the preponderance of scores were in favor of the latter. This led him to conclude that the cognitive maturity that naturally accrued with longer length of residence overrode any advantages that being exposed at a younger age might provide:

> The reanalysis of the Ramsey and Wright data is consistent with virtually all previous studies in showing that older learners acquire cognitive/academic L2 skills more rapidly than younger learners. Older learners also appeared to have an advantage in acquiring L2 sound discrimination and recognition skills but these findings should be treated cautiously due to the questionable validity of the tests. (Cummins, 1981:147–148)

There is nothing unique in Cummins's acknowledgment of the importance of cognitive maturation in second language learning success: Felix (1982), Genesee (1987), Menyuk (1977), Rosanksy (1975), and Snow and Hoefnagel-Hohle (1978) are some of those who have underscored the advantages of an older child, because more mature learners are better problem solvers than their more immature counterparts, but none of these authors have been able to come up with a solution to the Joseph Conrad conundrum: Why doesn't the same cognitive maturity which makes older children learn syntactic patterns faster and/or more effectively enable adolescents to overcome foreign accents? The concerns of Cummins and the other researchers just cited are correctly directed to the most important second language skills—the acquisition of vocabulary, the learning of grammatical patterns, the very demanding and academically crucial skills of literacy—and this is why so little has been written about any direct relationship between cognitive factors and foreign accents, but I think it is necessary to demonstrate that cognitive variables appear to be just as irrelevant as affective variables in trying to account for the emergence of accented speech after puberty.

To conclude this section, we ought to consider the possibility that improved cognition might actually interfere with successful language acquisition. This is contrary to the view espoused by the authors just reviewed, but it does seem to fit the stance that Krashen has taken in his model. Too much monitoring, too much tinkering with second language output, actually might do more harm than good. This is an idea that is also proffered in some recent research by Johnson and Newport (1987). They propose a biologically based explanation both for language acquisition and for the influence of cognitive changes in the maturing learner:

The traditional view of critical period effects in language learning has been that there is maturational change in a specific language acquisition device (Lenneberg, 1967; Chomsky, 1981). Such a view, with some modifications to incorporate the detailed points of maturational change, is consistent with our results. Also consistent with our results are views which hypothesize more general cognitive changes over maturation (see, for example, Newport, 1984). On this view, an increase in certain cognitive abilities may, paradoxically make language learning more difficult. (Johnson & Newport: 1987:49–50)

Their experimentation is restricted to tapping intuitions about syntactic phenomena; consequently, however pertinent their research and their ideas about language-learning constraints might hold for a better understanding of the acquisition of grammar, they do not help explicate the causes of foreign accents.

BACK TO BIOLOGY

The misgivings many researchers have about biological constraints for language learning with which we began this chapter and to which I will speak in the next chapter, have led most people interested in second language acquisition to look for sociocultural, affective, or cognitive reasons why a younger generation of language learners generally outperforms an older one, but we can see from a rapid review of these nonbiological explanations that important though they may be to morphological, lexical, grammatical, and communicative competence, they do not account for the excessively restricted goal of producing accentless speech in the target language. It is obvious that sociocultural, affective, and cognitive variables are relevant to the successful acquisition of phonology: Acton (1984), for example, has shown remarkable success improving the pronunciation skills of "fossilized" ESL learners, some many decades beyond puberty, not just by concentrating on teaching articulatory skills and awareness but by dealing with all the considerations above. Acknowledging the relevance of these to the learning and to the teaching of all facets of foreign language performance is not identical to admitting that any or all of them account for the existence of accents in adult speech. One can concede that rigorous physical training, strong motivation, and mental discipline are key ingredients to becoming a successful distance runner, to draw an athletic analogy, but the presence of these criteria do not obviate the importance of good genes—body build, muscle composition, and innate cardiovascular efficiency. So it is with second language acquisition: The influence of the variables we have discussed in this chapter on successful learning should not preclude the likely influence of biological constraints on certain types of language acquisition performance.

Now, to turn the tables on myself and ask how I would account for the Joseph Conrad phenomenon. Why is it that there is a critical period for accent, but no biologically constrained time limit on lexical and syntactic learning? As I have already suggested previously (Scovel, 1969), phonological production is the only aspect of language performance that has a neuromuscular basis. We can discount calligraphy or penmanship here because it involves comparatively little of the exquisitely intricate and complex neuromuscular programming that is demanded in human speech (cf. MacKay, 1987:Chapter 9; Tartter, 1986:Chapter 7). But if we look at any other level of linguistic skill—the ability to learn new words, to memorize new morphological inflections, to master even the most convoluted syntactic patterns, or to employ the right communicative message at the opportune sociolinguistic moment—none of these require neuromotor involvement; none of them have a "physical" reality. They are exclusively cerebral and psychological. This is why it is obvious to me that a neurologically based imprinting constraint on human behavior would affect only a highly complex *physical* phenomenon such as human speech and would not necessarily inhibit nonphysical, mental behavior. The ultimate explanation for the existence of foreign accents is that they are biologically based; they cannot be explained by variables that are derived from personality or environment. And this is why we have to look once again at the nexus of nature and nurture at a certain point of development and consider the tide of time.

6

THE TIDE OF TIME—THE EMERGENCE OF
PHONOLOGICAL CONSTRAINTS AT PUBERTY

About the time that Lenneberg's *Biological Foundations of Language* was published, several second language acquisition researchers came out with articles suggesting alternatives to the traditional view at that time, that almost all mistakes made by a learner of a new language came from the interference caused by the linguistic differences between the student's mother tongue and the second language being learned. The alternative view that was presented by these researchers, now some two decades ago, was that there were other reasons why second language learners made mistakes in addition to their natural tendency to fall back on their first language: They might overgeneralize a new rule; they might try to use a simple communication strategy; and they might even have been given the wrong patterns by their teachers (a source of errors that those of us who teach foreign languages are quick to reject). One of the influential publications in this era was by Selinker (1972), for it was he who coined the term *fossilization,* and who later, in a series of articles coauthored with Lamendella (e.g., Selinker & Lamendella, 1979), tried to account for the permanent presence of certain errors in the speech of even highly advanced second language learners. The best example of fossilization, of course, is a foreign accent, because it is so pervasive in speech and because it contrasts so starkly with the otherwise nativelike and errorless language use of superbly proficient foreign language speakers.

Selinker himself, incidentally, does not adhere to the claims I have made about the Joseph Conrad effect and differs with me in at least two respects. He has suggested that not all adult learners end up with a foreign accent: About 5% are able to pick up a new language sounding exactly like a native speaker (Selinker, 1972). He provides no experimental evidence for this number, however, and in this chapter we will see strong empirical support for my claim that virtually no adults can pass themselves off as natives in a new language. And in the final chapter of this book, we will return to discuss exceptions, but if they exist, they certainly do not come close to the 5% figure rather arbitrarily cited by Selinker. The second way in which we differ is that he believes there may be syntactic patterns which never get fully acquired by adult learners of foreign languages. For example, Selinker has suggested that certain English modals (e.g., could have, would have, ought to have) are extremely hard for nonnative speakers to master, and they may never be perfectly picked up. Again, there are few experimental data that I know of to support this view, but we will examine the possible presence of a syntactic "foreign accent" in the final chapter.

DIFFERENTIAL FOSSILIZATION AT PUBERTY

When we consider phonological accents as the archetype of fossilization, and when we compare their emergence at pubescence with the contrasting *improvement* in virtually all other skills being acquired by second language learners, we have an intriguing crossover effect between the learning of phonology (or at least the phonological features that are tied to sounding like a foreigner) and the linguistic skills of learning new words, new inflections, new syntactic rules, and so forth (Figure 6.1).

From Figure 6.1 we can see that linguistic skills learned in the new language, if viewed developmentally, are differentially affected at puberty. In the rough approximation of the skills that I have provided here, you can see that competence in the new language tends to increase with chronological development: There is a direct correlation between performance and age. This, incidentally, is what we expect of almost all human learning. All things being equal, we expect teenagers to be better bike riders, high jumpers, piano players, watercolor painters, and computer programmers than kids in kindergarten. The exception to this general upward flow of abilities is the phonological skill of sounding like a native speaker of a new language learned after puberty: We see in Figure 6.1 that there is a decrement in performance for this ability and that it is *inversely* proportional to age. Note that this graph is nothing more than a visual representation of the Joseph Conrad phenomenon, and it helps to reconcile some of the views which I reviewed in the beginning of Chapter 5 with the position I am taking throughout this book: It is hard to argue for a critical period for any aspect of

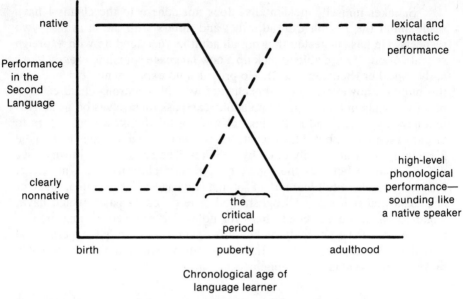

Figure 6.1 The crossover effect of linguistic skills acquired at puberty.

language learning from all the evidence we have—even for a constraint on general skills in pronunciation. What is being identified here is the isolated ability of being able to sound just like a native speaker of a language. For the sociobiological reasons I have already discussed in Chapter 4, this rare skill seems to be differentially affected by age, and it, alone among all the other things we learn when we pick up a new language after childhood, remains encrusted as a symbol of our evolutionary past and is forever fossilized.

THESIS: THE COLLECTIVE EVIDENCE FROM SCOVEL

We are now ready to look at the experimental evidence corroborating the crossover effect depicted in Figure 6.1. The collective support for this phenomenon and for the emergence and the irrevocability of foreign accent after about the first decade of life is copious and varied. Since I have been personally involved with some of this experimentation, you will forgive me if we begin with a review of my own work. We will use it not so much as a standard with which to compare other research on this topic as an introduction to other studies, and you are probably alert enough to see that researchers whose work both antedates and follows mine have frequently developed better experimental protocols or have been able to measure foreign accents in a more refined manner than I. Because of the comparative elegance of these other experiments, I view all of them as strongly supportive of my

104

thesis that, unlike any other aspect of foreign language learning, accented speech emerges as such a salient form of fossilization at about puberty that all native speakers of the target language can recognize it instantly.

Except for the informal junior high school survey which I reported on in my first paper (Scovel, 1969), the chief source of my empirical verification of a critical period for accents comes from a series of experiments which were reported in a paper delivered to the 5th International Congress of Applied Linguistics (Scovel, 1978). Using a tape of 10 native speakers of English and 10 very proficient nonnative speakers, I ran a series of identification experiments with four different groups of subjects: (1) adult native speakers of English, (2) child native speakers of English, (3) adult native speakers of English with varying degrees of aphasia, and (4) adult nonnative speakers of English. Let us look at the design, results, and conclusions of each of these four experimental studies.

Accent Recognition by Adult Native Speakers

The four studies which I am about to report on all deal with the perception of accents and with their production. All of the experimentation dating the emergence of accents to puberty that will be reviewed in this chapter deal either directly or indirectly with the perception or recognition of foreign accents because there is really no other empirical way by which to confirm their existence. We know virtually nothing about the acoustic and articulatory characteristics of how foreign accents are produced, so we are restricted in our research to the perceptual mode. A few second language researchers have tried to identify specific segmental and suprasegmental phonemic information about the production of non-native-sounding speech (Adams, 1979; de Bot & Malifert, 1982; Marks, 1980), and some have delved into the fascinating ways in which phonetic, paralinguistic features such as "voice setting" might contribute to the production of accented speech (Esling & Wong, 1982). However, until we have reached the stage where we can identify the physical "voice prints" of a foreign accent—say, on a spectrogram—we will have to rely on identifying accents via perceptual measures.

The four perception experiments I designed for the 1978 article were based on a tape of 20 speakers: 10 were native speakers of Standard American English and 10 were nonnative speakers. I took care in selecting only the most proficient nonnative subjects for this task because if even extremely fluent foreign voices were identifiable from their accents, the stronger the evidence would be for my claims that pronunciation was differentially fossilized. Although there were no Joseph Conrads in my subject pool, at least not to my knowledge, all 10 used English professionally in their daily lives, all had lived in the United States or an English-speaking country for at least five years, and all had completed or were completing their graduate studies in the

United States. In addition, I asked three experienced ESL/EFL teachers to listen to the nonnative subjects I had selected in order to eliminate any subjects whose pronunciation was not excellent. In keeping with my goal of choosing only superb speakers, I actually included two *native speakers* of English in this group of 10 nonnative speakers, but these two were not native speakers of American English but of Irish English and South African-Indian English. Remember that the task of the judges listening to this tape was not to pick out native English speakers but to select only those who spoke American English. It might also be noted that these 10 subjects were all comfortably acquainted with American dialects, having lived in the States and, in some cases, having married and raised families in America, and since all of them were students or teachers of linguistics and/or EFL, they were much better equipped to improve their own pronunciation and usage than the typical educated nonnative speaker. The subjects ranged in age from their 20s to their 40s and were balanced in their sexual distribution. The native language of the 10 speakers was Arabic, Swedish, Chinese, Romanian, Irish English, French, Portuguese, Lingala, Spanish, and South African-Indian English.

In order to get some confirmation of their overall ability in English apart from their pronunciation, I asked the nonnative subjects to write a brief essay on a selected topic—"the importance of sleep." I had also asked the 10 native speakers of American English to write the same composition, and these 20 essays were randomly distributed to a group of 31 adult American English judges who were asked to decide whether or not the compositions were written by an American. Although we will examine the results of the judgments about this written corpus in a moment, it probably should not surprise you to know that, on the basis of their writing skills, the *non-*Americans were perceived by the 31 judges slightly more often as Americans than were the 10 well-educated American subjects! The results should not astonish anyone who is cognizant of the Joseph Conrads and Henry Kissingers who use English as a medium of written as well as spoken communication.

Getting back to the pronunciation task that all 20 subjects had to perform: In a recording room I taped each subject separately reading the following sentences in as normal and relaxed a manner as possible; furthermore, they had as many trials as they wanted, and they recorded only their "best shot."

> Many now think the Steelers will win the Super Bowl for the third year in a row. The team is justly proud of its sure defense and its three zippy linebackers.

Because the study was done at the University of Pittsburgh, the passage was designed to be of some relevance and interest to the adults and children who would be asked to listen to it over and over again. Unfortunately for the football team, the selection did not prove prophetic, but my intent was more directed to its linguistic content. I purposely chose two sentences that would contain most of the segmental phonemes of American English. To load the dice slightly against my hypothesis—that is, to make it more difficult for the judges listening to the tape to identify natives from nonnatives accurately—I purposely chose a very brief passage and one that did not demand any suprasegmental gymnastics. Note that in terms of intonation, the two sentences can be read with normal rise-fall contour and do not force the speaker to use some of the more complicated suprasegmental features of English prosody that are required when you read transcripts of conversations, for example. Again, I wanted to ensure that identification would be difficult, so that the more accurate the judges were in separating the American from the non-American voices, the stronger would be my prediction of the indelibility of foreign accents, even in these highly competent nonnative speakers.

The same 31 adult judges, all speakers of Standard American English and, like the majority of the 10 taped native speakers, coming predominantly from Western Pennsylvania, listened to the 20 subjects randomly distributed between nonnative and native speakers on the tape. After the judges heard each subject, identified only by a number, they were asked to respond on an answer sheet to a simple yes/no question, "Does this speaker sound like an American?" The judges' answers for both the taped speech (the Oral Corpus) and the short compositions (the Written Corpus) are presented in Table 6.1.

The scores given by the 31 judges are divided into two categories: The column on the left, labeled Total Score, refers to the average raw score and percentage correct for all 20 subjects for both the oral and written corpora, while the right-hand column focuses only on the judgments of the 10 nonnative subjects for both the spoken and written texts. Note that we are more concerned with the correct identification of the nonnatives (true negatives) than we are with the correct recognition of the native language users (true positives). Thus, the results on the right are more telling than the ones on the

TABLE 6.1 Identification of Native and Nonnative English by Adults

	Total score		Identification of non-natives only	
	$\overline{X}/20$	%	$\overline{X}/10$	%
Oral corpus	18.94	95%	9.74	97%
Written corpus	11.42[a]	57%	4.71[b]	47%

[a] Approaching chance.
[b] Less than chance.
Source: From Scovel (1981).

107

left, though none of the data is irrelevant to our overall interests. The mean score of 18.94 for the oral corpus for all subjects shows that the experimental task was very easy; on an average, each judge misidentified only about 1 speaker out of 20 in the brief (less than 8 seconds) passages spoken. Since each subject was reading exactly the same material, note that the judges could make decisions only on the basis of the degree of accentedness in the speech and not of choice of topic, grammatical errors, or other nonphonological clues that sometimes might be used to identify a nonnative user of the language. Turning to the right-hand column, it is apparent from the difference between the percentage correct of the two columns (95% for all subjects vs. 97% for the nonnative subjects), that the judges were slightly better at making judgments about the nonnative speakers than about the native speakers. This means that there were more false positives than false negatives. That is to say that among the few mistakes that were made, there was a tendency for judges to say a native speaker was not an American (a false positive) than there was a tendency for them to classify a nonnative as native (a false negative). The results of this oral identification test are clearly supportive of the claim that even highly advanced adult second language users can easily be identified by their accent, even from only a brief amount of phonological data.

The ability of the judges to distinguish between the native and nonnative writers poses a remarkable contrast to the results with the oral corpus, however. In neither the total score given on the left nor the score for just the 10 nonnative subjects on the right were the adult judges capable of coming close to being accurate. Remember that all the judges had to do was to separate the two groups of writers on a yes/no task, so that even with random guessing, the judges would be able to achieve a 50% score on this recognition test; nevertheless, the total score percentage of only 57% approaches chance, and the nonnative score of 47% is *less* than chance. As already intimated, the nonnative users of English were so good in their writing that they were completely indistinguishable from educated native writers. Joseph Conrad himself probably couldn't have deceived the judges any more effectively than the 10 nonnative writers selected for this experiment, and so we see once more a solid endorsement of the differential fossilization of linguistic skills for these subjects who have acquired English (or at least American English) after their first decade of life.

I want to conclude this first experiment by mentioning that I have replicated at least the oral recognition component of this early experiment several times with classes of adult linguistics students, using the original tape, and the results invariably elicit the same degree of accuracy. For example, in 1982 I played the tape to a class of 37 native speakers of American English and found a 95% accuracy rate. There were 37 errors overall—1 per judge per subject, and they are about equally divided between false negatives (19) and false positives (18). An error rate of 5% or less is usually accepted in the social sciences as demonstrating that the results are "significant" ($p < .05$); thus, the ability to identify nonnative speakers seems to be consistent and significant when tapped experimentally. Note that recognition tasks like these are infinitely more rigorous than the claims some people make that "so-and-so speaks language X so well that native speakers consistently mistake her for a native speaker." It may be true that there are adult exceptions to critical period predictions, but anecdotal claims like this are exceedingly difficult to verify, and that is why experimental studies like the ones reviewed in this chapter are so vital to our understanding of second language acquisition. But if you do have anecdotal information about an adult exception that you ardently believe in, I will address the issue of experimental and anecdotal exceptions in the final chapter.

Accent Recognition by Child Native Speakers

Having fairly clear confirmation of the persistence of accents in adulthood and their ready recognition by adult judges, I was next interested in the ontogeny of this ability to recognize nonnative speakers. If adult native speakers are quick to identify accented speech, the developmental question that springs to mind is, at what age does this skill materialize? I decided to play my prepared tape of 20 speakers to 146 elementary school children of various ages to see at what age young native speakers of American English can accurately identify accented speech. The adult norm of 95% was chosen as the criterion for accuracy. Originally, I had hoped to begin with very young preschool children, but my naive hopes that they would participate cooperatively in my experimental enterprise were rapidly dashed when I discovered that 3- and 4-year-olds were more fascinated with the bright knobs and rotating reels of the tape recorder than with linguistic judgments about the voices they heard! For this reason, I started with 5-year-olds, who seemed to be reasonably aware of what I was asking them to do, and worked my way up year by year and grade by grade. Ideally, I would have had each age level contain roughly the same number of children, but owing to the uneven population of children in some of the grades in the suburban school where the experiment was conducted, the number of children fluctuated from age to age. The format for this second experiment was almost identical to the one undertaken with the adults. For this experiment, and for all subsequent ones, I did not use the written passages; they were used only in the first experiment as a kind of control to prove that judgments about authenticity of language use are ultimately made on phonological and not grammatical performance. Also, for the children, I made the instructions and the answer sheets a bit more explicit and more suited for this younger group of judges. Table 6.2 displays the results with the 146 school children of various ages.

TABLE 6.2 Identification of Native and Nonnative English by Children

	Total score		Identification of non- natives only	
	$\overline{X}/20^a$	%	$\overline{X}/10^b$	%
5-year-olds ($N = 8$)	14.50	73%	7.75	78%
6-year-olds ($N = 34$)	15.71	79%	7.56	76%
7-year-olds ($N = 47$)	17.04	85%	8.47	85%
8-year-olds ($N = 9$)	17.11	86%	8.11	81%
9-year-olds ($N = 38$)	18.76	94%	9.58	96%
10-year-olds ($N = 10$)	19.40	97%	9.90	99%

Jonckheere test for ordered alternatives. $H_o = G_1 = G_2 = G_n$ and $H_1 = G_1 < G_2 < G_n$ If $J^* > 2.58$, then null hypothesis can be rejected with $p < .01$.
a $J^* = 7.15$.
b $J^* = 6.64$.
Source: From Scovel (1981).

Again, I have divided the judges' answers into two columns: the Total Score reflecting their accuracy in identifying all 20 subjects, and their score for just the 10 nonnative speakers. You can see that except for the 7- and 8-year-old children in the right-hand column (cf. 85% and 81%), in every case, for both columns, the scores improve directly as a function of age. The identification scores are directly proportional to the age of the young judges. The exception just pointed out could be due to a statistical anomaly where with only half the subjects (10 instead of 20), the large discrepancy in numbers of children (forty-seven 7-year-olds vs. nine 8-year-olds) arbitrarily disrupts the normal progression of successively higher scores. Table 6.2 distinctly demonstrates how rapidly the adult criterion level of 95% identification accuracy is reached by these younger judges: It is clear from the data that the ability to accurately identify nonnative speakers is attained by the age of 9 or 10. Accent recognition appears to be an ability that culminates within the first decade or so of development.

We will see from other experiments to be reviewed in this chapter that the emergence of a foreign accent appears to come at about the ages of 10 to 12. Up to this point, I have given the approximate age of the critical period for acquiring accentless speech in humans as about puberty, but if we are open in our interpretation of how closely linguistic development and chronological age are linked, and the research shows us that the linkage is quite loose (Brown, 1975; Reich, 1986), then we can accept the ages of about 9 to 12 as being the time when both the accurate recognition of accents is achieved and the inability to speak without an accent emerges. Nature is seemingly fair: It gives us the ability to identify nonnative users of our mother tongue almost at the very moment it constrains us from ever learning a new language without an accent.

Accent Recognition by Aphasic Native Speakers

The third experiment I would like to report on deals with an entirely different population of judges: In terms of age, they are as old as, or older than, the adult judges used in the first experiment; in terms of level of linguistic development, in some ways they are as immature as the youngest children who participated in the second experiment. This third group were adult aphasics—men who, because of traumatic injury to the brain, suffered from varying degrees of linguistic deficit. There were 23 who participated in this experiment; all were native speakers of Standard American English and were inpatients or outpatients of two Veterans Administration hospitals in Pittsburgh. The mean age was 50, and with the exception of one left-handed patient who was left-hemiplegic and was diagnosed with a stroke to the right hemisphere, all of the men had incurred traumatic injury to the left hemisphere. As in the experiment done with children, a few minor adjustments in the directions had to be made to accommodate this particular group of judges to compensate for the possibility of the patients' not understanding the task they were to perform. Unlike the previous two studies, the test was individually administered to each patient, and, in addition to being asked, "Does this person sound like an American?" for each taped voice, the patient was given a picture of an American flag with the word YES printed underneath it, and a drawing of a blank square over the word NO. Responses could thus be given orally or by gesture, although most of the patients responded with the former. One further compensation made in sensitivity to this group was that each person was given a full 10 seconds to respond before the examiner moved on to the next speaker. Because many of these aphasics had severe comprehension problems, it was difficult to assess how much of the instructions they understood, even for this binary identification task, but it appeared to the examiners, who were all experienced therapists and who knew the patients well, that most of the aphasic judges understood perfectly the task they were to perform.

I wanted to assess the extent of linguistic disability these aphasics had incurred, especially in their auditory comprehension, so before they participated in the accent identification task, they were given the Token Test (DeRenzi & Vignolo, 1962), where subjects are instructed to identify and manipulate colored plastic chips of various shapes and sizes in a sequence of increasingly complex commands. The 23 aphasics displayed the full gamut of scores that can be obtained by this instrument—from a nearly minimal response (Group 1 in Table 6.3, with a range of only 3 to 5 points out of a

TABLE 6.3 Identification of Native and Nonnative English by Aphasics[a]

Group	No.	Token score[b]	Accent ID score[c]	Group	No.	Token score	Accent ID score	Group	No.	Token score	Accent ID score
1	1	3	7	3	9	15	9	5	17	41	8
	2	4	9		10	24	10		18	45	9
	3	4	9		11	24	10		19	46	7
	4	5	1		12	28	8		20	52	9
2	5	5	5	4	13	34	7	6	21	58	8
	6	12	9		14	34	9		22	58	10
	7	14	6		15	34	9		23	58	10
	8	14	8		16	35	7		24	59	10

[a] $N = 24$.
[b] Mean score for Token = 29.4 $(\overline{X}/62)$.
[c] Mean score for Accent ID = 8.1 $(\overline{X}/10)$.
Source: From Scovel (1981).

possible 62) to a nearly optimal score (exhibited by Group 6, with a range close to 100% level of performance: 51–59). Here I should stress that even non-brain-damaged, highly educated subjects (such as neurolinguists and aphasiologists) rarely achieve a perfect score of 62 on the Token Test, simply because of memory constraints and/or performance mistakes.

When we compare the results of the Token Test given in the leftmost column of Table 6.3 with the scores of the patients on the accent identification task in the two right-hand columns, we are actually more interested in the aphasics who scored poorly on the Token Test (say, those in the first four groups) than in those who came closer to normal achievement. To be sure, we know little about the nature of the receptive disabilities which inflict aphasics. Are the lower Token scores a reflection of disruptions in phonological processing, an across-the-board linguistic deficit, or even a higher constraint on cognitive processing at all levels? We do have evidence from the phonological production of aphasics that linguistic disruption in these patients can be circumscribed to phonology, and from this, it is fair to infer that low Token scores, for at least most of the aphasic judges in this third experiment, are a reflection of processing problems restricted to the phonological level. Given this inference, we would quite naturally assume that they would perform poorly on any accent recognition task, because such a test involves the decoding of extremely subtle phonological cues. However, the results in Table 6.3 are not consonant with such a simplified correlation. True, Group 1, the patients with the lowest Token scores, also performed most poorly on the accent identification test, and Group 6, the aphasics with the highest Token scores, did about the best on my accent recognition task, but other than these two observations, there are no other neat correlations between the two measures. Group 3, for example, did as well as Group 6 on the accent identification test, and a scatter diagram of the relationship between the two measures revealed no positive correlation between them.

Looking at the mean scores for all groups of the 23 aphasic judges, we can see that, collectively, they were only in the mid-80% range and did not reach the criterion of 95% established by the normal adult judges and matched by the 9- to 10-year-old children. In fact, this is only equivalent to the scores the 7- to 8-year-old children achieved. At the same time, given the severity of the loss in most of the adult aphasic subjects, the similarity among the adults, older children, and aphasics is more conspicuous than any dissimilarity, and the ability to recognize foreign accents does not appear to be dramatically impaired by the same neurological insult which can severely hamper other aspects of linguistic communication.

Accent Identification by Nonnative Speakers of English

The fourth and final experiment which tested accent recognition using my original tape of 20 speakers was undertaken by a former graduate student of mine at the University of Pittsburgh, Suzanne Poore. We were interested in testing the ability of ESL students to judge accented speech in English, the language they were in the process of learning. Ninety-two ESL students were chosen from beginning, intermediate, and advanced classes and representing the following native languages (in order of number of subjects): Spanish, Arabic, Portuguese, Japanese, Russian, Thai, Greek, and Italian. The expectation was that accent identification scores would correlate directly with ESL experience and proficiency, as measured by the three levels of ability grouping, and although the hypothesis was confirmed, it can be seen that the most advanced ESL students did not even come close to the adult aphasic criterion of 85% accuracy rate in accent recognition (Table 6.4).

Upon closer scrutiny, we can see an even sharper contrast between the ESL data in this table and the native-speaking judges: The overall mean

TABLE 6.4 Identification of Native and Nonnative English by ESL Students

English language ability grouping	Total ID score		ID of nonnative speakers only	
	$\overline{X}/20$	%	$\overline{X}/10$	%
Elementary $(N = 17)$	14.06	70%	5.65	57%
Intermediate $(N = 31)$	14.45	72%	6.29	63%
Advanced $(N = 44)$	15.45	77%	7.18	72%
$(N = 92)$	14.86	74.3%	6.60	66%

Source: From Scovel (1981).

TABLE 6.5 Correlations Between Accent Scores and Three Measures of ESL Skills

Correlation of Accent ID scores with	Mean scores X̄/highest possible score	Pearson product-moment correlations
Michigan Test—listening subscore	57.3/100	$0.255\ p < .01$
Michigan Test—written subscore	53.62/100	$0.241\ p < .02$
English Language Ability grouping (cf. Table 6.4)	14.86/20	$0.276\ p < .01$

Source: From Scovel (1981).

score for all three levels of ESL students for the correct identification of nonnative subjects was only 66%; this was dramatically lower than the 84% mean scored by the adult aphasic population and was even markedly lower than the 78% scored by the 5-year-old children, the youngest group tested. The nonnative judges, even the advanced ones, appeared unable to decipher in any consistent manner the phonological clues that so readily identified native from nonnative American speech for the various groups of native-speaking judges, and the response by many of the ESL students was little better than random guessing.

Interested in getting a slightly more quantifiable measure of the ESL proficiency of these nonnative judges, we were able to obtain their Michigan Test scores, administered at the beginning of their intensive ESL program at the University of Pittsburgh. Table 6.5 shows the results of three sets of Pearson product-moment correlation measures run on the accent scores with (a) the subscore of the Michigan Test that measures "listening comprehension" ability, (b) the Michigan subscore that reflects "writing" ability, and (c) the groupings into three levels already alluded to in Table 6.4.

Correlations were positive between accent identification accuracy and the three different ways of testing second language skills, and this suggests that no matter what measure you use to determine the ESL abilities of these students, the better students generally did better on the accent identification test and vice versa. We might almost be tempted to give the accent test as a quick and global measure of overall English ability, since it correlates so neatly with the three more laborious ways of assessing student ability levels. Be that as it may, it is clear that accent recognition is an important component of native speaker competence, and so early does it become engrained within our linguistic psyche, and so indelibly, that it takes the most traumatic form of neurolinguistic damage to disrupt its natural and remarkable course.

THE COLLECTIVE EVIDENCE FROM OTHER STUDIES

We have expended considerable time reviewing four sets of experiments I have devised to demonstrate the claims I made toward the end of Chapter 3 concerning a critical period for acquiring unaccented speech, but my work here is neither the earliest nor the most elaborate, and we should look at about 10 other experimental studies because they provide additional and impressive corroboration of a biologically based constraint on the acquisition of speech arising at about puberty.

One of the first empirical studies was carried out by Larew (1961), who selected 10 children for each age group, starting from 7 to 11 and including 14-year-olds. The pupils were all English speakers who had had no previous foreign language exposure, and care was taken to ensure that the intelligence levels in all the age groups were approximately equal. The subjects were taught four Spanish lessons which focused on the ability to reproduce certain phonemes in that language, and then an articulation test was given to measure the success the children had in learning these Spanish sounds. Larew interpreted the results as supportive of Penfield's "the earlier the better" philosophy, but the pronunciation scores reported in the experiment did not correlate neatly with the ages of the young learners, and there was no statistical confirmation that scores were clearly inversely proportional to the age of the children.

Larew's study confirms two points that are already implicit from our discussion thus far. First of all, it is rare to find any phonological measure where pronunciation scores actually *increase* with age. And second, when we examine phonological learning in terms of the ability to learn discrete points of pronunciation, and not in more global measures of segmental and suprasegmental success, the cognitive and linguistic maturity of older children helps them in these discrete phonological tasks just as ably as it assists them in the mastery of new morphological and syntactic patterns. The Larew data neither confirm nor disconfirm age-related constraints on second language acquisition.

One of the most well known early experiments was performed by Asher and Garcia (1969). This work is of historical interest because, as with Krashen, Asher's personal experimentation in this area of second language acquisition research convinced him that children are better learners than adults, and just as Krashen's belief that this was due to affect and cognition led him to the development of the "natural approach" method, Asher became convinced that the superiority of children was due to the physical movements they used in learning, and this led him to devise the "Total Physical Response" method. If nothing else, the critical period hypothesis has proved to be a fruitful spawning ground for popular new second/foreign language teaching methods.

Asher and Garcia tape-recorded the English pronunciation of 71 Spanish-speaking immigrant children, aged 7 to 19, and randomly mixed their voices with the pronunciation of 30 native speakers of American English. The results of their accent identification test provide a solid endorsement for the emergence of foreign accents at around puberty (Figure 6.2). The authors

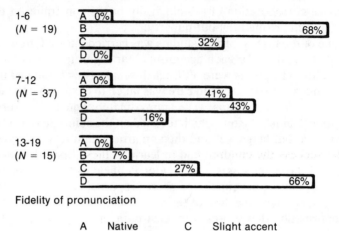

Child's age when
entering the
United States

1-6
(N = 19)
A 0%
B 68%
C 32%
D 0%

7-12
(N = 37)
A 0%
B 41%
C 43%
D 16%

13-19
(N = 15)
A 0%
B 7%
C 27%
D 66%

Fidelity of pronunciation

| A | Native | C | Slight accent |
| B | Near native | D | Definite accent |

Figure 6.2 English pronunciation of Spanish-speaking children. (*Source:* From Asher & Garcia, 1969:337.) © *The Modern Language Journal.* Used by permission of the University of Wisconsin Press.

found, like Cummins, that length of residence was an intervening variable and also that girls tended to receive higher scores than boys, although the latter effect seemed to dissipate at the older ages. Their conclusions about this data from Cuban immigrant children resonate favorably with the claims made in my article published the very same year as their experimental study:

> The implications from the data were that a Cuban child had the greatest probability of achieving a near-native pronunciation of English if he was six or younger and lived in the United States for more than five years. A child who came to America when he was 13 or older had a small chance of acquiring a near-native pronunciation even if he lived here five years or more. The child who was between 7 and 12 when he arrived here and then lived here five years or more had a 50–50 chance of achieving a near-native pronunciation. (Asher & Garcia, 1969:339)

We now look at a quite different study, because it is among the few that does not employ native speakers as judges of the accented speech but relies on the subjects themselves to assess the degree of their foreign accents. This survey by Seliger, Krashen, and Ladefoged (1975) was simple in design but telling in its implications. Immigrants to Israel and immigrants to the United States were asked several questions concerning their age when they arrived at the land to which they immigrated, and they were also asked to rate the degree to which their speech in Hebrew or English, depending on whether

TABLE 6.6 Self-Report of Accents in Israeli and U.S. Immigrants

Target language	Age of arrival	Accent	Don't know	No accent
English	9 and under	5	4	47
Hebrew		2	3	30
English	10 to 15	37	6	27
Hebrew		9	1	20
English	16 and over	106	4	7
Hebrew		50	1	5

Source: After Seliger, Krashen, and Ladefoged (1975: 21).

they had immigrated to Israel or the United States, sounded like that of a native speaker. Results of this self report survey are depicted in Table 6.6.

The authors broke down the age of arrival category for these subjects into three large groups: those who immigrated to Israel or the United States before 10, those who arrived in their early teens, and those who came after the age of 15. Self-report studies have certain inherent problems: For example, as the Internal Revenue Service well knows, people tend to report information that minimizes their cupidity and maximizes their good intentions! But this is a factor that cuts across the entire population of 364 subjects here, and it is hard to imagine why subjects who immigrated to Israel at a young age would tend to exaggerate their linguistic prowess in Hebrew, but that subjects who came to Israel in their mid-teens would view their Hebrew pronunciation more critically, to cite just one of several conditions necessary were the data entirely an artifact of skewed self-reporting. Therefore, the authors have demonstrated in this large survey of second language learners in two different nations that the presence of accented speech appears around puberty. Note in Table 6.7 how many of the youngest group report that they speak the target language without an accent and how few of the oldest group claim to have accentless speech.

One of the best-designed and most convincing experiments of the critical period hypothesis was performed by Oyama (1976). Her subjects were 60 adults who had emigrated from Italy to the United States at various ages, and they were asked to provide two oral samples of their speech in English: They were asked to read a paragraph (similar to my two-sentence reading task but longer), and they were asked to tell a personal story about some frightening anecdote from their own lives. Two graduate students in linguistics, both native speakers of American English, listened to the tapes of all the speakers and judged the degree of accent on a 5-point scale: from "no foreign accent" to "heavy foreign accent." Statistical measures of interjudge reliability confirmed that the two native speakers were extremely consistent in their accent judgments ($p < .001$; Oyama, 1976:267).

The presentation of Oyama's data is somewhat complicated. She has separate tables for the results of the paragraph selections and the story selections, and further, she presents the information in matrix fashion with the data about the age of arrival to the United States cross-referenced with the data about the number of years the subjects had lived in the United States. If you are a psychometrician, you will feel comfortable perusing her tables of statistical information, but for the general reader, I will summarize them briefly for you here.

Concerning the age of arrival data, Oyama, like Seliger et al. (1975), divides the subjects into three basic groups, those who arrived before 10, in the early teens, and after the age of 15. For both the paragraph reading and the spontaneous storytelling tasks, there was strong confirmation that age of arrival was the dependent variable, separating those subjects who were perceived as accent-free, or relatively accent-free, from those subjects who were perceived as having noticeable or distinct accents. Number of years residence in the United States did not emerge as a significant factor; in fact, from her statistical analysis of the interaction between age of arrival and length of residence data, it seemed that any effect of the latter was really an artifact of the former: "It appears, then, that accent is rather resistant to the effects of factors other than age at the beginning the language, and that the apparent influence of such factors is an artifact of their relationship with age at learning" (Oyama, 1976:271).

Oyama also addresses what I believe to be a peripheral issue in many of these accent recognition tasks, but since she has addressed the problem so carefully and so well, it is worth mentioning here. I have heard some people complain that tape-recording nonnative speakers is an unfair measure of their phonological potential in the target language, because they may be nervous and uptight about their accented speech, and this very concern enhances an accent that might be minimal or even nonexistent in a more natural setting. Oyama cites just such a possibility in her discussion of alternative explanations to her experimental results: "For those whose command of English phonology was shaky, increased attention seemed to have a deteriorative effect on performance. This recalls the Yerkes-Dodson law, familiar to psychologists, which states that high motivation enhances performance on relatively simple tasks, whereas it may hinder performance on difficult ones" (Oyama, 1976:270).

There are at least two counterarguments to this criticism. Oyama's choice of two different measures of speech is appropriate here because she chose a passage which all the nonnative speakers had to read, and which may have exacerbated the degree of accentedness in their speech because of their concern on form and not on content. But then she also recorded their spontaneous telling of a frightening anecdote in their lives, an old trick made famous in the sociolinguistic studies of Labov (1966), which gets subjects to focus on the content of what they are saying, sometimes in an animated and natural manner. Oyama's data seem to suggest that nervousness during recording is not a major concern, however. For both the paragraph and the story data, age of arrival was the only significant variable that accounted for the two judges' ability to distinguish accented from unaccented speech. That is, immigrants who came to the United States before the age of 10 had the least accent, and those who came after 15 had the most marked, and this was equally true whether the immigrants were reading from a prepared script or relating a spontaneous story. Although emotions obviously play a role in our linguistic performance, for both native and nonnative speech—a fact well acknowledged in the previous chapter, they do not appear to have any direct relevance to the presence of a foreign accent. Once again, we have confirmation that the marks of nature are present in what we say.

Although less directly concerned with accented speech, a study by Fathman (1975), at about the same time, of school-age children is yet another experiment that indicates that age of learning affects certain phonological skills differently from other types of linguistic performance. She tested the pronunciation, morphological, and syntactic skills of 200 ESL schoolchildren aged 6 to 15, using an oral response test she developed herself, and she found contrasting results between the 6- to 10-year-old group and the 11- to 15-year-olds:

> There appeared to be a difference in the rate of learning English phonology, morphology, and syntax based on differences in age. The younger children, aged 6 to 10 years, received significantly higher ratings on their English pronunciation, suggesting that preteen children are more successful at learning the phonology of a new language. (Fathman, 1975:120)

Conversely, Fathman discovered that the older children were better than their younger counterparts in the areas of morphology and syntax, a finding for which we have already seen support.

Dealing with a group of older learners than Fathman, Johansson (1978) examined the written and oral errors of Swedish university students of English and found that their spoken English was accurately distinguished from native speakers, but, as in the experiment on accent recognition by ESL students that I reported on earlier in this chapter, Johansson discovered that foreign judges (native speakers of Swedish) were only about half as accurate as native speakers in comprehending the spoken English passages made by the Swedish university students. His study suggests that nonnative listeners of a second language are not nearly as accurate as native speakers of that second language in comprehension. That is, Swedes are not as successful as native speakers of English in understanding the spoken English of other Swedes. Again, this implies that there is a certain phonological core underlying each language that is difficult to penetrate after puberty.

An experiment much more relevant to our quest for empirical evidence is one published by Tahta, Wood, and Loewenthal (1981). They conducted a well-designed study of 109 immigrants to Great Britain of a wide range of ages and from 20 different language backgrounds (from Arabic to Urdu). Information for each subject was gathered on their age, sex, mother tongue, years of residence in England, musical ability, and the way in which they learned English. The age at which they began to learn English was also noted. Tape recordings were made of each of the subjects reading a short passage of English, and three native-speaking judges then graded each subject on a 3-point scale: no accent, slight accent, or marked accent. The judges' total points per subject were summed so that a score of 0 indicated absolutely no accent but a score of 6 would indicate the most marked accent possible. Interjudge reliability was high. Of all the variables, the age at which the immigrants first began to learn English was the most crucial: "As expected, age at which L2 acquisition commenced was massively effective, accounting for 43.1% of variance in accent. Table 1 shows the dramatic changes in the likelihood of speaking accent-free English according to the age at which acquisition commenced" (Tahta et al., 1981:267).

The bottom line of Table 6.7 (the Table 1 referred to by Tahta et al., above) shows a conspicuous jump in accent scores, indicating an increase in the perception of an accent after the age of 11.

It is astonishing that so many of these studies pinpoint the conclusion of the first decade of life and the commencement of the second as a rather neat dividing line. Remember that in our discussion in Chapter 3 of the onset and completion of puberty, I tried to stress how misleading chronological age could be and that factors such as the "secular trend" could affect the age when puberty emerged in various societies. Remember too that studies of first language acquisition have shown that linguistic stages and chronological ages do not overlap neatly. With all this in mind, then, the remarkable unanimity among all the studies reviewed in this chapter provides, I think, a powerful testament to the consistency of the time when accents develop in second language acquisition.

One of the most recent studies verifying the existence of the critical period for accents is reported by Major (1987), who examined the pronunciation of a discrete set of English phonemes by 53 adult Brazilian EFL speakers. Seven native speakers of American English were used as controls.

TABLE 6.7 Ages of Acquisition and Emergence of Accents

	Age at which L2 acquisition commenced									
	6	7	8	9	10	11	12	13	14	15+
N	10	10	10	10	10	10	10	10	10	19
N of accent-free Ss	10	9	8	5	3	5	1	0	0	0
Mean accent score (0 = no accent; 6 = heavy accent)	0	0.30	0.60	1.80	2.20	1.80	3.9	4.8	4.4	5.16

Source: From Tahta, Wood, and Loewenthal (1981: 268).

Tapes of the pronunciation of these sets of phonemes were played to 10 native speakers of American English, who judged the pronunciation of the sounds on a sliding scale that was actually fine enough to represent scores from 0 to 256. Major's experiment is detailed and extensive, but for our purposes, it can be summarized in Table 6.8, which encapsulates the vast discrepancy between the pronunciation ability of the nonnative subjects, even the very good ones, and the native speakers.

Major's study is a remarkable demonstration of the pervasiveness of accented speech, limited in this case to a phonemic contrast between two vowels. Note that there is no overlap between the highest score obtained by a nonnative speaker (224.8) and the lowest score achieved by a native speaker (246.1). The gap is actually wider than it appears because the most highly ranked nonnative speaker, the one who scored 224.8, was almost 20 points higher than the second-best nonnative speaker, who received a 206.1. Note too that there is a vast difference between the means of the two groups: The native speaker group averaged more than double the score of the nonnative speakers (cf. 252.5 to 111.0)! Finally, it is obvious that the native-speaking group is more homogeneous and predictable than their nonnative counterparts because of the gross discrepancy in standard deviation scores (cf. 3.2 to 49.4). Major's study replicates and corroborates the findings of other experiments conducted by Flege and Eefting (1987) and contrasts and complements experiments like mine or the survey conducted by Seliger et al. (1975) because it is so narrow and discrete in its focus. Major was looking exclusively at the ability to distinguish between the vowel phonemes /ɛ/ (as in "bet" and /æ/ (as in "sat") pronounced in sentences. The other studies just referred to looked at very global, impressionistic measures (e.g., "Does this speaker sound like an American?"). It is revealing that using either perspective, discrete, "bottom-up" or global, "top-down" processing, native and nonnative speakers were accurately and consistently identified. Once again, we have evidence for the pervasiveness of foreign accents in adult learners of a second language.

TABLE 6.8 Degrees of Accentedness in Phoneme Pronunciation Between Native and Nonnative Speakers

	Range of accent score	Mean accent score	SD
Nonnative speakers (Brazilians) N = 53	15.9 to 224.8	111.0	49.4
Native speakers (American) N = 7	246.1 to 255.5	252.5	3.2

Source: After Major (1987).

CONCLUDING SYNTHESIS

After having read about these many experimental studies which have provided convincing and varied evidence for the emergence of accented speech for languages learned after about the first decade of life, for the ready and accurate ability of native speaker judges to determine native from nonnative speech (sometimes from the smallest snatches of phonological information), and for the uniqueness of accent phenomena in the face of all the other linguistic skills which seem to generally improve with social and cognitive maturity at adolescence, it must seem impossible to reconcile all this with the long litany of quotes and studies presented in the previous chapter arguing *against* biological constraints for language acquisition. Why does the accepted lore resist the lure of nature? The answer lies largely in our interpretation of what kind of "language" is actually circumscribed by biological constraints at puberty.

Unfortunately, almost all of the authors and researchers who doubt or deny the existence of a critical period have not been careful in describing how much of a second language is affected by possible biological constraints. Phonology, morphology, lexicon, and syntax are lumped together; the issue of differential fossilization of phonology, especially those complex segmental and suprasegmental acoustic features that identify nonnative speech, is left unaddressed; the Joseph Conrad phenomenon is ignored. In brief, these writers are talking about the acquisition of language, but not the acquisition of speech. Here, I am including virtually all of the references cited in the section on "The Night of Black Cows": Clark and Clark (1977), Ellis (1985), Hakuta (1986), Holmstrand (1982), Klein (1986), McLaughlin, (1978), Reich (1986), Steinberg (1982), Stern (1982), van Els et al. (1984), and Walberg et al. (1978). Given the foundation and the evidence provided so far, I think you can see that the contradiction between the two points of view can be reconciled if we distinguish between a critical period for language and a critical period for speech. I believe, and there are certainly many others who agree, that there is no evidence for a critical period for *language*—for the acquisition of all the global linguistic skills that go into human communication, but it is obvious that I do believe, quite strongly, in a critical period for speech—specifically for the ability to sound like a native speaker. The evidence for this is overwhelming and compelling. So overwhelming that I cannot see how its existence can be denied; so compelling that nonbiological factors alone cannot account for its etiology.

Finally, what about the few studies reviewed in the previous chapter that claimed there was no evidence for a critical period even at the *phonological* level? Olsen and Samuels (1973) drew this conclusion—that children in their teens had better pronunciation than their prepubescent subjects. If we accept their results, two things should be noted: First, the researchers did not look at intonation and other suprasegmental information, so the ultimate question of "accented" speech is left unanswered, and second, the evidence on the superior pronunciation ability of older children is mixed. Note that Major (1987), reviewed earlier in this chapter, found accentedness detectable in the English of adult nonnative speakers only on the basis of the phonemic contrast of two vowel sounds. I think we could agree that irrespective of the *rate* of acquisition, and in this case older kids are generally faster, younger children appear to emerge eventually with a higher degree of performance. This would also account for the study by Snow and Hoefnagel-Hohle (1978). Their teenage subjects were quicker in learning Dutch pronunciation, just as they were quicker in picking up inflections and grammatical rules, but this does not prove that the postpubescent children ended up at a higher level of pronunciation proficiency. Indeed, from the experimental studies covered in this chapter, we see that regardless of how quickly or slowly you acquire a second language, if you pick it up after about the age of 10 to 12, you end up easily identified as a nonnative speaker of that language. This is exactly the conclusion reached by Krashen, Long, and Scarcella (1979), who summarize the work of Snow and Hoefnagel-Hohle, Walberg et al., and several other studies which had been published on child and adult second language acquisition to that date, and find confirmation for the following generalization:

> In other words, adults and older children in general initially acquire the second language faster than young children (older is better for rate of acquisition), but child second language acquirers will usually be superior in terms of ultimate attainment (younger is better in the long run). Distinguishing rate and attainment, then, resolves the apparent contradictions in the literature. (Krashen et al., 1979:161)

This has been a tedious, and perhaps even toilsome, accounting of the experimental work in support of a critical period for the attainment of accentless speech, but it is necessary in the face of the popular contention that either it does not exist at all or, if there are age constraints on language learning, they are caused exclusively by nonbiological factors. The detailed examination of the research in this chapter was necessary, however, because I feel that the empirical record should be known, and that the apparent contradictions between the literature reviewed in the previous chapter and the claims and proofs that have been proffered in this one can be resolved. However, now it is time to consider stories that are not so experimentally exacting, but, or because of this, these accounts are absolutely enthralling. Let us look for critical period evidence in the bizarre, almost unbelievable reports of children who grew up on their own and never had a chance to learn a human language until they were captured and removed from their inhuman habitats.

7

NATURE'S CRUEL AND UNUSUAL EXPERIMENTS—LIMITATIONS ON LANGUAGE LEARNING IN FERAL CHILDREN

From the hills of Rome, the forests of India, and the jungles of Africa, we have the stuff that myths are made of: the twins, Romulus and Remus, raised by a wolf; the young Mowgli, befriended by a bear; and the muscular Tarzan, swinging in the trees with his fellow apes. There is something innately captivating about the idea that humans can recapitulate their evolutionary origins and return, once again, in communal harmony to our fellow creatures that share this planet. This sentiment is not new, of course, and is found in the writings of a previous age:

> I am as free as Nature first made man,
> Ere the base laws of servitude began,
> When wild in woods the noble savage ran. (Dryden, 1968)

There is something innocuous and innocent about these accounts of wild, or feral children, and note how they contrast emotionally with other legends like those about "werewolves" (literally, "man wolves"). A child raised by wolves or in the wild attracts our sympathy and admiration; a grown adult that behaves like a wild wolf instills fear and revulsion! For the philosophers, when actual cases like Romulus and Remus are discovered, the question of the moment is: Are these wild children, "inhuman" because of their deprivation from society, or are they "noble savages," pristine examples of man-

124

kind before its fall? Regardless of the emotions we may harbor, and irrespective of the philosophical queries we may have, stories like these are worth telling here because they are basically tests of the impact that imprinting might have on human behavior. Nature has provided us with sometimes cruel, but always unusual experiments dealing with the existence of a critical period for the acquisition of speech and language, and we must scrutinize these accounts and see if we can sift facts from legends and come up with additional evidence to accompany the "unnatural," manipulated data gleaned from our carefully controlled scientific experiments.

WILD CHILD OR NOBLE SAVAGE?

When we examine these cases from the viewpoint of second language acquisition research, it is useful to place them into a psycholinguistic context. They attract our professional interest because they deal with the boundaries of our normal schema. Although they are technically cases of first language acquisition, they could be considered "second" language learning because of the way the feral children have to be taught and formally instructed. And the children themselves are sort of in the middle of a neat dichotomy between infants and adults. Using Brown's (1987) useful two-by-two matrix showing how important it is to distinguish between first or second language acquisition in children from second language learning in adults, we can see that the learning of a human language for the first time by these wild children presents a situation that is both peripheral to our normal classifications and yet central to our examination of how language is learned (Figure 7.1).

More than with any other topic discussed in this book, the accounts of children raised by animals or living alone in the wild is by far the most difficult to base empirically or even to substantiate. The very nature of living alone in nature, or at least isolated from human contact, means that there are no records, no observations, no facts which we can go on. We are dealing, in a real sense, with contemporary prehistory; we have no attested historical documents to verify human conditions which we believe to be true. Compounded to the absence of detail is our natural tendency to view these stories with fascination and, in some cases, embellish them with speculation. We all know people who never let truth stand in the way of a good story! I quote, at some length, a typical newspaper account of a feral child, this one much more recent than many, but it aptly illustrates the promise and problem of using this sort of evidence to help us better understand second language acquisition:

Boy Raised by Wolves in India Dies

New Delhi, India (UPI)—Ramu, the "wolf boy" raised by a pack of wolves in a jungle where he was found in 1976, has died at a home for

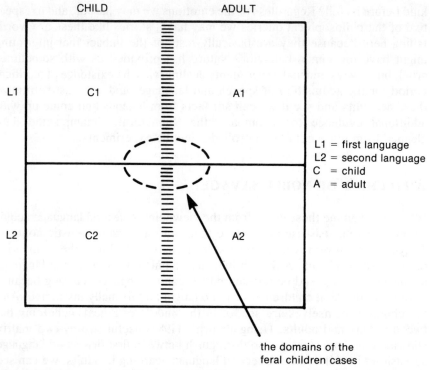

CHILD   ADULT

L1   C1   A1

L1 = first language
L2 = second language
C = child
A = adult

L2   C2   A2

the domains of the
feral children cases

Figure. 7.1 Language acquisition in normal children, adults, and wolf children. (*Source:* After Brown, 1987:41.) Adapted by permission of Prentice-Hall, Inc., Englewood Cliffs, New Jersey.

paupers run by Nobel Laureate Mother Teresa. He was 19 and never learned to speak. . . .

His death last Monday—reported by the *Times of India* yesterday—leaves his jungle origins and his life with the wolf family a mystery. The *Times of India* said he developed cramps about two weeks ago and failed to respond to medical treatment. . . .

When Ramu was discovered in a jungle forest near Musafirkhana in 1976, he was naked and walking on all fours, rescuers said. The nails on his fingers and toes had grown to the length of claws, they said, and his palms, elbows, and knees were calloused. His hair was matted. He fought to avoid capture, reports said, but was restrained and taken to the Little Flower convent in Sultanpur district.

Zoologists from throughout India were called to examine him. They agreed that his survival in the jungle was made possible by the wolf family that treated him as one of its cubs. The boy was later moved from the convent and placed in the care of Mother Teresa's Missionaries of Charities Prem Nivas home in Lucknow. Under the nun's tutelage, he learned to bathe and dress himself but never learned to speak. (*San Francisco Examiner & Chronicle,* 1985:A16)

The emotional side of us is intrigued: long nails, matted hair, calloused limbs from running on all fours. But if we step back from the story and examine it as behavioral scientists, a host of unanswerable questions arises. How do we know his age? He was reportedly 19 years old when he died, but how was it possible to determine this without a birth certificate, public testimony, or the boy's own corroboration? How long had the child lived with wolves? We among all creatures are born the most premature; we alone must spend months and months learning to walk and eat, and years and years learning how to fend and forage for ourselves. Indeed, I have heard some parents in modern American society complain that some of their human offspring have *still* not learned how to survive independently even after three decades of upbringing. Be that as it may, it is an undeniable fact that Ramu was not sired by wolves, and it is a logical assumption that he was not raised by them as a tiny infant but, at some point in his young human life, was somehow abandoned in the wild and fell into the company of another species. At what age all of this occurred is beyond our ken, but, at the very least, Ramu had some contact with humans at a tender age, and though the contact itself may not have been tender, it is inconceivable that he had grown up never having had any interaction at all with humans. Other questions abound. How healthy was Ramu as a tiny baby? Was he abandoned by his human parents because they coldly refused to care for an infant whom they perceived to be retarded or physically disabled? We will see in the final case to be reviewed in this chapter that such a misperception by a parent led to even graver consequences than the unfortunate events which affected Ramu. Knowing full well that wolf cubs grow independent from a pack in a season or two, we wonder if Ramu wandered year to year, ever seeking or being sought by a bitch with a new litter. We are simply powerless to answer any of these vexing queries, but without any answers at all, it is difficult to determine what these cases can tell us about the importance of early socialization for normal human behavior.

These reports, as I have said, have captured the public's imagination over the years, and they are not as uncommon as you might expect. To my knowledge, the best compendium of cases is found in Lucien Malson (1972), *Wolf Children and the Wild Boy of Averyron,* for he cites 53 reports, some of which, I am sure, are of dubious authenticity. Still, the names of the children themselves display a great geographical variety and an almost whimsical character. To give you a flavor of this variety, here is a list of a few of the cases in chronological order: the first Lithuanian bear-child (1661); the Bamberg calf-child (about 1680); the Karpfen bear-girl (1767); the Salzburg sow-girl (1843); Clemens, the Overdyke pig-child (1863); the Jalpaiguri girl (1876); the Justedal snow-hen (1895); Lucas, the South African baboon-child (1904); the Indian panther-child (1920); Assicia of Liberia (1930); the second leopard-child (1940); the Mauritanian gazelle-child (1960); the Teheran ape-child

(1961), etc. Regardless of their veracity, the names themselves are connotative and colorful.

Malson's book is interesting in another way because, as a Marxist author, he has used this compilation of cases to prove that we are not innately "noble savages" but are conditioned by our social environment; thus, the wild children are proof positive that it is not nature but entirely nurture that shapes our behavior. I began this book by stressing the fallacy of looking to either extreme as the source of human action, but regardless of his bias and his conclusions, Malson's historical review of this topic is useful. Useful too are occasional quotes he cites in support of the importance of early socialization, and some of them make explicit mention of the critical period:

> There is a period during which a child is particularly sensitive to language during which he can learn to talk. It has been shown that if the child . . . is not in an environment in which there are people to talk, then he will never be able to talk with the same ease as those who have learnt to speak during the period in question. (Merleau-Ponty in Malson, 1972:56)

Curtiss (1980) divides all the cases of feral children into three categories in terms of their relevance to assessing the critical period for language acquisition: children raised alone—or, more properly, who raised themselves; children raised by animals; and children raised by insane parents or caretakers. Because there are only three well-attested reports of wolf children from all the curious cases cited in the literature, because these three cases are fitting examples of each of the three categories listed by Curtiss, because the three occur chronologically in the same sequence as the one just mentioned, and since they are accounts from three different continents, I will use Curtiss's classification to introduce three studies that reflect enormous diversity but are united in their support for the notion that language must be imprinted early or not at all.

VICTOR—A BOY RAISED ALONE

The two most famous cases in Europe are of Victor, who was found in southern France during the first few days of the nineteenth century, and Kaspar Hauser, who was discovered a few years later in Germany. But I am excluding the second case from the ones on which we should focus our attention in this chapter because it is a much less believable story than Victor's. Kaspar was supposedly imprisoned for many years as a younger child, reputedly without much human contact, and after many years, he was somehow discovered wandering around free. Subsequently, he was taught for several years and cared for, and seemed to be progressing successfully until the memory of his earlier travails came back to him, and he allegedly was able to remember the identity of his captors. Shortly after this, he was found half dead and seriously wounded, and could only mutter the word *man* when asked what had happened. Evidently, his unknown enemy returned, four years later, and in 1833 Kaspar was found stabbed to death in a park. Later, according to some accounts, it was discovered that Kaspar was a distant contender for the crown, and he was first imprisoned and then done away with to remove him from royal competition. Although this story has all the ingredients of a novel and has, in fact, been turned into a movie (*Every Man for Himself and God against All,* directed by Werner Herzog), it is a much more confusing and suspicious tale than the case of Victor, or the other two accounts which I would now like to share with you.

Kaspar Hauser is not the only feral child to inspire a film. Francois Truffaut, the great French director, produced *L'Enfant Sauvage* ("The Wild Child") in 1969 to capture on film the poignant story of Victor, discovered in the district of Aveyron. The story of Victor is best recounted in two highly readable and informative books by Lane (1976) and Shattuck (1980), and these are my references for the subsequent discussion of this case. Victor's story is really a tale about three people, for he is not the only character. Well known to those who have read about this case, and certainly prominent in the books by Lane and Shattuck, is Jean Itard, the doctor who devoted several years of his life to the ambitious but ultimately unattainable goal of turning Victor into a linguistic, socialized, and civilized human being. Less famous by far was the dedicated Madame Guerin, the housekeeper who took care of Victor from the time he was moved to Paris, only a few weeks after his capture, until the time of his death, almost three decades later. One of the ironies of this case is that Victor was practically the toast of postrevolutionary Paris during the first few years of the new century, when the scientific community laid odds on whether Itard could tame the savage beast or whether the years of early conditioning in the wilds would win out, and then, after a few years, when Itard's interests shifted and high society's attention waned, perhaps because Victor did acculturate somewhat and became less of a curiosity, the wild child literally dropped out of sight, and except for the barest of details, we know nothing about his last 17 years. We do know that he spent the remainder of his life with Madame Guerin, and so we can conclude that she provided him the affection he was denied as a child and the humanity that Itard tried to teach, but which Victor was able to learn only from her.

There are so many intriguing aspects of these accounts of feral children that it is easy to get diverted from our central concern with language and become tangentially preoccupied with the sometimes sad and sometimes amusing anecdotes about attempts to change Victor's eating habits, to develop his cognitive powers, or to deal with his latent sexual drives. But there is enough that is interesting about his language use and disuse alone. From the beginning, it was clear that he was literally *l'enfant sauvage*—the French word for "child" being a cognate of "infant"—from the Latin, "without speech." The description of the child, soon after discovery and capture, by Bonaterre, a professor of natural history in Aveyron, makes this clear:

> Although the tongue of this young wild boy is normally formed, and does not cleave to the palate, he has no language other than some inarticulate sounds. His expressive sounds, rarely emitted unless he is emotional, are rather noisy, especially those of anger and displeasure; when joyful, he laughs heartily; when content, he makes a murmuring sound, a kind of grunting. (Bonaterre, in Lane, 1976:38)

Even in the depths of misery in his early years in Paris, where he appeared to long for the quiet confines of the fields and forests to the south, and where a thunderstorm would evoke an almost hypnotic longing in his demeanor, Victor was never seen to cry. It even appeared that he did not sneeze until Itard had trained him to discriminate a wider range of smells. When he did sneeze, his reaction of fright suggested that it was a completely new response to him. For a long time, he displayed all the symptoms of an autistic child: He had no language and rarely made vocalic sounds; he spent hours alone, often rocking back and forth in an almost catatonic state; he would ignore voices and faces; and he seemed impervious to other changes in his environment. There are two conflicting views on whether Victor, or any of the other legitimate cases of feral children, was autistic. Bettelheim (1959) claims that he was, and that his autistic behavior, like autism in the normal population, stemmed from extreme emotional deprivation in early childhood. As Lane puts it so well, "But the salient fact about Victor is not that he lived in the wild, but that he lived there alone." (Lane, 1976:174) I hasten to emphasize that Bettelheim's explanation for the etiology of this illness is nowadays rejected by most people, but I cite him here because he thinks the feral children are afflicted with this syndrome. Lane considers the arguments both pro and con and concludes that autism alone does not adequately explain Victor's condition:

> Victor's symptoms, then, including his mutism, may overlap with those of congenital retardation or autism, but are explained by neither; instead they are the result of his isolation in the wild, as Itard maintained all along. (Lane, 1976:179)

Another, though even less likely, affliction that Victor might have been subject to was epilepsy. Several times in the accounts written by Itard, he describes states of anger or disruption that progressed into a fitful behavior closely resembling epilepsy:

His outbreaks of anger became more frequent and more violent and resembled the fits of rage I have already referred to. But they were directed less against people than against things. In this destructive state he rebelled by chewing his sheets and blankets, biting the mantelpiece, throwing andirons, ashes, and burning coals around his room. He would then fall into convulsions. As in an epileptic fit, he would end up by losing consciousness. (Itard, in Shattuck, 1980:122)

Concerning his language development, despite all the hours of instruction and conditioning on linguistic learning by Itard, Victor did not fare much better than Vicki, the chimp that was reared in a home in an effort to teach it human communication. Do not misunderstand me; I am not at the very least implying that Victor was anything but completely human in the physical, moral, and spiritual senses of the word, but when we look at his meager linguistic development, his productive vocabulary was extremely limited. One of Victor's few words, pronounced very indistinctly, you might note, was *lait* ("milk"), but his mentor soon discovered that even this modest success was not without drawbacks:

Itard perceived two serious flaws in the way Victor used his first word. First, Victor would not detach the word from the presence of what it meant—from its "referent." There is no true language without that separation. Second, what lait referred to for Victor was extremely imprecise. Clearly, it did not mean "white liquid produced by a female mammal, anywhere, anytime." His behavior suggested something closer to: "my pleasure in drinking this white water, right here, right now." Itard watched his triumph turn to ashes. (Shattuck, 1980:148)

Itard was so influenced by his failure to teach Victor any substantive linguistic communication that it prompted him to come close to defining a critical period for language acquisition a good century and a half before the publication of the writings of Penfield and Lenneberg. Itard summarized most of his long association with Victor in a short list of five "truths" that emerged from his research on his ingenuous but frustrating pupil:

In behalf of a critical period for language acquisition, "That this imitative force, whose purpose is the education of his organs and especially the apprenticeship of speech, and which is very energetic and active during the first years of his life, wanes rapidly with age, with isolation, and with all the causes which tend to blunt nervous sensitivity. We may conclude that the articulation of sounds, indisputably the most unimaginable and useful result of imitation, must encounter innumerable obstacles at any age later than early childhood." (Itard, in Lane, 1976:129)

Itard's lack of success was not solely confined to language development, but it became obvious that the early isolation from normal human interaction prevented Victor from maturing cognitively, socially, and emotionally, and Itard became disenchanted with transforming Victor into a civilized citizen of Paris, and simultaneously grew interested in advocating the teaching of sign language to the deaf. His frustration is aptly captured in several expressions of doubt and dismay, one of which reveals an explicit admission that his young wild child was really an incarnation of Rousseau's noble savage. Such outbursts by Itard sprang in response to emotional fits of despair by Victor:

> I cannot describe the pained expression on his face with his eyes closed and every so often a tear coming out between the lids. Oh! at that moment as at many others when I was ready to give up the task I had imposed on myself and when I looked on all my time as wasted, how deeply I regretted ever having known this child, and how I condemned the barren and inhuman curiosity of those men who first uprooted him from an innocent and happy life! (Itard, in Shattuck, 1980:146)

Like Ramu, the reputed wolf child of India reported in the recent newspaper account, Victor's age was unclear. From his appearance and a thorough physical examination, he seemed to be about 12. He became pubescent early after his capture, and so we know that all of these attempts to teach him language came at the time the critical period was completed. His failure to learn language partly substantiates the claims I am making for language acquisition, although I think you can see even in this first story that the wild children present only negative proof. Neither Victor nor any other wild child that I am aware of who was socialized after about the first decade of life learned to speak, let alone learned to sound like a native speaker of the target community. This will be evident from all of the cases investigated in this chapter. However, the supposed cases of feral children who were socialized at very young ages—say, 6 or 7,—before the advent of puberty, but also never learned to talk, does not disprove the hypothesis. In some cases, like that of Isabelle of Ohio (Curtiss, 1980), who was resocialized at about the age of 6½, the improvement has been remarkable, but, of course, there are no cases of feral children learning to sound exactly like native speakers. They, like some autistic children, represent a tiny minority who are prevented from learning language even though they are still young and have the opportunity. The reason that young feral children might not ever learn to talk normally is quite logically due to the extreme psychosocial pathology of their early childhood isolation or, in the most cruel cases, to the traumatic abuse of demented parents. I think it was the American humorist Robert Benchley who said that you can't prove a platypus doesn't lay eggs by taking a picture of it not laying eggs. The fact that all children do not grow up speaking perfectly does not prove that there is no critical period.

After five years of study, Itard gave up on Victor in 1806. For some years, Victor and Madame Guerin continued to live at the Institute for Deaf

Mutes, where Itard had undertaken his investigation of the wild child from Aveyron, and then in 1811 they moved to an ordinary residence in Paris for the rest of Victor's life in complete anonymity. We have no death certificate and no records of where he was buried. We do know he died in 1828, at about the age of 40, in the same year Kaspar Hauser was found wandering in the streets of Nuremberg. One final footnote of historical interest. A famous French author with the same first name lived four houses down the street from where Victor and Madame Guerin spent their last 17 years together, and it is not at all improbable that the frequent sight of the socially crippled noble savage inspired this writer to produce his most famous work, *The Hunchback of Notre Dame.*

KAMALA—A GIRL RAISED BY WOLVES

We move to a different century, a different continent, and a set of rather different conditions, to the story of actually two wolf children found in eastern India in the fall of 1920. Having lived in India as a boy myself, I can appreciate how accounts like these are more common in South Asia than in some other areas of the world; the region is generally rich in vegetation, the climate is largely hospitable to living without shelter, and the human population is so large that the boundaries between animals and people are constantly challenged. Humans and animals are reincarnations of one another in the myths and rituals of that colorful country, and it is easy to see how stories of feral children, both real and fanciful, are perpetuated. Kamala of Midnapore is the best-documented case to emerge from that part of the world in several centuries, and though her story provides some interesting contrasts to Victor, it leads us to the same unsurprising conclusion. My primary reference for the following account comes primarily from the readable book by Maclean (1979).

In the fall of 1920, Rev. J. A. L. Singh, an Indian missionary who ran an orphanage in the eastern province of Bengal, was out on a hunting expedition about 50 miles south of his hometown of Midnapore. The locals living around the jungles of that area had been talking for some time about strange *manush bagha* ("man beasts") seen furtively stalking the forests at night, and Reverend Singh, who pursued hunting with the same missionary zeal that he displayed running his orphanage, spent several nights watching an abandoned termite mound where these supposed man beasts were lurking with a pack of wolves. One night, they were able to surprise the animals, and the locals who accompanied Reverend Singh killed the mother wolf as she emerged from the mound, and began digging inside the den where a furry ball of cubs had bundled together in terror. Imagine their surprise after they were able to force the cubs apart when, with much snarling and nipping, they discovered two of them to be little girls, aged about 3 and 6, though again we

133

really are quite unsure. Reverend Singh arranged to have them transported to the orphanage and gave them the names Amala and Kamala. Both girls were sickly, malnourished, and infested with parasites, and Amala, the younger of the two "sisters" (though we have no record that they were actually siblings), never did recover completely and died almost a year after their capture. Mrs. Singh, who had devoted her attention to both children, now directed much of her time to nurturing Kamala, and she became to the surviving sister what Madame Guerin had been to Victor—the anonymous yet faithful human caretaker who was the mother they never really knew when they lived in their natural state.

Like Victor, these children were fascinating creatures to observe during the early months of their captivity because every one of their actions seemed to be conditioned by the specific influence of their natural environment. Unlike Victor, who was by and large herbivorous and was especially fond of nuts, the Midnapore children were voracious carnivores, nocturnal by nature and snarling and testy by temperament. For a long time, they would eat nothing but raw meat, something the Singhs, but not the girls, found particularly distasteful, and among the delicacies Amala and Kamala enjoyed during their nocturnal forages around the yard were cockroaches and mice. You can imagine what the other children in the orphanage felt: They probably believed the new residents were truly werewolves! The Singhs were gradually able to wean the wild children from meat to a diet of vegetables and rice, and after months of laborious conditioning, Kamala slowly acquired a minimally acceptable level of social behavior.

Kamala outlived her wolf "sister" almost nine years and, in 1929, died of nephritis at about the age of 15. Neither of the two Indian girls lived nearly as long as Victor, and the frailty of their physical condition probably tells us more about the impoverishment of Asia, especially at that time and place, than it does about the natural physical strength of the sexes or the relative merit of different kinds of diet. We would expect that the course of her language development would be comparatively successful because she was found only about halfway through the first decade of life and, unlike Victor, who was around 12 at his apprehension, was far from the constraints of the critical period. But remember that these natural experiments are not just measures of linguistic deprivation; they are tests of all sorts of limitations, and the opportunity to learn a language before puberty is a necessary, but not sufficient, condition for the complete and accurate acquisition of a primary language. It is a great loss that we have only haphazard references to Kamala's language development:

Unfortunately, Singh is less informative on this subject and less consistent with the information he does offer than on many other not so critical aspects of her behaviour. As a schoolmaster polyglot and amateur philosopher, one might have expected him to take particular interest in

Kamala's efforts towards acquiring language, and indeed the careful logging of her first attempts at speech indicate that he was interested, but he lacked both the time and the close relationship that his wife enjoyed with Kamala to make a detailed study of her linguistic unfolding, such as it was. However, it emerges clearly that Kamala did learn to speak and to understand considerably more than she could express, and that the progress she made with language, as recorded by Singh, follows a pattern which matches the overall picture of her development. (Maclean, 1979:166–167)

Almost from the beginning, Reverend Singh was besieged by the public curiosity that Kamala had aroused, and it was not very long before international reports circulated and foreign scholars became interested in the wolf girl of Midnapore. One of these, an American anthropologist, worked most closely with the Indian missionary, and together they published the diary account of Kamala's years at the orphanage (Singh & Zingg, 1942).

From this account, it is evident that Maclean's observations are accurate and that there is precious little in Singh's diary that gives us an accurate picture of Kamala's linguistic development. The most information we have is a list of some 40 words that represented part of her vocabulary at about the age of 10 (Singh & Zingg, 1942:103–104), and from the fragmented information that we possess, we can see that Kamala appeared to use the same processes of phonological simplification and lexical overgeneralization employed by normal children, though at a far earlier age. Maclean briefly describes some of her lexical and phonological learning:

The new words came in quick succession: Bha(t) (rice), Bhal (alright), Am(I), Khai (eat), Papa (Rev. Singh) and Lal (red). She learnt the names of some of the other children, but could only get out the first syllable or a one-syllable approximation of their names. She would say "Soo" for Saraju, for instance. Later on, when she began putting two words together, she would run the sounds into each other so that "Ami Jabo" (I will) became "Amjab," or "Toommy" (I am) became "Toom." It was hardly an impressive performance, but in the circumstances it was an encouraging start. (Maclean, 1979:170–171)

Even as she got older, it appeared that the cognitive, emotional, and social deprivation she had endured as a younger child took its toll on her ability to develop significant interpersonal relationships and to communicate effectively:

By the beginning of 1926, at an age of approximately eleven or twelve years, Kamala still had a vocabulary of no more than thirty words, which she made sparing use of, not always answering when spoken to and rarely initiating speech, except to jabber away to herself as she walked

135

under the trees in the garden, or sat in her corner alone. (Maclean, 1979:182–183)

It is a shame we do not have a tape of her private moments of glossolalia. I doubt if we would have found any evidence for improvement in her acquisition of Bengali, but those inarticulate soliloquies could have given us a glimpse into her own little mental world, and I suspect that her babbling might very well have been a recapitulation of the grasping for sounds and syllables that a human infant makes and that Kamala herself once made. She continued very slowly in her linguistic development until her death, and at this stage, she apparently used snatches of syntax with several words strung together. For instance: "*Ma Ma chota bulu fullachbe* ("Mama, the little one hurts") (Maclean, 1979:218).

Kamala died in 1929 of complications resulting from kidney failure, the same malady that befell her younger "sister" eight years previously. She was buried in the churchyard under a banyan tree next to Amala, and, unfortunately, all of the mystery that shrouded the children's early life from our understanding lies buried with her. She never learned enough of language to tell us about where she came from or who she really was.

GENIE—A CHILD RAISED IN INSANITY

Tragic as the accounts of Victor, Amala, and Kamala may be, the tale of the third wild child which I have chosen to relate strikes us with pathos and pity. The ironies in the case of Genie are profuse and vexing: She is by far the most assiduously examined feral child for whom we have records, and yet her case adds little to our understanding of early childhood deprivation; she is the only child for whom we have accurate birth records and descriptions of neonatal development before social and language deprivation, and yet this information only obfuscates our comprehension of how genetic or neonatal influences might affect the developmental prognosis of feral children. Ironic too is the fact that when the news broke about this story in Los Angeles in the fall of 1970, it was seen as an unbelievably grotesque event, but unfortunately, some two decades later, reports of severe abuse and deprivation are no longer unique. All of this is a way of repeating an earlier warning—that human behavior is so extremely complex and complicated that it is doubly difficult to extract from it clear-cut, dependent variables to which we can attribute certain measures of performance. For Genie, we are able to quantify many of the factors that surround her attempts to acquire language, but she is not a living Rosetta stone from which we can decipher the exact ways that nature and nurture come together in time to create human speech.

The details of Genie's childhood deprivation are so sordid that they need not be detailed here. Suffice it to say that for a period of almost 12 years, from the time she was 2 until her discovery by the outside world at 13½, she was confined by her crazed father to a small bedroom, where she spent most of the time strapped in a harness and out of touch with the sights, sounds, smells, and tastes of a normal world. You may wonder why or how Genie's case can be lumped together with the other feral children as an example of a "natural" experiment. The key issue is early deprivation from normal social and linguistic intercourse, and, in Genie's situation, she was almost as isolated from the world of people, or at least of sane people, as Victor and the children of Midnapore. Surely, something inside us rebels so strongly at the frightful abuse that Genie endured that, by contrast, we find ourselves almost admiring the other feral children: Their situation is spontaneous and wholesome, and their conditions seem comparatively human; though Genie lived with people, the inhumane treatment she suffered makes her case the inhuman one. The first two situations I described were nature's unusual experiments; now we consider one that is unusually cruel.

The single most useful source for psycholinguistic information about Genie is Curtiss (1977), a book based largely on her doctoral dissertation at UCLA. Curtiss's work summarizes competing ideas about the critical period hypothesis, so she is obviously interested in this modern-day wild child for the identical professional reasons we are. The book follows Genie's social, psychological, cognitive, and, above all, linguistic development for a period of about five years (1970–1975) and provides additional information about neonatal development from hospital records, with this, and a brief description from Genie's mother about what occurred during the intolerable years of bestial captivity (her deranged father committed suicide shortly after her rescue), we have the most evidence ever assembled about the conditions surrounding a child who has been isolated from language before puberty. These two separate sources of information cloud the picture somewhat. Because Genie did not live alone and because she was visited and fed at least daily, it wasn't that she had no exposure to humans but that her contacts were very limited and perverted. According to the mother's testimony, her father never spoke to her and punished her if she made any noises whatsoever. From her hospital records, we know that she was not a completely normal baby. She had a congenital hip problem, which was corrected by a splint worn during her first year, and soon after the splint was removed, she contracted acute pneumonia, and the attending pediatrician observed possible signs of mental retardation. It was this diagnosis that triggered her insane father to subject Genie to the long and cruel confinement. Even though we have much more information about Genie than we have for any other feral child, certain issues are almost as unclear about her as they are about her predecessors. For example, we are not positive that she is a perfect "test" case because she may have already had some genetic or congenital weaknesses that were exacerbated by the appalling brutality to which she was subjected. Do not think I am saying that her problems stemmed largely from nature and not nurture, but I am asking you to be open-minded about the likelihood that many other children may have emerged from an identical experience of pathetic treatment with more success and resilience.

In light of the psychological and neuropsychological measures made of Genie's development and lack thereof, Curtiss contends that Genie's isolation from language and her simultaneous exposure to a narrow world of sensorimotor movement and perception gave her a proclivity to process information through her right hemisphere. Accepting the somewhat simplistic dichotomy that the left hemisphere is the synthetic, "linguistic" side of the brain and the contralateral hemisphere is the analytic, "perceptual" half (Springer & Deutsch, 1981), then it is natural to assume that Genie's condition doubly reinforced a tendency to use the right hemisphere. It is relevant to note that prisoners confined in isolation for long periods of time and who are also restricted in their physical movement, appear to spend a great deal of time scrutinizing the few objects that surround them and engaging in other "right hemisphere" imaging (Weir and Weir, 1987). Curtiss claims that Genie was a "right hemisphere" thinker and language user because of her abnormal early conditioning, and she apparently substantiates this claim with results from an impressive battery of neuropsychological and neurolinguistic tests (e.g. dichotic listening, tachistoscopic measures, and a wide range of "paper-and-pencil" tests). She finishes her book with a particularly apt conclusion:

> From our observations and testing, Genie appears to be a right-hemisphere thinker. Most importantly, she uses her right hemisphere for language. Genie's language is abnormal in specific ways. Her language resembles that of other cases of right-hemisphere language as well as the language of those generally acquiring language outside of the "critical period." Her case, therefore, supports Lenneberg's "critical period" hypothesis and furthermore suggests specific constraints and limitations on the nature of language acqusition outside of this maturational period. (Curtiss, 1977:234)

Given the neurolinguistic tests alone, Curtiss voices an even more specific and intriguing speculation:

> The dichotic listening tests indicate that her language *is* right-hemisphere language. Thus, Genie's case may indicate that after the "critical period," the left hemisphere can no longer assume control in language acquisition, and the right hemisphere will function and predominate in the acquisition and representation of language. (Curtiss, 1977:216)

Since I find the evidence for Genie's reputed right hemisphere processing not nearly as convincing as Curtiss does, I will not hurry to endorse this speculation about lateralization and the critical period, comfortably though it

138

may accommodate the views that have been advocated thus far, but we should remain open-minded about the possibility. In some ways, it is similar to the idea that Seliger (1981) suggests for exceptions to critical period constaints, which will be brought up in Chapter 9.

Curtiss devotes most of her book to an assessment of the growth and plateauing of Genie's language. Although her phonology improved, her pronunciation never has come close to approximating that of a native speaker of English, and when we compare her overall pronunciation with the little data that we have for Kamala's Bengali, the similarities are apparent. For instance, Genie also would delete final consonants and syllables: /pu/ for "pool," /pi/ for "pink," and /pir/ for "period" (Curtiss, 1977:73). She also had difficulty acquiring appropriate suprasegmental sounds; for example, she used accurate word stress but not phrasal stress (perhaps because the latter involves phrase structure information), and she was not able to acquire normal intonation patterns (Curtiss, 1977:90). Her lexical and syntactic learning was constrained in a variety of ways, so we can see that, like all of the other feral children, Genie suffered from the fact that she was not exposed to human language and interaction for a sufficient period of time in early childhood. She is like Victor in that her socialization began late, at about the same age as the nineteenth-century wild child, for she was just into her teens, although her progress is clearly better than that found in the fragmentary records of the feral boy.

All this said and done, the evidence from Victor—a boy raised alone, Kamala—a girl raised by wolves, and Genie—a child raised in insanity *indirectly* supports critical period limitations for speech, and quite possibly for language too, although you may remember that my contention is that a strong version for imprinting before puberty in humans can ultimately be found only in speech. What we obviously have *direct* evidence for is that early and natural socialization and interpersonal interaction is crucial to human development, irrespective of the acquisition of communicative skills. We can see this clearly in Victor, Kamala, and all the other unusual natural cases. And from the cruel cases like Genie, we know that it is far better to be abandoned than to be abused.

8

ARGUMENTS AND COUNTERARGUMENTS—MORE NONBIOLOGICAL EXPLANATIONS FOR A CRITICAL PERIOD

Fascinating as nature's cruel and unusual experiments may be, we can see that studies of feral children lack rigor and incisiveness because they are usually poorly documented, and their naturalness makes it inherently difficult to quantify the relative influence of various stimuli. We are constantly asked to compare apples and oranges. One can surely sympathize with Lenneberg's laconic summary of the wild child cases he reviewed:

> The only safe conclusions to be drawn from the multitude of reports is that life in dark closets, wolves' dens, forests, or sadistic parents' backyards is not conducive to good health and normal development. (Lenneberg, 1967:142)

This is why I would like us to return to the empirical stance I have adopted for this examination of the critical period and look at more quantifiable evidence. In this chapter, we will consider arguments against the views I have espoused throughout the book and which were introduced in some detail in Chapter 3. At the start of Chapter 5, you were already alerted to the fact that my views on the critical period reflect the minority opinion among second language acquisition researchers, and now you will be presented with even more evidence against my biological perspective—evidence which I will attempt to refute. You alone are responsible for deciding whose data is more compelling and whose arguments are most convincing.

KRASHEN'S LATERALIZATION BY FIVE HYPOTHESIS

In a paper published three years after my early article on this subject, Krashen coauthored a short study (Krashen & Harshman, 1972) that set the stage for his more widely read publications and for his now well-known "monitor" model of second language acquisition. In this article, the authors reexamine much of the data which Lenneberg gave to suggest that lateralization of language to the left hemisphere (in most cases) was completed about puberty. From their reanalysis, the authors conclude that lateralization is actually completed much earlier, around the age of 5, thus vitiating the idea that loss of neuroplasticity is a probable cause for the language learning difficulties of people past puberty. By arguing against a biological etiology for such phenomena as foreign accents, the authors effectively open up the possibility that nurture and not nature is responsible. They do see nature (lateralization) and nurture (the linguistic environment) interacting in the first few years of development, but they assume that this interaction is finished long before puberty begins:

> Perhaps the best interpretation is neither that late lateralization causes poor language nor the reverse, but rather that external linguistic behavior and internal linguistic lateralization are parallel manifestations of crucial processes of linguistic development normally taking place in the first five years of a child's life. (Krashen & Harshman, 1972:17)

In less than a year, Krashen published "Lateralization, language learning, and the critical period: Some new evidence," (Krashen, 1973), which was his reply to my first *Language Learning* article (Scovel, 1969), and in the next two years, he followed up with two other publications which reiterated and expanded upon the ideas that were first articulated in Krashen and Harshman, 1972. Both papers (Krashen 1975a, 1975b) were read at conferences and subsequently published in the conferences' proceedings: the Georgetown University Round Table on Developmental Psycholinguistics: Theory and Applications, and the New York Academy of Sciences conference on Developmental Psycholinguistics and Communication Disorders. Central to all of these articles are the following claims: (1) A reanalysis of Basser's work on aphasics (cited in Lenneberg) suggests that lateralization for language is completed at about 5, (2) results from dichotic listening studies and other kinds of experiments also implicate this early age for lateralization, (3) the case of Genie (based on the first few years of investigation) suggests that successful language acquisition can take place after puberty, and, finally, (4) nonneurological factors such as cognitive maturity may more adequately account for any language learning constraints which arise at puberty. I would like us to consider each of these in reverse order, giving particular scrutiny to (1), because it is the issue of lateralization that is of the most relevance to my 1969 article and to the whole notion that neuroplasticity is programmed and timed genetically as part of the innate releasing mechanism responsible for the normal and accurate acquisition of human speech.

I have already acknowledged in Chapter 5 that cognitive and affective variables play an important role in language learning, first or second, but, at the same time, you have read in the sections titled "Cognitive Causes" and "The Effect of Affect" that because of their failure to account for the Joseph Conrad phenomenon, among other things, these factors do not explain foreign accents. Yes, as Krashen has emphasized continually, cognition and affect are exceedingly important to successful language acquisition, but this, of course, is not the issue. The issue is whether either variable can account for the emergence of foreign accents after the first decade of life, and here, the answer is clearly no.

In the same way, we can discount the claim made about Genie. The publications cited here (Krashen, 1973, 1975a, 1975b) were based on the early work with her, not too long after she was found. Krashen himself was a coauthor of one of the first scholarly articles to come out on Genie (Fromkin, Krashen, Curtiss, Rigler, & Rigler, 1974), and that publication was quite optimistic about Genie's progress to that date and about the possibility of her eventual linguistic success. As we know from our perusal of Curtiss's work in Chapter 7 (Curtiss, 1977) and from the apparent and unfortunate lack of substantive linguistic progress up to the present, Genie is not a counterexample to any critical period claims.

The dichotic listening data Krashen presents is more pertinent to our discussion. This is a procedure developed by Kimura (1961) where competing signals are played to both ears via headphones, and a subject tries to respond to signals given in only one ear. The accuracy achieved for a particular ear is a reflection, supposedly, of the involvement of the contralateral hemisphere. That is, more accurate results with the left ear in music apparently indicate that the *right* hemisphere is more active in processing nonlinguistic sounds, whereas more accurate results with the right ear in remembering sequences of numbers suggests that the *left* hemisphere is responsible for sequential processing. After reviewing several dichotic listening studies using a special percentage scoring system he developed with Harshman (Krashen & Harshman, 1972), he argues that dichotic listening measures of children of different ages do not vary significantly and appear to plateau at about 5, or even 4 (Krashen, 1973; 66–67). On the basis of this calculation, then, Krashen concludes that lateralization for language is completed at a much earlier age than that posited by Lenneberg and others.

The dichotic listening data is not that simple, however. In his George-town Round Table paper, Krashen (1975a) himself presents contradictory data. He mentions a study by Satz, Bakker, Tenunissen, Goebel, and Van der Vlugt (1975) where their dichotic listening experiment with 24 children aged 6 to 14 revealed that the strength of right ear advantage (and hence the reputedly increased involvement of the left hemisphere) actually *increased* with age and became significant at 9 and levelled off at 11. Porter and Berlin (1975) also found correct scores improving with age. This directly contra-dicts Krashen's early lateralization hypothesis, and he tries to explain away the discrepancy by saying that it conflicts with the *aphasia* data, which Krashen sees as pointing to age 5. But such reasoning is illogical because it is not fair to validate the results of dichotic listening experiments on normals with the results of aphasia tests run on brain-damaged patients. Besides, it seems odd to accept the dichotic listening measures as proof when they are similar to the aphasia data but to reject them as "inconsistent" when they conflict. The dichotic listening experiments should be accepted or rejected as relevant to the issue at hand, regardless of whether the findings of the experiments are in complete agreement and irrespective of whether the ex-periments as a whole are consistent with another set of psycholinguistic measures. My own view is that dichotic listening tests are much more sus-ceptible to inconsistency than other measures (see, for example, Berlin & Cullen 1977), and I do not see this kind of evidence giving us clear corrobora-tion of the age at which lateralization has completed. Springer and Deutsch (1981) seem to share this same hesitation about giving dichotic listening studies as much credence as other techniques of assessing changes in latera-lization:

> Given the variability in outcome of studies using different methodolo-gies, as well as the variability found in studies using the same measure of lateralization, it is clearly premature to draw conclusions regarding change in asymmetry with age. Further research using more refined measures of lateralization should provide the answers. (Springer & Deutsch, 1981:141)

This brings us to the most important argument underlying Krashen's lateralization by five hypothesis—the aphasia data. Much of his reassess-ment of the aphasia data is based on Lenneberg's citation of Basser (1962) and is illustrated by Table 8.1 and also referred to earlier (Table 3.1). Lenne-berg used these data to demonstrate that left hemisphere dominance for language is present during the early years, before the age of 10, but he went on to conclude importantly that the completion of this lateralization for language did not take place until about puberty. We can see that there is a distinct tendency for speech to be disturbed if the left hemisphere is injured (13 vs. 7 cases), whereas speech tends to be normal if the right hemisphere is

143

TABLE 8.1 Lesions After Onset of Speech and Before Age Ten

	After catastrophe speech was:	
	Normal	Disturbed
Left hemisphere	2	13
Right hemisphere	8	7

[a] Based on Basser, 1962.
Source: From Lenneberg (1967: 151).

affected (8 vs. 2 cases). Krashen does not disagree with this conclusion but with the age at which this hemispheric difference is manifest, and in looking back over the Basser data, he contends that the data is really for cases before the age of 5 and not 10 (Krashen, 1973:65). But this is only a small part of the overall data. When we go on to consider the other cases that Lenneberg collected from Basser, we have more cases and more consequential evidence that the younger brain (i.e., from birth up to puberty) is less lateralized, more flexible, more plastic, than that of an adult (Table 8.2).

A hemispherectomy is performed when there is serious illness or damage to one hemisphere (e.g., a malignant tumor), and most of the hemisphere is removed by surgery. Largely because the young brain is more resilient, this operation is not uncommon among children but quite rare among adults. From Basser's data, summarized in Table 8.2 by Lenneberg, we can see that if this drastic surgical procedure is performed before the teen years, rarely do we encounter permanent speech deficit. Remember that language be-

TABLE 8.2 Speech in Children and Adults After Hemispherectomy

Lesions acquired	Hemisphere operated on	Speech not affected or improved postoperatively	Permanent aphasia
Before teens[a]	Left	49	3 (had aphasia before operation)
	Right	38	5 (had aphasia before operation)
Adult[a]	Left	None	6 (1 had aphasia before operation)
	Right	25	None

[a] Based on Basser (1962).
Source: From Lenneberg (1967: 152).

comes lateralized to the left hemisphere in most subjects, so we are essentially interested in the occurrence or absence of aphasia for patients who have undergone a left hemispherectomy. For children operated on before puberty, 49 emerged without any speech loss while only 3 experienced permanent aphasia. The data on the postpubescent patients is dramatically different: None of the six left hemispherectomies emerged without aphasia. This evidence is not discussed by Krashen, but let us examine it using his lateralization by five metric. We might imagine that the "before teens" population was really *before 5*. But if we look at the individual cases cited in Basser, we can see that the hemispherectomies were performed at ages ranging from 1½ years to about 13. Basser's reports on Case 5 and Case 30 are particularly illustrative. Both children had their left hemispheres removed well after the age of 5 but before the onset of puberty, and both children seemed to emerge from the hemispherectomies with little or no linguistic deficit:

> *Case 5* He was aged 11 years at operation on January 19, 1950. While still in hospital after the operation he was talking more than he had done for years. He knew peoples' names and described activities in the ward and his parents were "amazed." Within two months of the operation his speech was observed to be clear and he had a repertoire of songs which he sang with correct words. His speech continued to improve over the next five years. He became left-handed following the operation. His seizures continued. (Basser, 1962:452)

> *Case 30* Hemispherectomy was performed on July 15, 1954, at the age of 10 years. Her speech was normal pre-operatively and the pre-operative verbal intelligence score was 94. Speech was unaffected by the operation and remained normal in the follow-up period. There was no change on post-operative psychological testing. Seizures were frequent pre-operatively and had ceased after operation. (Basser, 1962:456)

The presence of cases like these—of children who have had their left hemispheres removed *after* 5 but *before* the teenager years provides undeniable evidence, I believe, that 5 is just too early an age to posit for the completion of lateralization of language to the left cerebral hemisphere.

LATERALIZATION AND NEUROPLASTICITY

Notice that the questions of when lateralization or dominance for language is completed and how left hemisphere dominance is possibly related to a critical period for accent acquisition are issues we have already introduced in Chapter 3, where I spelled out the claims that Penfield, Lenneberg, and I had made. Krashen's reassessment of some of these claims has forced us to reconsider the role of the brain and to update the evidence we have used to argue for or against the influence of neurological changes on language acquisition. The survey compiled by Basser (1962) and Krashen's own papers of the mid-1970s are considerably dated, and so it is timely to review the relevant literature of the past dozen years or so. First, let us look at data concerning the early or late lateralization debate, and then let us consider other possible measures of brain plasticity that may be related to the emergence of foreign accents, irrespective of the role played by the timing of lateralization of linguistic processing and production to the left hemisphere.

Much of the misunderstanding and many of the contradictions that are found in the research on lateralization for language can be resolved if we divert our attention from specific disagreements we may harbor (e.g., is lateralization completed by 5 or by puberty?) and direct it to points of common agreement. In doing this, I hope the neurolinguistic literature on this particular topic, which is already nearly incomprehensible to those of us in language teaching, will become more understandable and more consistent. Please remember, however, that neurolinguists and neuropsychologists are just as much prisoners of their personal and professional points of view as linguists and language teachers. Neurophysiological facts in and of themselves do not point to one consistent "truth" pure and simple. It is healthy for us to remember the line from *The Importance of Being Earnest* that reminds us, "the truth is rarely pure and never simple!"

Impure and complex though it may be, there is quite a bit we have learned about lateralization in the past two decades that can apply to a clearer understanding of possible neurological constraints on language acquisition. We now know, for example, that the propensity for the left hemisphere to process language, for which we have had over a century's worth of evidence from the study of aphasia in adults, has been corroborated in experiments with very young infants (e.g., Morse, 1976), and that it may well be based in neuroanatomy. That is, as Geschwind and Levitsky (1968) have discovered, the left hemisphere tends to be slightly larger than the right hemisphere in some of the areas of the brain which are responsible for linguistic processing, and this, of course, implies that the foundations for language lateralization are embryological and, hence, biological. This evidence was not well known when Penfield and Lenneberg wrote, but note that this new information does not suggest that they were wrong and that lateralization is completed at birth or shortly thereafter. It simply means that lateralization for language, and probably for other complex behaviors, is part of our innate releasing mechanisms as humans. It is present at birth but it does not achieve its complete potential until much later. I know of only one published speculation (Kinsbourne, 1976) that left hemisphere specialization might be complete and unchanging from birth, but this notion is without the slightest empirical support.

For a better idea of for what all the evidence means, we might consider a similar phenomenon—the propensity for right-handedness. It is obviously genetically based, and it may even be related to the kinds of neuroanatomical asymmetries discussed by Geschwind and Levitsky, but no one would wish to claim that a young infant or a 5-year-old is "completely" right-handed; it is more reasonable to make this claim about an older child, perhaps a child who has become a teenager. We can see that any recent data that reveal a *propensity* for lateralization of functions at prepubescent ages do not ipso facto prove that the allocation of these functions to the left or right hemisphere is necessarily *completed*. I think this is a misconception some people have about Krashen's reanalysis of my lateralization by puberty position: Dichotic listening studies which show a strong right ear advantage for language at the age of 5 do not prove that children that young are completely left-hemisphere-dominant for language; they are probably much more indicative that lateralization has taken place, is taking place, and will continue to take place. The fact that speech and language survive intact after the removal of the left hemisphere of children older than 5 proves that lateralization for language has not yet been completed and that the brain is still flexible in how it can recover from trauma and reallocate functional duties. Thus, there is no real conflict between the position I have taken along with Lenneberg and all of the collective neuroanatomical and neurolinguistic findings that have accumulated in the last score of years.

Another misunderstanding arises over the question of how much, if any, permanent linguistic damage remains in young children who have had left hemispherectomies. Again, recent research has increased our knowledge about this issue but has also fueled the potential for confusion. In a series of experimental reports, Dennis and Whitaker have shown that contrary to some earlier assumptions, children born with congenitally incomplete or missing left hemispheres have not ended up with perfect linguistic abilities but are often left with subtle yet measurable linguistic deficits (Dennis & Whitaker, 1976, 1977). For example, these children seem to have great difficulty learning syntactic/semantic relations in clauses marked by "before" or "after," and this loss would indicate that although these young patients have had many years to acquire these relations during their prepubescent years—when, ideally, the normal right hemisphere would pick up the linguistic slack, so to speak, for the missing left hemisphere—these concepts are not readily picked up. Again, I do not see this as evidence against gradual lateralization until puberty or against the plasticity of the young brain. It is not surprising that under highly adverse neurological conditions—a left hemisphere missing from birth due to congenital defects or the surgical removal of the left hemisphere subsequent to severe brain injury—a child will exhibit some slight syntactic or semantic linguistic deficits.

Regardless of these limited constraints, we can note with some interest that phonology seems to be left comparatively intact and undamaged. Dennis (1981) describes syntactic and pragmatic difficulties exhibited by a young adult who was born without a *corpus callosum*—the association pathways that connect the left and right hemisphere and that share the information in each with the other. Despite this major neurological deficit, the patient did not appear to have problems discriminating or producing all the sounds of English. This nudges us to believe that if linguistic problems do happen to emerge in children who are brain-damaged before puberty, the limitations are only for complex syntactic/semantic/pragmatic information and not for phonology. In fact, it may be that the later a hemispherectomy is performed, the more chance there is that a slight but general cognitive loss will become evident. This is one of the suggestions made by Hoffman et al. (1979). Recent confirmation of a similar notion is found in Riva (1987), who sees the young brain as flexible for all but very elaborate cognitive tasks. Therefore, any language problems occurring in children who progress through life without a left hemisphere may actually be more cognitive in nature than linguistic. Since the sound system of a language is the least likely to be associated with the mental processes we normally call cognition, the speculation made by Hoffman et al. seems related to an idea proposed by Schnitzer (1978). He noted that phonological processing and articulatory production seem unaffected in any of these cases, and he suggested that perhaps phonology is ultimately lateralized or processed separately from other linguistic skills. So even if there emerge subtle cognitive and/or linguistic problems in people who have no left hemisphere from a very young age, this finding does not vitiate the claim that the prepubescent brain has great neurological plasticity when it comes to phonological programming.

In this review of various research on plasticity and lateralization, it is time to look again for case studies of children who have had severe left brain damage or left hemispherectomies between the ages of 5 and puberty simply to underscore the validity of the claim that I have made, based on Lenneberg, that the loss of the neuroplasticity that allows for native speaker phonological production and that occurs around puberty is probably based on the completion of lateralization. Gott (1973) has studied the case of a girl who first had left hemisphere surgery for a tumor at the age of 8 and then subsequently had a left hemispherectomy at the age of 10. Two years subsequent to this major operation, she appeared to have normal auditory processing and speech production, and measures of her overall linguistic competence were far superior to those of adult left hemispherectomy cases reported on in the literature (Gott, 1973:107). Lebrun and Leleux (1982) cite two similar cases: Children with left hemispherectomies performed at ages 7 and 10 suffered no linguistic impairment when their language was assessed in adulthood. Recent studies and research summaries appear to reconfirm the belief that the prepubescent brain has extraordinary linguistic flexibility:

148

Nonetheless, the present findings provide additional confirmation that early language development, although predominantly subserved by the left hemisphere from birth in the majority of neurologically normal individuals, can occur in the total absence of the usual neuroanatomical and neurophysiological substrate. (Byrne & Gates, 1987:432)

Another way of reconfirming the earlier claims that lateralization for language was completed around puberty and thus might be a possible neurological or biological cause for the appearance of accents in speech would be to look at the other hemisphere. Is there any evidence that lateralization of visual and spacial skills to the right hemisphere tends to finalize after the first decade of life? Carey (1978) in a review of data gleaned from experimental and clinical studies of subjects of varying ages concludes that the contralateral hemisphere seems to undergo the same timing as the linguistic side of the brain:

A preliminary search of the literature reveals that over a wide range of right hemisphere functions, a landmark in the development of the right cerebral hemisphere appears to be reached between ages 10 and 12. Such regularity would support the maturational view of the developmental course of face recognition. (Carey, 1978:199)

The fact that the right hemisphere seems to enjoy the same neuroplasticity as the left at young ages, at least as far as lateralization of higher level functions is concerned, leads us back to the contention made by Curtiss (1977) about Genie. Recall that she claimed that Genie's pathological upbringing in a nonlinguistic environment shunted language processing from the left to the right hemisphere during her prepubescent years. Similarly, the child with severe left hemisphere damage, or one who has had a left hemispherectomy, obviously has had the right hemisphere assume responsibility for all the linguistic and cognitive functions normally served by the contralateral hemisphere. The remarkably normal performance of these children (excluding the wild children, of course) in virtually all aspects of behavior implies that the *corpus callosum* allows for the free-and-easy transfer of most information back and forth between the two hemispheres before puberty. It is almost as if the young brain is a computer with two disk drives: Programs and files can be copied back and forth with impunity. Damage to drive A does not interfere with the retrieval of the same information found in drive B. After lateralization is completed, however, each drive has stored its own set of files, and damage to either drive leads to loss of information that has no longer been copied into the other drive. Witelson (1977), in an excellent review of the hemispheric and plasticity research, cites evidence in support of the shifting of language to the right hemisphere in children with early brain damage (Witelson, 1977:255).

Yet another piece of evidence concerning the time of life when lateralization appears to be completed is found in experiments with visual field processing. Neuropsychologists measure the differences in speed and accuracy in recognizing information presented to the left and right visual fields of each eye as a way of tapping hemispheric processing. Usually, verbal information is processed best when presented to the right side of each eye, thus implicating contralateral or left hemisphere control. Reviewing results of visual field experiments with children, Barroso (1976) noticed that the biggest difference among the age groups was at 10. Children under 10 tended to be less consistent in their visual field responses, whereas children 10 and older tended to have the generally expected pattern of left hemisphere processing for verbal visual information and right hemisphere control for nonverbal visual stimuli (Barroso, 1976:170).

The more we examine this ever-growing body of neurolinguistic evidence, the more we realize that the fact that the propensity for language to be processed is present at birth and can be readily measured by dichotic listening experiments at 5 does *not* imply that lateralization for language and other higher-order functions is *completed* at birth or at 5, and the more we consider the conclusions voiced by neurolinguists and neuropsychologists who have reviewed all this research for us, the more confident we can feel about the claim that hemispheric specialization is a genetic investment that nature has deposited in our species and that grows with compounding interest under proper linguistic and cultural nurturing until the teenage years. At that time, the investment has matured, at least for certain skills like acquiring accentless speech, and we are free to acquire other investments, like the development of writing skills or the acquisition of technical and professional vocabulary. Witelson (1977) and Stillings et al. (1987) provide fitting summaries to conclude this section:

> Obviously, learning occurs during adult life, but this hypothesis suggests that adult learning is more a matter of quantity than quality, and that it involves further learning based on already acquired cognitive or mental abilities. If this is so, then puberty may well be the age, as Lenneberg (1967) suggested, when left-hemisphere specialization stops developing, albeit indirectly—as a result of no further increase in the acquisition of relevant new skills. And perhaps it is at this stage of final acquisition of such species-specific cognitive skills, that neural localization of functions becomes firmly established. Specifically, it may be that it is this time that left-hemisphere cognitive functions can no longer be assumed by other neural areas, such as the right hemisphere. (Witelson, 1977:270)

> Why some people recover and others do not is not yet understood. Nevertheless, one major principle about recovery and plasticity that seems to be well established is that they are greatest in the young. Thus,

a child who suffers a lesion in the area of the brain that controls speech is more likely to fully regain the ability to speak or understand language than an adult who suffers a lesion in the same area. Probably for related reasons, a child learning a second language is more likely to speak it like a "native" than is an older individual. (Stillings et al., 1987:287)

OTHER MEASURES OF NEUROPLASTICITY

A completely different manner of looking at the concept of early neuroplasticity is to attribute its existence not so much to the completion of lateralization but to a combination of other neurological developments taking place in the maturing brain. From this point of view, hemispheric specialization is just one measure of the neurological flexibility that a child enjoys; other brain changes that could be equally related to plasticity are (1) the proportionately rapid growth of the brain compared to body growth, (2) the rapidly increasing presence of chemicals that assist in the synthesis of neurotransmitters, (3) the process of myelinization—where neural axons responsible for transmitting information from nerve to nerve become insulated with myelin, a substance that improves the speed and efficiency of interneural communication, (4) the proliferation of nerve pathways themselves in the young brain—especially in the cerebral hemispheres, and (5) the speeding up of synaptic transmission among nerves owing to the increasing presence of neurotransmitters. Many of these changes were already noted by Lenneberg; processes (1) and (2) which I have listed above are illustrated in his 1967 work (Figures 8.1 and 8.2). Note how both neurological growth curves mark an exponential rate of development and how both plateau at the end of the first decade of life, making attractive the assumption that both may be related to the tapering off of neuropsychological plasticity at around puberty.

The last three processes are discussed by Lecours & Lecours (1980) and are reviewed by Satz (1983), who finds all of these processes along with lateralization interacting and most probably collectively responsible for what Lecours calls "quasi-embryonal plasticity" (Lecours & Lecours, 1980). From our brief scanning of this additional neurophysiological information, I think we can conclude that lateralization alone cannot be the unilateral cause of plasticity, nor can it even be viewed as the only accurate measure of whether plasticity has been lost. If there is one consistent theme I would like to maintain in this book, it is that the acquisition of one or more languages by humans is so complex and complicated that it defies explanations that are based on a single variable. Thus, I would agree with Satz and others who see obvious links between the neurophysiological changes just listed and the mysterious but very real ability of young children to recover linguistic and

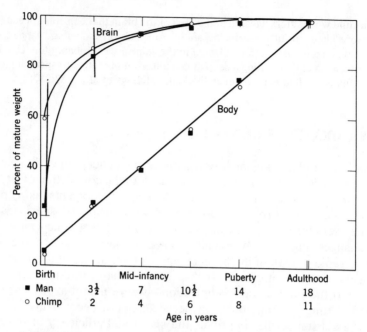

Weights are expressed in terms of per cent of mature weight. The parameter is *rate* of growth. Notice that the rate of body-weight increase is practically identical in man and chimpanzee, whereas the rate of brain-weight increase is quite different during the first quarter of the maturational histories.

Figure 8.1 Comparative brain/body growth rates. (*Source:* From Lenneberg, 1967:173.)

cognitive skills despite catastrophic brain damage, but who are circumspect about the precise nature of this relationship:

> Lecours points out, however, that despite continued advances in the biological foundations of hemispheric specialization, many substantive questions remain which often foster premature speculations as one attempts to integrate the multi-faceted chemical, psychological, and morphological aspects of brain maturation and hemispheric specialization. (Satz, 1983:296)

Whatever the relationships that exist between developing form and maturing function, and accepting the spirit of restraint suggested by Satz and which I myself have advocated, especially in applying neurolinguistic research to language pedagogy (Scovel, 1982), I would like to conclude our assessment of the arguments and counterarguments about plasticity and foreign accents by going back to the original 1969 article on lateralization:

> It seems reasonable to me that the ability to master a language without a foreign accent before the age of about twelve is directly related to the

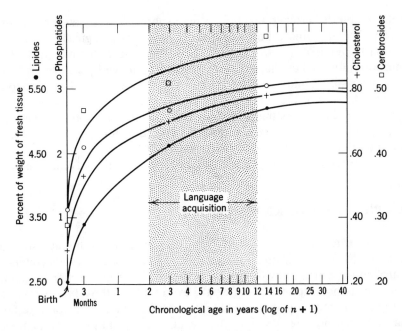

Chemical composition of human cerebral cortex plotted as a function of chronological age. (Based on data by Brante, 1949, and Folch-Pi, 1955.)

Figure 8.2   Increases in neurochemical production in the growing brain. (*Source:* From Lenneberg, 1967:164.)

fact that lateralization has not yet become permanent; similarly, it seems apparent that the *inability* of adults to master a language without a foreign accent after the age of about twelve is directly related to the fact that lateralization is permanent. By this I do not mean that children have the ability to store a second language in the right hemisphere and thus have, in effect, two dominant hemispheres. Nor do I mean that adults cannot learn the sound patterns of a language completely because the dominant hemisphere is completely occupied with one language system already. Rather, I mean that the same plasticity that accounts for the ability of the child's brain to relocate speech to the non-dominant hemisphere accounts for the plasticity that must be evident in the neuropsychological mechanisms underlying the production of the sound patterns of a second language. (Scovel, 1969:252)

The evidence that has accumulated over the past two decades and which I have reported on thus far in this chapter reaffirms, I believe, the claims that people like Lenneberg and me had made earlier. Specifically, we see solid support for language lateralization as a dynamic phenomenon, present at birth, maturing through childhood, and finalizing as the teen years begin. We see equally firm evidence for young children being able to recover linguistic abilities after traumatic left hemisphere damage, all the way up to puberty. We also find other measures of neurophysiological maturation in addition to hemispheric specialization. In sum, the collective body of evidence strongly implies that nature has endowed us with an innate releasing mechanism—the ability to program complex behavior like language to one hemisphere, so that the other can be free to program other complex tasks; that nurture allows this maturing linguistic system to respond to and learn from a community of language speakers (whether mono-, bi-, or multilingual); and that the timing of this interaction, at least for certain skills (e.g., sounding exactly like a native speaker), is preset by the advent of puberty.

CAN PRACTICE MAKE PERFECT?

I would like to avert our interest from that area of psycholinguistics that deals with the brain and direct it now toward the more traditional confines of controlled experiments with human behavior. Here it is easier to quantify what is or is not happening—after all, even with all the advances made in neuropsychological technology, we can still be much more precise about what happens outside the skull than what may or may not be happening inside it. And it is here, I think, that we meet the most compelling counterarguments about my notion that there are critical period constraints on accentless speech. In his useful review of all the variables that can be used to distinguish between child and adult second language acquisition, and which may be specifically tied to accents, Brown discusses what he refers to as "psychomotor considerations" (Brown, 1987:45), and it is under this general umbrella that I would like to place the remaining counterarguments to be introduced and refuted for the remainder of this chapter. Certainly the most challenging counterargument comes from the work of Neufeld at the University of Ottawa, who has possibly proven that practice does indeed make perfect, and that all you need is a good model, proper training, and a bit of time to pass yourself off as a native speaker in a language with which you have only the minimal acquaintance. Neufeld has published so prolifically on his work in this area that it would be exceedingly time-consuming to review his publications chronologically, but because much of what he writes pivots around the results of a few important experiments, I will try to address all of his writing by focusing on a report and review of his empirical research, and largely ignore his general claims and comments, however useful they might be. The spirit that I have adopted throughout this book is best reflected in a popular Chinese apothegm: *jian le zhi ma, diu le xi qua!* ("In trying to pick up the sesame seeds, you drop the whole watermelon!").

Surely there have been places throughout this book where you have believed I have filled your hands too full with sesame seeds, but despite the range and detail of specific information I have tried to cover, I hope you

154

have continued to be provided with a firm grip on my overarching focus despite the slipperiness of much of the data. My concern is on the fruitful, not the seedy! For this reason, I will present an abbreviated summary of Neufeld's counterarguments to my claims about the critical period and collapse all his publications on the topic into one discussion (Neufeld, 1977, 1978, 1979, 1980, 1987; Neufeld & Schneiderman, 1980).

One of the key components of Neufeld's view of language acquisition is that we are all born with the same innate abilities to acquire language and that these abilities are not curtailed in any major way, by biological constraints:

> The unique difference I see between the very young child, who learns his first language as a matter of course, and the older child, confronted with a new language, is that in the first case there is a unconscious desire to learn, and in the second there may not be. In other words, the disparity we observe in school-age children learning a second language is likely due to psycho-sociological factors which have nothing whatsoever to do with innate linguistic aptitude. (Neufeld, 1978:19)

> Although it may be somewhat early to suggest that we replace the critical period hypothesis with cognitive-socio-psychological hypothesis discussed above, I believe we should encourage further research in this area. Premature as this hypothesis may be, it is compelling from a scientific standpoint since it adequately accounts for much of the variation we see in adult second language learning. This hypothesis neither forces us into the untenable position of disregarding exceptional cases nor does it oblige us to restrict our perspectives to simplistic dichotomies as embodied in the critical period hypothesis. (Neufeld, 1980:297)

You will immediately recognize a familiar argument. It is the same one raised, discussed, and dispensed with in Chapter 5—that affect, cognition, and similar factors account for all language-learning constraints. What is of import to us, however, are not claims like these which Neufeld and others have propounded, but the actual evidence which leads him to espouse these views. The most impressive data he has mustered come from a unique and fascinating experiment he undertook to train native speakers of English to sound like native Japanese and Chinese speakers.

Twenty native speakers of English participated in an 18-hour training program in which they watched and heard videotaped lessons on short passages of Japanese, Chinese, and Eskimo. The Eskimo data were later discarded because of difficulty in getting native-speaking judges who all shared the same dialect. The program was based on the now popular idea of delayed oral production and early training on comprehension (e.g., "The Natural Approach" of Krashen & Terrell, 1983). For the first few hours, subjects watched and listened to videotaped passages made by native speakers. Subjects were asked not to make any oral responses to this initial material. In the second stage, listening continued but was supplemented with such activities as having the subjects trace intonation contours of the phrases they were listening to. In the third stage, for the last few hours of instruction, subjects first whispered repetitions of the materials they had been hearing and then finally repeated them out loud during the last three hours of training. The subjects appeared to participate actively throughout the program, partly, perhaps, because they were young college students who had been told (without substantiation) that they had been preselected for the experiment because of their language-learning ability. Neufeld hoped that this small bit of fabrication would be helpful in motivating the participants in the experiment. At the end of the program, each of the 20 subjects practiced repeating passages from the eighteenth lesson five times, and only the last, and presumably best, recording was used for evaluation. Each subject recorded 10 phrases of four to eight syllables in length for Japanese and Chinese. Three native speaking judges were selected to evaluate the two languages, and they were asked to score the subjects they heard on a 5-point scale.

1. Heavily accented with nearly all English-like sounds.
2. Noticeably foreign with many English-like sounds.
3. Near-native with frequent English-like sounds.
4. Appears native with occasional English-like sounds.
5. Unmistakably native with no signs of interference.

Remember that the subjects were all native speakers of English (though this fact was kept from the judges) and the judges were native speakers of Japanese or Chinese, and so that a 5 on this scale would mean that the judges perceived the subject as a true native speaker of one of the two Asian languages and a 1 would mark the subject as having virtually no phonological ability in Japanese or Chinese. Scores for each subject were based on majority opinion (i.e., a subject would be given a 5 if two judges marked 5 regardless of whether a third judge gave a 4 or even a 3). Neufeld's results are presented in Table 8.3.

In reporting on the results of this experiment, Neufeld expresses great confidence in the large numbers of native speakers of English he was able to train to speak Japanese and Chinese without a foreign accent. It should be noted that the subjects ranged in age from about 19 to 22, so they were all well past puberty: "Eleven of the 20 subjects were judged to be native speakers of Japanese and nine were judged to be native speakers of Chinese, based upon their ability to imitate ten target utterances" (Neufeld, 1979:234).

Thus, from Neufeld's perspective, his theoretical presupposition that psychosocial constraints and not biological barriers account for imperfect language learning in older children and adults is substantiated by this data

TABLE 8.3 Judgments on Accentless Speech for English Subjects Trained in Japanese and Chinese[a]

Subject number	Japanese	Chinese
4	5	4
8	5	5
23	5	4
2	4	3
5	4	4
12	4	4
15	4	3
16	4	4
17	4	4
1	3	3
21	3	3
10	3	4
11	3	3
19	3	3
20	3	3
6	2	2
22	2	3
14	2	2
25	2	1
7	1	2
	$\overline{X} = 3.30$	$\overline{X} = 3.20$
	$SD = 1.12$	$SD = 0.95$

[a] Composite scores with means and standard deviations for Japanese and Chinese.

Source: From Neufeld and Schneiderman (1980: 108).

because, through intensive and appropriate training, he was able to overcome an accent problem for about half of his subjects. One might even go so far as to claim that he demonstrated that practice can indeed make perfect. As you might surmise, I find the data and conclusions unconvincing for at least three reasons, and these will be discussed in ascending order of importance.

First, we can look at the data in Table 8.3, and without challenging the measures on which it is based, we can try to answer the question: Were the subjects generally successful in passing themselves off as native speakers on the basis of judgments of their pronunciation of a few brief snatches of the target languages? The mean scores for both languages is about 3.3. This means that the average judgment about all 20 subjects for both languages is category 3, "Near-native with frequent English-like sounds." Note, then, that the mean score was nowhere near category 5, "Unmistakably native with no signs of interference." Next, we can see that although Neufeld is right in pointing out that many subjects got high scores (4s and 5s) on both languages, almost an equal number did not fare so well, and a few (subjects

25 and 7) got at least one 1. Realizing that all subjects spent 18 hours in a well-designed and carefully sequenced training program whose *only* goal was to enable the participants to repeat a few target language sequences with perfect pronunciation, I find the scores in Table 8.3 less than impressive. It is worth noting too that Neufeld never told his subjects anything about the structure or meaning of the brief Japanese and Chinese passages—this was a rote repetition task, and so I feel the scores are unusually low since all of the subjects' efforts should have been expended on parroting the proper phonology.

Second, and more demaging, is the way Neufeld chose to define how a subject is "judged to be native speaker." As you can see from Table 8.3, 9 subjects received scores of 4 and 5 for Japanese and 8 subjects received those scores for Chinese. This does not add up to the 11 and 9 subjects cited in the quote above, so we have a discrepancy between the actual data reported and the claims made about the data. I suspect that the number of "native speakers" cited in the quote is based on any scores of 4 or 5 given by any judge to any subject, and this might be the reason why the numbers in the quote do not match the numbers listed in the table, which is based on the average score the three judges gave to each subject. Be that as it may, the relevant objection I would like to raise is Neufeld's definition of "native speaker." You might remember that in the studies that I and other researchers used as reported on in Chapter 3, the accent recognition task was binary, and there was no "near-native speaker" category. To me, Neufeld's category 4 is tautological: "Appears native with occasional English-like sounds" is simply another way of saying, "very good *non*native speech." Henry Kissinger is a 4 if we apply this same rating system with English as the target language. "Native speech" cannot have "nonnative" sounds intruding into it. With this recategorization in mind, then, we have only a few subjects who scored 5s in Neufeld's important experiment: Subjects 4, 8, and 23 all got perfect scores in Japanese, and subject 8 was perfect in Chinese. Note that only subject 8 was judged "native" in both languages. Although 3 subjects out of 20 seems to represent a paltry success rate considering the intensity of the training session and the limited information perceived by the judges, still it poses a challenge to the claim I have been consistent with throughout this book—that language learners cannot pass themselves off as native speakers after the age of puberty.

This leads to the third, and most robust, criticism of Neufeld's experimental protocol: I think the results of his study are flawed because of the instructions he gave to his judges:

> Judges were interviewed individually, at which time they were told that our study consisted of detecting linguistic interference resulting from learning English as a second language. The assistant responsible for this phase of the project explained that they were to hear tape-recorded

speech samples of twenty persons, some of whom, as recent arrivals, might not yet have learned English. Still others, it was explained, might be fluent speakers with detectable traces of interference. (Neufeld, 1977:53)

Unlike the instructions that I or Oyama and others used, where judges were told the exact truth about what they were to hear, the judges in this experiment were led to believe that they were listening to native-speaking immigrants with speech that was nearly pure (recent arrivals with no knowledge of English) ranging to speakers whose native language had been contaminated by English. As Neufeld readily acknowledges, the judges "expressed surprise and disbelief" when told after the experiment that all the subjects they heard were nonnative speakers of the two languages (Neufeld, 1977:54). Since the Japanese and Chinese judges were literally set up to hear native speakers of their mother tongues, it does not amaze me that 3 of the 20 subjects were rated as "native speakers." Indeed, it is astounding that, given the instructions to the judges, so few 5s were recorded, and this detailed study ends up simply underscoring the saliency of foreign accents. So pervasive are they that they can even override the expectations of judges who are predisposed not to hear them. From this we can conclude that practice cannot make perfect what nature has already made permanent.

DO ACCENTS ARISE FROM A PSYCHOMOTOR MISMATCH?

The final counterargument to my contention that accents stem from biological constraints is based on psycholinguistic research in yet another arena of evidence. Flege has been the most exacting, articulate, and productive proponent of this viewpoint and has supported his claims with experiments which focus on acoustic analyses of discrete features of pronunciation in the mother tongue and the target language. Like those of Neufeld, his publications are profuse and cover several years of inquiry (Flege, 1980, 1981, 1986; Flege & Hammond, 1982; Flege & Hillenbrand, 1987).

Flege (1981) reviews much of the critical period literature and then examines some possible nonbiological explanations for accented speech emerging in older learners. I would place his attempts to explain the advent of accents in the same psychomotor approach as Neufeld's in that both researchers look at their emergence in adult speech as a problem of first language interference that can or might be overcome if learners could somehow modify their phonetic model of what the phonemes in the target language should sound like. Instead of the somewhat vague and sweeping criterion of whether or not a speaker sounds like a native, Flege relies on data from the other extreme: He examines what he calls "subsegmental" phonetic features (Flege, 1981:449), like voice onset timing, to compare differences between a "French/t/," and "English/t/," and an "accented English /t/" produced by a native speaker of French. Voice onset timing refers to the differences in time (measured in milliseconds on a sound spectrograph) between the moment when a syllable begins and when voicing can actually be seen on a spectrogram. What we call a "voiceless" consonant like /t/ usually has a long onset before voicing begins, whereas a voiced consonant like /d/ usually has a short lag before voicing can be seen. Languages differ as to the VOT lag for consonants, and so the difference between a French /t/ and an English /t/ can be quantified quite precisely by using the VOT: French /t/s are less aspirated and hence have shorter VOTs than their English equivalents. It is this phonetic contrast that Flege is interested in utilizing to explain why nonnative adult speakers have trouble acquiring the phonology of a second language perfectly. In light of his review of the literature and his initial work with VOT contrasts among speakers of different languages, Flege comes up with the following hypothesis:

> It has been postulated here that children and adults possess the same general capacity for learning to pronounce foreign languages and that one important cause of foreign accent is phonological translation between languages by speakers who already speak a first language. According to the phonological translation hypothesis, an individual may be completely successful in his/her phonetic learning of a second language and yet still retain an accent because pronunciation of the foreign language is based on pairs of corresponding sounds (or non-segmental phonetic dimensions) found in the native and target language. The hypothesis rests on the assumption that both children and adult language learners modify native-language patterns of phonetic implementation, and that superordinate acoustic models based on pairs of corresponding sounds or phonetic dimensions in two languages serve as input for phonetic learning in second language acquisition. (Flege, 1981:451–452)

The existence of a psychomotor superordinate acoustic model leads Flege to posit two predictions:

> First, it predicts that bilingualism is not possible at the phonetic level since it posits that pronunciation of a foreign language is, for most speakers, eventually shaped to conform to an acoustic model provided jointly by the native and foreign languages. An individual might learn to speak a foreign language without apparent accent, but a fine-grained acoustic analysis should reveal differences between the language learner and native speakers of the target language along those parameters where phonetic differences exist between the native and target language. . . .
> Second, one would expect phonetic learning in a second language to affect pronunciation of a learner's first language. (Flege, 1981:452)

These two predictions lead me to two observations. I really see no conflict between Flege's superordinate acoustic model of first and second language acquisition and my own biological interpretation. Flege is justifying the existence of subsegmental phonetic interference in second language acquisition with a mental model; I, in turn, would simply say that this is another way of talking about neuroplasticity. Accurate models *or* pronunciation can be achieved before puberty, while the neural substrates for exquisitely fine neuromuscular programming are still "flexible." The overwhelming evidence we have reviewed which demonstrates the ability to pick up accentless speech before puberty, on the one hand, and the inability to avoid it after puberty, on the other, proves that regardless of whatever is happening in the abstract and high-level realm of mental models or at the concrete low-level world of voice onset timing, there is convincing proof that language learners perceive and produce two different forms of linguistic behavior if language is acquired before or after the first dozen or so years.

As for my second observation, it is ironic that Flege argues for the contention that second language learners can acquire a new tongue without an apparent accent and still have measurable subsegmental phonetic differences between their pronunciation and that of native speakers of the target language. I find interesting some of his recent experimental work that verifies the existence of this phenomenon (Flege, 1987; Flege & Hillenbrand, 1987). The data suggest to me that minute differences in voice onset timing, since they apparently do exist among different groups of speakers, and since they are also apparently not part of the acoustic information people use to make judgments about whether a person speaks with an accent, are not essential to whatever constitutes the learning of the sound system of a language. In a sense, they are the same kinds of measurable but phonologically irrelevant paralinguistic features like voice pitch or volume (Esling & Wong, 1982) which vary from language to language but do not in and of themselves identify a speaker as native or nonnative. And this is why I also find Flege's second prediction not directly relevant. If learning a second language well does imply certain minute subsegmental phonetic changes in the pronunciation of some of the phonemes in your mother tongue (and again, Flege seems to have shown this with voice onset timing), since these differences are never or rarely perceived, they are paralinguistic not linguistic phenomena. In the next and final chapter, I will briefly mention just the reverse of what Flege is talking about here—our inability to pinpoint the exact phonetic features that characterize foreign accents. We have witnessed abundant evidence that the nativeness of an accent can be immediately and correctly identified, even by very young native speakers, but as far as I know, no one has been able to specify what constitutes foreign accents phonetically: Are they distinguished by subsegmental phonetic features (perhaps those identified by Flege), by segmental features (suggested in a study by Basson, 1986), by suprasegmental features (suggested in a study by Jansma, 1987), or by some combination among the three? Flege has supposedly clear information about the opposite problem—phonetic differences in the pronunciation of certain consonants by native and nonnative users of a language—differences which are not heard as distinctive. It is my contention, then, that until a superordinate phonetic model and the measurements of slight voice onset time differences can account *directly* for the differences in perception and production of what native speakers recognize as native and nonnative speech under experimental conditions, Flege's work does not contribute to our understanding of the etiology of foreign accents. As it now stands, I see his meticulous experimentation and his overall model as representing the perspective of acoustical and articulatory phonetics in our study of interlanguage and fossilization; it does not pertain to the issue of whether or not accents have a neurological or biological basis.

There is one more psychomotor approach that merits mentioning, and this is the idea proffered by Bever (1981) that it is not a maturational change in the brain that accounts for foreign accents but the gradual dismantling of the internal language acquisition device that is with us at birth but then disappears at around puberty, when cognitive ability is sufficient to meet most language-learning needs. Bever is almost tart in his assessment of a biologically based critical period: "the critical period is a redoubt for a diehard nativist" (Bever, 1981:178). Bever suggests that it is not biology but the loss of the innately specified language acquisition abilities which he refers to as a "psychogrammar" that accounts for the emergence of accents at about puberty, the age at which this psychogrammar is automatically dismantled:

> My proposal is this: the reason that a psychogrammar exists is because of the vital role it plays during language acquisition, much of which occurs during the first five years of life. The psychogrammar is needed during that period to mediate between the systems of speech production and perception. It is the internal translator that regulates conflicting capacities which arise as each of the two systems of speech behavior develop separately. (Bever, 1981:185)

In some ways, Bever's "translator" mediating between speech perception and production is similar to the way that I understand Flege's "superordinate phonetic model" to work. But unlike Flege, Bever does not try to relate his model to any empirical data, and, even more troublesome, it is hard to see justification for his belief that innate linguistic abilities of an abstract nature are lost or dismantled at a certain time in life as a normal, maturational process. How would this dismantling affect the acquisition of other second language skills, like lexical and syntactic learning? If these are affected, then how does one account for the Joseph Conrad phenomenon? I find, unfortunately, that more questions are raised than answers provided with Bever's version of a psychomotor explanation for foreign accents.

We can conclude this chapter by readily acknowledging a wide and imaginative range of counterarguments against the position to which I have adhered throughout the book. But from the review we have taken together of the lateralization by five hypothesis, the possibilities that there are other ways to measure neuroplasticity, the attempts to train people to pass themselves off as native speakers, and the psychomotor models just examined, I find no attractive alternative to the conclusion that accents are a pervasive and permanent symbol of our biological foundations. This does not mean that there are no loose ends to tie up, and it is to this one remaining task that we now turn for our final chapter.

9

QUESTIONS, CONSEQUENCES, AND CONCLUSIONS—A SUMMARY OF WHAT WE KNOW AND WHAT WE HAVE YET TO LEARN

We have come a long way from the Pleistocene age discussed in the very first chapter of this book, both in human history and in the range and depth of issues covered, but that does not mean that the bulk of questions have been answered, the majority of consequences been considered, and the chief conclusions been drawn. This is the way with applied science. It must somehow steer a compromise between the unfudging finality of the *"quod erat demonstrandum"* of geometry, which leaves no lingering doubts or haunting suspicions, and the overused triteness of the "further research is obviously necessary" of the social sciences, frequently employed to encourage future funding for the experiment that should have originally been undertaken. This final chapter, then, is a balance between QEDs and lacunae. Because almost all of the research reported on in this book has been devoted to the complex and complicated speech behavior of human beings, there are questions to raise and consequences to consider; nevertheless, because I believe much of the evidence presented to be cohesive and irrefutable, there are certain conclusions to be made. And so, from the perspective of applied psycholinguistics, the discipline most aptly equipped to deal with the merger of nature, nurture, and time in human speech behavior, let us think about some questions, mull over several consequences, and face up to a few conclusions, as our time to consider a time to speak draws to an end.

164

WHAT MAKES A FOREIGN ACCENT FOREIGN?

Somewhere in this discussion of a critical period for the development of human speech, you must have wondered, however briefly, about what makes an accent sound alien. We will stop to consider, in a moment or two, the remote possibility that in addition to phonetic interference, there is some sort of lexical and/or syntactic evidence for nonnative speech, but looking just at the data reported on in this book, we can accept the fact that there is overwhelming support for some form of phonological interference arising at about puberty, and we are thus left with the question: What exactly is it in the phonetic signal that tells us almost instantly that the person talking to us is not a native speaker? Is it a segmental problem?: an /r/ for an /l/ which I once heard, for example, aboard a certain Asian airline of impeccable credentials just as the 747 began to thunder down the runway for takeoff and the steward, in otherwise superb English, wished us all a "good fright"! Is it a suprasegmental phenomenon—a problem with stress, rhythm, tone, and intonation?: for example, the frequent tendency of English speakers to superimpose English falling intonation as the "tone" for each word in a tonal language like Chinese. Or is it a phonetic feature that characterizes what Esling and Wong (1982) refer to as "voice setting"?: the tendency to retroflex stops that typifies the nonnative (or the dialectal) quality of Indian speakers of English. Very few researchers in second language acquisition have begun to deal with these questions empirically, but I suspect that a combination of all of these characteristics collectively marks a speaker phonologically with a kind of *gestalt*. Just as an individual phoneme cannot be broken down into specific, invariant features (Tartter, 1986), I cannot see how we can hope to decompose an accent into specific phonetic characteristics which are consistently identifiable and which invariably identify all nonnative speakers. At this stage of our understanding of phonetics and speech perception, this is not only a night in which all cows are black, it is also a night in which all researchers are equally blind. Despite the opacity of the problem, there are several people who have provided hints and glimpses of what we do or do not hear in accented speech.

Adams (1979) has written a full-length monograph which attempts to identify the rhythmic and stress problems faced by foreign learners of English. Her elaborate study involved the use of judges to separate native from nonnative speakers by identifying the stress patterns of the phrases they heard. It also used an electromyographic analysis of the thoracic muscles responsible for expiration, to see if native speakers of English used a different pattern of muscular movement from nonnative speakers and thus to try to account for differences in stress and rhythm between the two groups of subjects; and finally, the study examined the speech of the two groups acoustically, seeking to determine if there were invariant features of pitch, amplitude, or duration that might consistently identify the rhythm and stress patterns of the nonnative speakers. Not surprisingly, the judges could easily identify the nonnative speakers and also mark down how their stress differed from that of native speakers. However, the electromyographic analysis revealed no differences in the actual use of expiratory muscles between native and nonnative speakers, and there was no evidence from the acoustic analysis that native and nonnative speakers of English employ acoustic features differently. In sum, Adams was unable to discover an anatomical or an acoustic correlate of the clear rhythm and stress differences manifest in the speech of native and nonnative English speakers, despite the fact that she was careful to use rigorous and quantifiable measures of suprasegmental speech.

In a little known but meticulously analyzed study of the speech of two highly fluent nonnative speakers of English, Marks (1980) examined only the segmental sounds that appear to characterize accented speech. His analysis includes a detailed phonetic description of the vowel and consonant production of the two subjects, an attempt to account for the dynamic nature of their phonological production through the writing of "variable rules" (Dickerson, 1975), and an account of when and where the two subjects would sometimes slip back into using phonological variants that they normally did not use; that is, he tried to consider the effects of "backsliding" (Selinker & Lamendella, 1979). One of the few questions which Marks was able to answer concerned the relative importance of consonant versus vowel errors in identifying the accented speech of the two subjects:

> It is clear, that from the point of view of foreign accent, native language transfer can only be a negative influence on target language output. It is most noticeable in both subjects in their production of vowels. However, a small segment of vowel production can be seen to play a much larger role than might be supposed. In both subjects, transfer of native language patterns of vowel reduction results in there being little or no vowel reduction in their target language output. This contributes a great deal to the foreignness of the subject's accent.
>
> As far as consonants are concerned, native language transfer makes a much smaller contribution to foreign accent. However, it is interesting to note that the consonants which do seem to be affected by native language transfer are the sonorants: /l,r/. Both these consonants are the closest consonants to vowels in terms of the distribution of distinctive feature values on a distinctive feature matrix. This may indicate that perhaps native language transfer contributes most to foreign accent where it affects vowels and vowel-like sounds. (Marks, 1980:114–115)

Marks has certainly provided some clues as to what the phonetic features are that identify nonnative speech, but intriguing though his suggestion about the relative prominence of vowels may be, we should remember that his study involved only two subjects, that their native languages were both

European (Spanish and Hungarian), and that he did not examine the comparative influence of suprasegmental features. Consequently, Marks has left us with a plausible but certainly inconclusive answer to the question about what marks a foreign accent phonetically.

Besides segmental and suprasegmental influences, nonnative speech may also be marked by the general, paralinguistic characteristics of speaking which Esling and Wong (1982) refer to as voice setting. In their review of the literature on this topic, they suggest that the following features frequently typify the English spoken by an American male adult (Esling & Wong, 1982:90).

1. spread lips
2. open jaw
3. palatalized tongue body position
4. retroflex articulation
5. nasal voice
6. lowered larynx
7. creaky voice

It is possible that these paralinguistic qualities are also used by native speakers to help pick out foreign from native speakers, but I personally suspect that they play a less salient role in accent identification than the segmental and suprasegmental sounds of a language. It appears to me that even though voice quality is an aspect of pronunciation to which foreign language teachers should pay more attention, a point well illustrated by Esling and Wong, it does not in and of itself separate native from nonnative speakers because it is influenced by so many variables that are extraneous to the phonology of a particular language. It is greatly affected by such nonlinguistic phenomena as age, sex, body size, emotional state, and even whether or not the speaker is suffering from a cold. Voice setting must surely be useful in acting, and manuals for actors make frequent mention of them in suggesting how to feign an accent (Herman & Herman, 1943), but once again, they alone do not give us the necessary and sufficient phonological evidence of why a person does not sound exactly like a native speaker.

In an experiment in which 61 nonnative speakers of English were examined to see what variables seemed to account for their relative success or lack thereof in pronunciation accuracy, Suter (1976) mentions the range of variables and the difficulty in trying to determine which of them is most prominent in accounting for a foreign accent:

> One would have to consider not only the phonemes and allophones of the languages involved, but also such things as the placement of stress, intonation patterns, tempo (i.e. the speech at which syllables succeed one another), and any characteristic patterns of loudness, continuity (the incidence of pauses), and register (the quality of voicing). Furthermore,

some determination would have to be made as to which of these qualities the judges are most sensitive to, i.e. distortions of some things presumably influence judges more than distortions of others. All of these complex considerations combine to affect the judgements of the accuracy with which a non-native speaker pronounces English. (Suter, 1976:248)

IS THERE A CRITICAL PERIOD FOR SYNTAX?

Throughout this book, I have proceeded on the premise that foreign accents are a phonological phenomena and that the Joseph Conrad effect, discussed most thoroughly in Chapter 3, decisively demonstrates that exceedingly competent learners of a second language can easily pass themselves off as native users of the target language in their ability to acquire words, morphological patterns, or grammatical rules. Although this premise is accepted by most second language acquisition researchers, it has certainly not gone unchallenged, and this is why it is important for us to try to answer this question with some degree of finality: Is there a critical period for syntax? I know of at least three experimental studies that have focused specifically on this query: Patkowski (1980) concluded from his research that the answer is yes, and Ioup (1984) drew the opposite conclusion from her inquiry into the matter, and Coppieters (1987) came up with the same answer as Patkowski, but for constraints on syntactic competence, not syntactic production.

Patkowski's study is well designed and statistically sophisticated, being, in essence, a summary of his doctoral dissertation. Taking 67 non-native-speaking adult immigrants to the United States, he made a written transcript for each from a half-hour-long interview which was conducted in English. The transcripts were then given to two native-speaking judges who were trained ESL teachers, and they judged the degree of English proficiency for each subject on a Foreign Service Institute-type 5-point scale. The two judges also assessed written transcripts from 15 native speakers who acted as control subjects. From personal information he was able to glean from the nonnative speakers, Patkowski was able to determine the age of arrival and the years' residency in the United States for each subject. After the subjects were graded by the judges and the results were analyzed statistically, he found that the most important variable that affected the lexical and syntactic accuracy of the subjects' English was whether or not they had learned English before or after the age of 15:

> Thus, all of the results discussed above seem to be strongly consistent with the notion of an age limitation on the acquisition of syntax in a second language. Descriptive statistics reveal strikingly dissimilar population distribution characteristics for the pre- and post-puberty groups on syntactic proficiency; analyses of variance show strong main effects on syntactic proficiency for age at which learning begins and no significant

effects for instructional and practice variables; correlational analyses further reinforce this picture. (Patkowski, 1980:459)

Patkowski concludes his article by reviewing some of the critical period research, reflecting on my notion of the Joseph Conrad phenomenon, and discussing the overall advantages of long-range second language acquisition as opposed to picking a language up primarily through formal instruction. While I accept the evidence which he has ably presented, and while I acknowledge the importance of exploring the pedagogically useful question of whether there is a critical period for acquiring syntax, there are a few comments I have on the validity of Patkowski's conclusions.

It should be noted that he incorporated judgments about the spoken English of these immigrants into his experiment too, and that they clearly confirmed the results that I and others reported on in Chapter 3 have achieved. He also used another measure of syntactic ability, a test of syntactic intuition called the Linguistic Intuitions Test (the LIT), and it is worth quoting Patkowski about the strong confirmation of the Joseph Conrad phenomenon he found for at least one subject, when we consider the great discrepancy between the subject's execrable pronunciation ability but his excellent syntax:

> The subject's spoken output was very difficult to comprehend and his tape proved excrutiatingly hard to transcribe. Of course, since the judges were working from written material, the subject's poor phonological performance did not affect the rating. On the LIT, however, the subject scored at the native level, making only one mistake (on the item which had also proven the most difficult for the native controls). Thus, there is little doubt that there can be great disparity among various aspects of linguistic proficiency in individual cases. (Patkowski, 1980:464)

We have, then, in Patkowski's very own data, an apt example of a mismatch between phonological and syntactic ability that goes against the general direction of his experimental data.

A question also arises about the design of the experiment. The oral transcripts of all the subjects (both native and nonnative speakers) were not taken down verbatim but were edited to exclude mispronunciations and references which might have given away the subjects' national background (Patkowski, 1980:452). It is therefore possible, since this was not a "blind" transcription where the transcriber did not know which subjects were native speakers and which were not, that the editing process allowed for the appearance of nonnative lexical and syntactic clues that might not have been manifest if the transcripts remained unedited. It is also instructive to note that unlike the phonological studies, Patkowski's experiment dealt exclusively with nonnative subjects, so his judges were never asked to compare the syntactic performance of these subjects with that of native users of English. It would be useful to see, for example, if the performance of his younger-than-15 group would be indistinguishable from transcripts of native speakers, for if this were true, his data on syntax would be similar to the results that some researchers have achieved with comparisons of phonological performance. Until more studies like Patkowski's are undertaken, we must assume that there are few if any constraints on the possibility of native-like lexical and syntactic performance for people who learn a language after puberty.

Coppieters (1987) has examined the acquisition of syntax by adult learners from a slightly different perspective. Through extensive interviews, using judgments of grammaticality, he discovered profound differences between 20 native and 21 near-native adult speakers of French in their underlying competence about the language. So great was the divergence between the two groups in their grammaticality judgments in fact, that none of the near-native speakers had scores that overlapped with any of the native speakers. Coppieters concludes that the native speakers, who had acquired French from childhood, obviously had a different set of intuitions about French syntax and usage than the near-native speakers, all of whom had begun to learn French intensively only after early childhood. We might thus surmise that Coppieters' results suggest the chance that there might be a critical period for syntactic competence, even if none might exist for syntactic performance. I think several issues must be resolved before we can reach this conclusion however.

For example, although Coppieters tried to ensure that all grammaticality judgments were based on natural language use and not on prescriptive "grammar school" usage, it is impossible to rule out the influence of formal language training on the linguistic intuitions expressed by the native speakers. What all of the native speakers had in common and what none of the near-native speakers possessed was early and rigorous training in French schools. If early prescriptive training does play a substantial role in the difference between the two groups of subjects, this intriguing experiment tells us more about differences in "competence" for linguistic usage rather than for linguistic use between native and very good nonnative speakers.

If, however, Coppieters has actually been successful in tapping competence for language use, and is among the first to show that adult second language learners can never truly match the ability of native speakers to make accurate grammaticality judgments, we might have a syntactic analogue to the results I discovered about the relatively poor ability of even good nonnative speakers of English to make accurate judgments about foreign accents. If Coppieters is indeed correct about the possibility of intrinsic constraints on linguistic intuitions about a language learned after childhood, this is an excellent example of an area of second language acquisition where we have much to learn.

170

Ioup (1984) confirms many of the claims reviewed thus far, even though her experiment was not specifically constructed to counter the position that Patkowski has taken or to support the perspective that I have adopted. She conducted two studies, both involving the assessment of compositions which were written by nonnative speakers of English by judges who were native English speakers and ESL teachers. In the first study, the judges were unable to tell which of the English compositions were written by native speakers of Hebrew and which by native speakers of Spanish. Surprisingly, even the judges, who were somewhat experienced in contrastive linguistics, could only randomly guess at the native language of the writers solely on the basis of their syntactic errors. In the second study, which much more closely replicated Patkowski's experiment and which is more germane to our interest, judges had to decide which of 13 subjects were Arabic and which were Korean on the basis of compositions which the subjects had written and also of taped oral passages. Intriguingly enough, the judges again were making virtually random guesses about the subjects' native language when they were forced to rely only on syntactic information via the compositions, but when they could hear the subjects speak, their accuracy improved enormously, and it was much easier to identify the Arabic and Korean subjects. Ioup concludes from her experiments and from her own review of the research that interlanguage phonology, the pronunciation characteristic of a learner who is a native speaker of one language and is in the process of picking up a new one, is much more likely to be influenced by interference from the mother tongue than interlanguage syntax (Ioup, 1984:14). This is, in effect, another way of describing the Joseph Conrad phenomenon. A more recent study of 182 schoolchildren in various classes from fourth to eleventh grade, contrary to the findings of either Patkowski (1980) or Snow and Hoefnagel-Hohle (1978), there did not appear to be consistent differences in successful acquisition of syntactic or semantic features in second language learning that could be attributed to the children's chronological age (Morris & Gerstman, 1986). And consequently, from the studies which I have concentrated on here, and from all the other research reviewed in earlier chapters, I can only conclude that the existence of the Joseph Conrad phenomenon is confirmed and that the answer to whether there exists a critical period for syntax ranges from a potential maybe to a probable no.

IS THERE A CRITICAL PERIOD FOR DIALECTS?

A question of much greater complexity and, therefore, one more difficult to answer conclusively concerns whether the critical period constraints we have been discussing for a language community can be extended to dialects. In my 1969 paper, it was suggested, somewhat facetiously, that the difference between a language and a dialect might be defined as whether or not you could pick up a new variety of speech after puberty and still sound like a native speaker: If you could accomplish this task, the new variety would be simply a dialect of your mother tongue, but if you could not learn this new variety without an accent, it was obviously a completely different language. The distinction between languages and dialects, though, is exceedingly difficult to delineate because along with linguistic criteria, one must also bring to bear sociolinguistic, historical, religious, and political factors. Up to this point, I have assumed, argued, and demonstrated that the learning of a new language is constrained phonologically after puberty, but I have skirted the issue of whether this constraint exists for picking up a new dialect too. Evidence of the complexity of the dialect issue comes from some data gleaned in my 1976 study on nonnative speakers who were misidentified as native speakers. In that study, I culled and grouped together in one table the relatively few times (less than 2.5%) that non-Americans were mistakenly identified as native speakers of American English by the child or adult native-speaking judges. Of the 10 non-American subjects, two were actually native speakers of English, but their mother dialects were Irish English and South African Indian English. Table 9.1 shows how frequently these two dialect speakers mistaken for Americans compared with the other eight subjects, all of whom were nonnative speakers of any English dialect.

The table lists the number of misidentifications by each of the different age groups (in the vertical columns), and quite obviously, the youngest judges (especially the ones aged 5 to 8) made by far the most misidentifications, whereas the older children and the adults made the fewest (e.g., of the 31 adult judges, only eight misidentifications of the 10 subjects were made, and five of those were for 1 subject). The horizontal rows list the 10 subjects by their mother tongue in order of how easily they were misidentified—from the most to the least. From Table 9.1, we can see that the native speaker of Arabic was the one who appeared to sound most like an American and the South African Indian English speaker sounded the least. The Irish English speaker is found about in the middle of the other subjects, so we can conclude that being a native speaker of English does not ensure that you will have an inordinate advantage in sounding like a native speaker of another *dialect* of English. From this table, it is apparent that perceptions about whether a speaker is a native or a nonnative speaker of a particular dialect do not represent a neat linguistic continuum, where linguistic varieties that are historically or typologically closest to the variety of speech used by a person making accent judgments are most readily misperceived as being unaccented. My intuitive guess about this problem is that there are many other variables that can override whether the linguistic differences are great or small, and so a speaker of another dialect of your mother tongue might actually be easier to spot as "foreign" than a speaker of a language that comes from a completely different language family from yours. Some of

TABLE 9.1 Number of Misidentifications per Nonnative Speaker Made by Each Age Group of Judges

No.	Native language	Sex	Age groups							Total no. of misIDs
			5 N = 8	6 N = 34	7 N = 47	8 N = 9	9 N = 38	10 N = 10	Adults N = 31	
6	Arabic	M	3	26	20	3	5	0	0	57
11	Swedish	F	3	13	17	2	2	0	5	42
7	Chinese	F	3	12	12	3	2	1	0	33
4	Romanian	F	4	13	13	0	0	0	1	31
15	Irish English	M	2	6	8	3	5	0	1	25
16	French	F	2	11	9	2	0	0	1	25
14	Portuguese	F	1	7	6	2	0	0	0	16
19	Lingala	M	0	7	5	1	0	0	0	13
10	Spanish	M	0	5	4	0	0	0	0	9
12	South African Indian English	M	0	4	3	1	0	0	0	8

Source: From Scovel (1978).

these variables might be the presence of perceptually salient phonetic features (e.g., the retroflected consonants of the South African Indian English speaker seemed to provide an immediate tipoff that he was not an American); an unusually low and resonant speaking voice (e.g., the Arabic speaker had had experience in radio broadcasting and was particularly smooth and almost avuncular in his speaking style); and the length of residence and the intensity of language use in the target language community (e.g., the Swedish speaker had resided in the United States for many years and had used American English almost exclusively during this period of time for both personal and professional needs). These are just a few of the factors which must have bearing on the degree to which a nonnative speaker might sometimes be misperceived as speaking without an accent in the type of experimental study which I conducted. From Table 9.1 and from the variables that were just cited, I do not see any reason why it would necessarily be easier for a speaker of another dialect to overcome a "foreign" accent than it would be for a speaker of an altogether different language.

This is tantamount to claiming that the same biological mechanisms that constrain the learning of the phonology of a new language after puberty also restrict a person's ability to acquire a new dialect without a "foreign" accent. The evidence in support of this particular application of the critical period hypothesis is not as copious or as strong as the evidence which we have reviewed for the learning of a new language. Support for a critical period for dialects comes from a survey performed by Krashen and Seliger (1975) that was modeled after their foreign language acquisition survey (Seliger et al., 1975). Native speakers of American English who had immigrated to the New York City area at various ages were asked, "When you travel outside of New York, do non-New Yorkers take you for a New Yorker by your speech?" Table 9.2 provides the answers the 214 subjects gave in this self-report study.

The results of this dialect recognition task seem to mirror those that the authors found in the language recognition task with American and Israeli immigrants: There is a definite tendency for the subjects who moved to New York before puberty to be perceived as New Yorkers, and there is the reverse trend for the subjects who immigrated there after puberty not to

TABLE 9.2 Self-Reports of Presence of
Native or Nonnative New York
City Dialect

Age moved to New York	Yes	No
3 to 9	40	27
10 to 15	27	40
over 15	15	65

Source: From Krashen and Seliger (1975).

sound like New Yorkers. This study seems to confirm a suggestion that Labov (1970) has made that puberty might be an important turning point for the acquisition of a new dialect—a notion which appears to have some empirical support from a study done by one of Labov's students on the acquisition of a second dialect by children of different ages (Payne, 1980). Krashen and Seliger conclude with a firm claim that dialect acquisition is no different from language acquisition:

> Nevertheless, the findings indicate that the critical period hypothesis is relevant for both second language and dialect learning; there is a general constraint on the learning of a new phonological system even if that system is recognized as still belonging to the same language. These results also suggest that learning a new dialect, at least on the level of learning to utilize new phonological rules is similar to learning a new language. (Krashen & Seliger, 1975:28–29)

The picture is clouded, however, by studies designed to test the accuracy of people's ability to distinguish different social dialects solely on the basis of their speech. Hewett (1971) found that although her subjects were fairly accurate in distinguishing white speakers of standard American English from black nonstandard speakers, they were not so adept at separating social class from ethnic group and thus misidentified standard black speakers as white. A similar phenomenon is clearly evident for two black speakers, out of about a dozen white and black speakers of various socioeconomic classes, in a dialect recognition task undertaken by Fraser (1973), where social and educational factors seem to interact with judgments about a speaker's ethnic group.

Related to the question of dialects is the tangential issue of whether or not there is a critical period for the acquisition of sign language, and though I plead ignorance about this fascinating medium of human linguistic expression, there are hints at dialectal differences and potential critical period constraints for this complex form of nonverbal communication. For example, Philip Reeves, an actor in *Children of a Lesser God,* claims, "Did you know people can tell where you're from by the way you sign? . . . There's a Texas accent for signing, we found. Many signs are regional." But as for spoken dialects, there may be a difference between our ability to learn a new geographical dialect and our skill in acquiring a new social dialect, if such a dialectal distinction is really valid, but the question about a critical period for the acquisition of a second dialect is one that I am not equipped to answer. It can only be pointed out that compared with the strong evidence we have for a critical period for the acquisition of accentless speech at around puberty for a new language, the evidence we have to support a similar barrier for a new dialect is comparatively scarce. It is up to other sociolinguistis or second language acquisition researchers to gather more substantive evidence and come up with a more definitive answer.

IS PHONOLOGICAL LEARNING CONSTRAINED AT THE AGE OF 6?

Another challenge to the perspective that I have adopted for this book is raised in a comprehensive and insightful review of maturational constraints on language development by Long (1987), where in his reading of the experimental literature, a more plausible age for the emergence of accents is only halfway to puberty—at about the age of 6. In the studies he reviewed by Newport (1984), Payne (1980), Ramsay and Wright (1974), and Tahta et al. (1981), there appeared to be a general decline in pronunciation accuracy after about the age of 6, well before the completion of a learner's first decade.

Certainly, there is no evidence to suggest that second language learners cannot acquire accentless speech after the age of 6 as long as they are prepubescent—the survey studies suggest this. Further, recall that my 1982 recognition experiment with children of increasing ages did not show a consistently high criterion level (95% accuracy) with any group of children younger than 9. Assuming that there is some correlation between a child's ability to recognize accented speech and to produce accentless speech, it would seem counterintuitive to expect that children *decline* in their ability to speak three years before they actually *improve* in their recognition ability. It is apparent, though, from Long's analysis of the data that there is still much we do not know, and here it is obvious that more research is needed.

ARE THERE EXCEPTIONS THAT DISPROVE THE CASE?

Moving from questions to consequences, one of the most pressing issues with which I have been confronted when I discuss the critical period hypothesis with language teachers and people interested in second language acquisition research is the probable existence of exceptions to my claim that it is impossible to learn a foreign language without an accent after puberty. The presence of even a few exceptional adults who can pass themselves off as native speakers of a language which they have acquired after their adolescence severely challenges the strong version of the critical period hypothesis which I have been adhering to throughout this book. One consequence of my claims is that if there are exceptions, either my version of the critical period hypothesis is discredited or that it is simply too strong and should be scaled down from a theory to a general principle about language acquisition. In the following consideration of this particular consequence, I hope to avoid either modification of my views and accommodate what we know about exceptions, if they do exist, into my continued advocacy for a strong version of the hypothesis.

First, we must dispense with the widespread belief that there are many adult second/foreign language learners who can easily pass themselves off as native speakers. This impression is popular but difficult to corroborate empirically. I have had many Americans tell me that they have frequently been mistaken for a foreigner because of the authenticity of their pronunciation of a language they have learned after puberty (most commonly a Romance language). I do not, for a moment, dispute the accuracy of their accounts, for I myself have had occasionally encountered the same claim about my own pronunciation of Thai, but this kind of anecdotal information is exceedingly misleading when it is compared with the high level of judgment and the empirical sensitivity of the kinds of experimental studies on accent recognition that I and others have performed and that were introduced in Chapter 3. It is my impression that very often, these anecdotal affirmations of excellent speaking ability are almost a reverse form of endorsement for the existence of a nonnative accent in the speech of the foreigner being complimented, for often these congratulatory comments entail two implicit claims about the foreigner's speech: One is that the native speaker presupposes that nonnative speakers like you (especially American) do not or cannot learn to pronounce the native language superbly, and the other is that since you are such an obvious counterexample of the presupposition, the native speaker overexaggerates your actual prowess in the language. It is my impression that if we ask the native speakers who are complimenting us whether or not they could pick out our voice as that of the nonnative speaker from a tape of about four other native speakers of their mother tongue, the answer would usually be strongly affirmative. Thus, what people often mean when they say, "I'm amazed that you sound just like a native!" they are really saying something like "You speak my language brilliantly—especially for a foreigner!"

An ancillary consequence of these anecdotal impressions about the relative success of adult nonnatives to sound almost exactly like native speakers is the question of how important a role the similarity and differences between mother tongue and target language plays in terms of eventual success. Are languages that are linguistically and historically similar (e.g., Spanish and French) easier to learn without an accent than languages where there is a much greater linguistic contrast (e.g., English and Chinese)? Referring back to Table 9.1, you will note that there is no logical relationship between the degree of linguistic similarity of the native languages of the various speakers and English and the speakers' relative success in being misidentified as native speakers of English. As already observed, the nonnative most frequently mistaken for an American was an Arabic speaker, and the one virtually never mistaken for an American was a native speaker of English of a non-American dialect. The haphazard ranking of the languages linguistically (e.g., non-Indo-European languages like Arabic and Chinese rank higher than languages which are historically closer to English like Portuguese and Spanish). I am not trying to imply, of course, that there is no correlation at all between the linguistic relatedness of two languages and the relative ease it is for speakers of one to learn the other: My personal and professional experience leads me to assume that the correlation is strong. But when we look specifically at whether this correlation also pertains to the highly specialized skill of learning to sound *exactly* like a native speaker, the amount of linguistic similarity between the mother tongue and the target language is apparently irrelevant.

Assuming that there are indeed some exceptions to my claim that *no* adult can learn a language after puberty without some trace of a foreign accent, what could possibly account for such an ability? Seliger (1981) has provided a possible clue in the witty title of an article dealing with foreign accents which he called, "Exceptions to critical period predictions: A sinister plot." Reviewing the neuropsychological research on the general distribution of right- and left-handed people and the assumptions that neuropsychologists make about what percentage of the entire population has the potential for right hemisphere processing of language if there is damage to the left hemisphere, Seliger claims (p. 55) that "almost 36% of a normal population may be said to have *potential* for hemispheric plasticity beyond puberty." From this, he draws the following conclusion:

> Where does all of this leave us with the critical period prediction? It leaves us in the paradoxical position of not trying to do away with the exceptions by claiming they are false but rather trying to explain why there are not more exceptions. In order to explain such exceptions, we must proceed beyond the implicational level of investigating the critical period effects on second language acquisition to methodical research. The problem may be investigated from two opposite but complementary directions—the individual language acquirer and the intrinsic linguistic characteristics of that which must be acquired. (Seliger, 1981:55)

I have already alluded to possible linguistic and paralinguistic characteristics that might influence judgment on whether or not an adult learner might sometimes be mistaken as a native speaker of a second language, but as for the neurological characteristics of the individual, I am less certain than Seliger about the possible relationship between potential hemispheric plasticity in adults and the ability to pick up accentless speech. As I noted in a brief reply article to Seliger, the question here is: "Which demands greater neurophysiological plasticity, the ability to recover from aphasia or the ability to sound exactly like a native speaker in a language learned after puberty?" (Scovel, 1981:61). What I mean to imply in this almost rhetorical question is that I see no *direct* link between the ability to recover from aphasia and the ability to acquire accentless speech. Furthermore, the overwhelming majority of the neurolinguistic research I have reviewed suggests that there is little neuroplasticity after about the first decade of life, so if there are adults who can pick up a new language without an accent after puberty, the chances are slight that the precise reason for their linguistic precocity is continued neuroplasticity. Novoa and Obler (1985) have written a detailed description of a superb adult language learner whose linguistic talents as a competent polyglot, they speculate, may be related to an unusual pattern of brain lateralization resulting from a combination of neurological, immunological, endocrinological, and genetic factors which Geschwind and Behan (1982) have identified as possibly affecting hemispheric lateralization. Novoa and Obler's study is the only one I know that is supportive of Seliger's ideas about lateralization, but as Satz and Soper (1986) have been able to demonstrate, the Geschwind and Behan model is completely untenable, and thus I would conclude that the linguistic ability of Novoa and Obler's subject is due to a wide variety of natural and nurtural factors but is not specifically attributable to a neurolinguistic substrate.

I would like to postpone any further discussion of possible neurological or environmental explanations for precocious foreign language learning ability and look at exceptions in a different light. Let us assume, for the moment that there are a few adult exceptions to my claim that people cannot pass themselves off as native speakers if they have acquired a language after puberty, even though there is no empirical evidence that such individuals exist. Coppieters (1987), incidentally, claims that some of his near-native French speakers spoke without a distinguishable nonnative accent. Given the very few adult subjects who have been tested for authentic native accents, it is quite likely that anecdotal impressions that people have voiced are valid, and that there are indeed adult learners who would pass muster even if their voices were taped and they were judged along with native speakers of the second language they had learned. The number of these exceptions would be quite small, and, if we follow a normal distribution for our guidelines, these exceptions would probably constitute 2.14% of the population, if they fell within 2 standard deviations of the norm, or more probably would constitute only 0.13% of the population, if they were within 3 standard deviations of a normal distribution (Glass & Stanley, 1970:101). Figure 9.1 displays this statistical information, along with my speculations about how exceptions to a critical period may fit in with normal and other abnormal linguistic behavior.

The bell-shaped curve typifies the range of individual behavior one would expect to find in any large biological grouping. ''Normal'' behavior is typical for at least 68% of the population: This means that the large majority of individuals fall within ±1 standard deviation of the norm—the exact middle of all variation. On either side of this majority, atypical exceptions are found, tapering off exponentially into increasingly smaller fractions for each standard deviation from the norm. From a genetic point of view, these

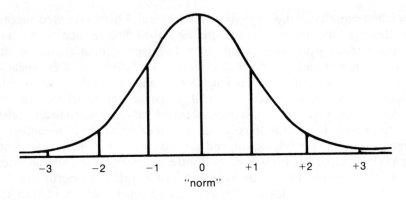

"Normal" language learning occurs for about 68% of the population (+ or − 1 standard deviation from 0).

True exceptions to the innate language learning ability of our species may be represented by severely autistic children (about .13% of the population: −3 standard deviations).

True exceptions to the critical period constraint for accentless speech after puberty in our species may be represented by a few individuals (about .13% of the population: +3 standard deviations).

Figure 9.1 Exceptions to the critical period as part of a normal distribution for a population of speakers.

exceptions display phenotypical or individual behavior, which contrasts sharply with the genotypical or expected behavior of the majority of individuals for any given species. Notice that there are two kinds of phenotypical behavior. To the left, or −1, −2, or more standard deviations, are phenotypical exceptions that fail to match the behavioral norm of the species: For example, ducks which might never imprint for following behavior, even under the most optimal time and conditions, would fall into these categories. To the right, or +1, +2, or more standard deviations, are phenotypical exceptions that exceed the behavioral norm of the particular species: Ducks which might imprint on almost any moving object under the most unfavorable time and conditions would fall into this categorization.

Applying this figure to the acquisition of language by humans, for the phenotypical exceptions to the left, we would certainly want to include autistic children, those fortunately rare individuals who seemingly fail to acquire even a mother tongue, despite all the apparent advantages of nature and nurture. I am not including the feral children in this category because they are such bizarre exceptions to the natural development of children in our species that they really should be considered separately from any discussion of a normal distribution. Thus, many cases of autism (and possibly of dyslexia as well) would fall into the 2.14% range of −2 standard deviations, and the most severe cases (children who grow into adulthood without ever acquiring any language?) would fit only into the 0.13% category of −3 standard deviations.

When dealing with exceptions to the critical period, however, we should not neglect the other side of the bell-shaped curve. Exceptional language learners would naturally fall into the 2.14% of the population that comprises +2 standard deviations, and I would be willing to concede that superexceptional language learners, that is, adults who can learn a foreign language well enough after puberty to be misidentified as native speakers on a tape, would fit into the category of +3 standard deviations. From this, we can infer that about 0.13% of any population of adults, or about 1 out of 1000, are not bound by critical period constraints. The information illustrated in Figure 9.1 is inferential, not empirical, but to me it provides a plausible explanation for any exceptions to the strong version of a biologically based critical period which I continue to espouse.

I might add a footnote to this discussion by saying that the distribution does not account for what happens to adults as they grow old. Selinker and Lamendella (1979) have suggested that senescence marks an upper bound on language learning abilities, and Seright (1985) ran an experiment which indicated that younger adults (aged 17–24) outperformed older adults (aged 25–41) in certain measures of second language learning ability, most prominently, in aural comprehension. These claims or findings say almost nothing about the phenotypical ability of any single individual; they cannot be viewed in any way as showing that increasing age is an unsurmountable constraint to the learning of a new language—this I mention solely to reassure all of us who have already surpassed the uppermost age of Seright's study!

CAN YOU HAVE A FOREIGN ACCENT IN YOUR NATIVE LANGUAGE?

Another consequence of the claims that I have been proffering about critical periods is that because I have looked only at possible mother tongue interference on a second language, I have totally ignored the chance that interference may actually also work retroactively and affect a speaker's native language. One of the early and misguided fears of bilingual education in North America was that language capacity was somehow limited, so that the more you learned of a second language, the less you would remember of your mother tongue. Although this fear is completely without foundation, recent sociolinguistic research has determined that there are unfortunate linguistic situations where children appear to grow up learning neither their first language nor a target language completely. Scandinavian researchers who have studied Finnish guest workers in Sweden have claimed to have discovered this phenomenon, which they call "double semilingualism" and which is aptly reviewed by Carlson (1981). The work on double semilingualism does not focus specifically on whether or not individuals can grow up without sounding like a native speaker of any language, but this is a distinct possibility for bilinguals who are reared in a constantly fluctuating bilingual environment where there is no consistent linguistic norm for either of the two predominant languages.

We should also recognize that the presence of a third language in the environment (or even several) might serve to cause further interference. The study by Sorenson (1967) of multilingualism in the Amazon basin suggested that Indian children in that area grew up with no complete sense of what a mother tongue was. Tomaszczyk (1980) has shown that Polish immigrants to the United States often acquire a "foreign accent" because of their long exposure to English and because their Polish intercourse is unnatural because it is with other American Polish immigrants and not with monolingual native speakers who have no English-speaking contacts. This means that under certain situations, albeit rarely, the acquisition of one or several languages before puberty, *if* the linguistic models are inconsistent and/or inaccurate, can prevent an individual from progressing into adulthood with a native-sounding accent. And it may be that even after adolescence, continual and prolonged exposure to a second language without opportunities for restitution of the mother tongue can lead to the loss of a native-sounding phonology in the first language. I do not find either consequence to vitiate claims about a critical period for language acquisition; they simply underscore a point that I have already stressed in this book—language acquisition is a complex phenomenon that is constantly affected by a wide range of natural and nurtural variables.

WHEN THE BRAIN PLAYS TRICKS ON THE VOICE

Monrad-Krohn (1947) relates the fascinating account of a young Norwegian woman who had suffered a severe head injury from a shell fragment during World War II. She first came to see the author about two years after her initial trauma, almost completely recovered from the aphasic symptoms and physical disabilities which had first beset her:

> She walked into hospital without any noticeable limp and she spoke quite fluently but with such a decided foreign accent that I took her for German of French. She complained bitterly of constantly being taken for a German in the shops, consequently the assistants would sell her nothing. One must bear in mind the hatred of everything and everybody German that had developed after the German assault and occupation without any declaration of war, further accentuated by the atrocious behavior of the "Gestapo." She was born in Nordstrand, outside Oslo. Her parents

came from the district of Solor and her husband from Oslo. She had never been outside Norway and never had anything to do with foreigners. (Monrad-Krohn, 1947:410)

The neurological damage sustained was to the left frontal region, and at the time of Monrad-Krohn's examination, there were virtually no other linguistic deficits except for what he termed "altered melody of language" or "dysprosody." The case, though rare, is not unique. Whitaker (1976) reviews some of the early cases in this century and gives a brief report of one "foreign accent syndrome" patient he observed, and Kent and Rosenbek (1982) provide a spectrographic analysis of the speech of brain-damaged patients with apraxia of speech and identify some broad phonetic features that because of their aberrancy may create the impression that the patient is speaking with a foreign accent. The authors allude to the difficulty of pinpointing the exact phonetic nature of accented speech in the following observation:

It should be remembered that impersonators can imitate another person's speech by reproducing certain salient aspects of that person's speech patterns. It is not necessary that the impersonations be exact acoustic replicas. Similarly, a foreign accent might be perceived primarily on basis of a small number of deviations from the standard dialect. "Foreign accent" probably is a broad perceptual category and it is entirely likely that two speakers, each of whom appear to have a German accent, can have rather dissimilar speech patterns. (Kent & Rosenbek, 1982:270)

None of the neurolinguists cited above have come close to localizing a neurological site where foreign accents might be triggered, and especially given the comments by Kent and Rosenbek, in all likelihood there is no single area of the brain which innervates accented speech. These unusual but well-documented cases of accents emerging in the speech of otherwise normal adult native speakers again have no direct consequence on the proposal that there are biological constraints on learning accentless speech by a certain age. They are appropriate to review because they are such highly atypical cases of accented speech. In the case of Monrad-Krohn's Norwegian patient, for example, we have a woman who is a complete monolingual and has never learned another language, but because of her brain injury, she does not sound like a native speaker of the only language she knows!

CRITICAL, OPTIMAL, OR SENSITIVE?

Several authors have attempted to make a distinction between a *critical* period and a *sensitive* period for language acquisition, and because there are certain consequences to the choice of either term, perhaps here is where I can defend my selection of the former throughout this book. Colombo (1982) in his comprehensive review of critical periods from the perspective of developmental psychology, mentions that the adjectives *optimal* and *sensitive* are used as well as *critical* in the literature on this topic, and it is instructive to note that in the references I have cited, all three terms are employed: Asher & Garcia (1969) use *optimal,* Oyama (1976) uses *sensitive,* and I and others have used *critical.* Colombo states that the last term usually connotes a strong version of the effects of nature and time on behavior and that it should be employed only under the following conditions:

> The term *critical period* should not be used unless it is accompanied by (a) an approximate onset and terminus of the period, (b) the most exact specification of the critical stimulus to which the organism is most sensitive, and (c) a correspondingly exact specification of the critical system that will be affected later on by exposure to, or deprivation of, the stimulus during the period. (Colombo, 1982:270)

I believe that I have satisfied the three requisites that Colombo has listed: (a) The approximate span of time for humans is from birth until about the age of 12—plus or minus two years, depending on individual and environmental factors; (b) during the given time the individual must have a great deal of exposure to consistent and accurate models of at least one language; and (c) such exposure of (b) during time (a) will ensure that the individual will have the opportunity to acquire all the phonetic, phonological, and paralinguistic features necessary to sound exactly like a native speaker of at least one language.

Because these criteria are met, because the acquisition of human speech seems so similar to the imprinting behavior of other animals discussed in Chapter 2, and because the empirical evidence for this phenomenon is so strong, I have chosen to refer to this time constraint as a *critical* period for speech development. Returning to a suggestion I made at the end of Chapter 5, it may well be that the role of affect and cognition, so crucial to the successful learning of almost any skill but especially of a second or foreign language, is more important in the early years—important enough to say that the first 15 or so years of life is a "sensitive" period for language acquisition. I personally do not feel comfortable with this suggestion because I see affective and cognitive factors playing a significant role in language learning at any time in life, but if this claim is made, note how it differs in terminology from what I have been talking about throughout this book. It is a *sensitive* not a *critical* period, and it is a time for the acquisition of *language* not of *speech.* Recall that, from the very beginning, I have been saying that only speech is constrained by the kind of early imprinting behavior that is found in other animals. It seems that other aspects of language—

vocabulary and syntax, for example—are free from any ultimate learning limits. For these reasons, I have chosen to adhere to the term *critical period,* although I assume that in most cases, the adjectives *optimal* or *sensitive* can be used as synonyms without much loss of concision.

A TIME TO CONCLUDE

Just as I hope it has become quite obvious to you that there does indeed exist a "time to speak," it may also be apparent by now that there needs to be a "time to keep silent." One danger of writing a book that flirts with so many wide-ranging issues is that things simply do not get tied neatly together at the end and no real closure is reached. Nevertheless, despite the enormous diversity of the disciplines covered, I hope you have sensed that three separate themes have played a consistent and unifying role in all of our discussion: the impact of nature, the influence of nurture, and the effect of time on how nature and nurture come together. It may be useful to restate some of the most relevant insights from all of the different ways these three themes have been manifest.

    1. The acquisition of nativelike speech appears to be very similar to the types of imprinting behavior found in the so-called lesser animals, and thus the idea that Lenneberg so firmly propounded, that human language has biological foundations, is strongly reaffirmed.

    2. But in contrast, I find no evidence for a critical period for vocabulary or syntax, and, consequently, I do not see the existence of a critical period for accentless speech providing any proof either for or against the efficacy of early foreign language teaching in the schools. Arguments on this complex issue must be based on other criteria, not on the biological constraints for speech on which I have focused our attention.

    3. And at the same time, the inability of adults to sound exactly like a native speaker of another language after puberty by no means implies that language learners cannot improve their ability to speak a foreign language as adults. Postpubescent learners can and should work on improving their phonological ability; the critical period for accentless speech simply means that adults will never learn to pass themselves off as native speakers phonologically—a fairly useless linguistic goal to begin with.

    4. The existence of a critical period does not mean that mere exposure to a language before puberty will ensure a native accent; it is a necessary but not sufficient criterion for ultimate linguistic success. Here is where affective, social, and motivational variables, among others, are of great import.

    5. There seems to me solid evolutionary evidence to explain why accents emerge at around puberty, and Chapters 1 and 4 in particular provide good arguments for the reason we are marked by our speech at the very

age we begin to join a social group and are mature enough sexually to contribute to the gene pool of the group we become a member of.

There are other insights which might be listed here to conclude with, but I would begin to violate the very sense of timing which is so important to this book were I to continue. So allow me to finish with a brief apologia for writing a book that spends so much time proving something that we cannot do! It is a great strength of American society that we conduct our lives as if anything were possible. Our history is filled with Walter Mittys; our skies are filled with Jonathan Livingston Seagulls; and our homes are emblazoned with apothegms like the motto used by the U.S. Army Corps of Engineers: "the difficult we do immediately; the impossible takes time!" For this reason, we have enjoyed enormous economic and technological success, and I do not want for one minute to denigrate this accomplishment or the philosophy which is largely responsible for it. But I feel that it is this very philosophy that has made acceptance of the critical period for speech so difficult and so generally unpopular, at least in North America. If anything is to be learned from this psycholinguistic discourse into the effects of nature, nurture, and time on the acquisition of a new phonology, it is that there are certain constraints on our behavior, and success, in whatever terms we seek to measure it, is not just dependent on our ability to rise above and beyond the genotypical expectations in which we are raised, but it is equally dependent on our ability to recognize what we can never do. For me, the acquisition of a new language will remain a phenomenon of natural fascination and mystery, not simply because it is a special skill of such incredible complexity that it remains one of the greatest achievements of the human mind, but because it also is a testimony of how much we can accomplish within the limitations that nature has placed upon us. We among all animals possess the gift of tongues because we have a time to speak.

REFERENCES

Abbs, J., & Sussman, H. 1971. Neurophysiological feature detectors and speech perception: A discussion of theoretical implications. *Journal of Speech and Hearing Research,* 14:23–36.

Acton, W. 1979. *Second Language Learning and Perception of Difference in Attitude.* Unpublished doctoral dissertation, University of Michigan, Ann Arbor.

Acton, W. 1984. Changing fossilized pronunciation. *TESOL Quarterly,* 18:71–85.

Adams, C. 1979. *English Speech Rhythm and the Foreign Learner.* The Hague: Mouton.

Aitchison, J. 1976. *The Articulate Mammal: An Introduction to Psycholinguistics.* New York: Universe Books.

Andrew, R. 1976. Use of formants in the grunts of baboons and other nonhuman primates. In S. Harnad, H. Steklis, & J. Lancaster (Eds.), *Origins and Evolution of Language and Speech* (pp. 673–693). New York: New York Academy of Sciences.

Ardrey, R. 1970. *The Social Contract.* New York: Dell.

Asher, J., & Garcia, R. 1969. The optimal age to learn a foreign language. *Modern Language Journal,* 38:334–341.

Barroso, F. 1976. Hemispheric asymmetry of function in children. In R. Rieber (Ed.), *The Neuropsychology of Language* (pp. 157–180). New York: Plenum.

Basser, L. 1962. Hemiplegia of early onset and the faculty of speech with special reference to the effects of hemispherectomy. *Brain,* 85:427–460.

Basson, S. 1986. *Patterns of Pronunciation Errors in English by Native Japanese and Hebrew Speakers: Interference and Simplification Processes.* Unpublished doctoral dissertation, City University of New York.

Berlin, C., & Cullen, J. 1977. Acoustic problems in dichotic listening tasks. In S. Segalowitz & F. Gruber (Eds.), *Language Development and Neurological Theory.* New York: Academic Press.

Bettelheim, B. 1959. Feral children and autistic children. *American Journal of Sociology,* 64:455–467.

Bever, T. 1981. Normal acquisition processes explain the critical period for language learning. In K. Diller (Ed.), *Individual Differences and Universals in Language Learning Aptitude* (pp. 176–198). Rowley, MA: Newbury House.

Boy raised by wolves in India dies. 1985, February 24. *San Francisco Sunday Examiner & Chronicle*, p. A16.

Brewster, T., & Brewster, E. 1981. Bonding and the missionary task. In R. Winter & S. Hawthorne (Eds.), *Perspectives on the World Christian Movement: A Reader*. Pasadena, CA: William Carey Press.

Brown, H. D. 1987. *Principles of Language Learning and Teaching*. Englewood Cliffs, NJ: Prentice-Hall.

Brown, R. 1975. *A First Language: The Early Stages*. Cambridge, MA: Harvard University Press.

Bryden, M. 1965. Tachistoscopic recognition, handedness and cerebral dominance. *Neuropsychologia*, 3:1–8.

Byrne, J., & Gates, R. 1987. Single-case study of left cerebral hemispherectomy: Development in the first five years of life. *Journal of Experimental and Clinical Neuropsychology*, 9:423–434.

Carey, S. 1978. A case study: Face recognition. In E. Walker (Ed.), *Explorations in the Biology of Language*. Montgomery, VA: Bradford Books.

Carlisle, R., & Siegel, M. 1974. Some problems in the interpretation of Neanderthal speech capabilities: A reply to Lieberman. *American Anthropologist*, 76:319–322.

Carlisle, R., & Siegel, M. 1978. Additional comments on problems in the interpretation of Neanderthal speech capabilities. *American Anthropologist*, 80:367–372.

Carlson, P. 1981. *Field-testing the theory of double semi-lingualism: An evaluation of Toukomaa's findings*. Unpublished master's thesis, University of Pittsburgh.

Chromsky, N. 1965. *Aspects of the Theory of Syntax*. Cambridge, MA: M.I.T. Press.

Chomsky, N. 1976. *Reflections on Language*. New York: Pantheon Books.

Chusid, J. 1973. *Correlative Neuroanatomy and Functional Neurology*. Los Altos, CA: Lange Medical Publications.

Clark, H., & Clark, E. 1977. *Psychology and Language: An Introduction to Psycholinguistics*. New York: Harcourt Brace Jovanovich.

Coleman, R. 1971. Male and female voice quality and its relationship to vowel formant frequencies. *Journal of Speech and Hearing Research*, 14:565–577.

Colombo, J. 1982. The critical period concept: Research, methodology, and theoretical issues. *Psychological Bulletin*, 91:260–275.

Connolly, K. 1972. Learning and the concept of critical periods in infancy. *Developmental Medical Child Neurology*, 14:705–714.

Cook, V. 1978. Second-language learning: A psycholinguistic perspective. *Language Teaching and Linguistics: Abstracts*, 2:73–89.

Coppieters, R. 1987. Competence differences between native and non-native speakers. *Language*, 63:544–573.

Corballis, M., & Morgan, M. 1978. On the biological basis of human laterality: I Evidence for a maturational left-right gradient. *Behavioral Sciences*, 2:261–336.

Crelin, E. 1976. *Development of the Upper Respiratory System*. Summit, NJ: CIBA.

Cummins, J. 1981. Age on arrival and immigrant second language learning in Canada: A reassessment. *Applied Linguistics*, 11:132–149.

Curtiss, S. 1977. *Genie: A Psycholinguistic Study of a Modern-Day "Wild Child."* New York: Academic Press.

Curtiss, S. 1980. The critical period and feral children. *UCLA Working Papers in Cognitive Linguistics*. 2:22–31.

Day, M. 1970. *Fossil Man*. New York: Bantam Books.

de Bot, K., & Mailfert, K. 1982. The teaching of intonation: Fundamental research and classroom applications. *TESOL Quarterly*, 16:71–77.

Dennis, M. 1981. Language in a congenitally acallosal brain. *Brain and Language,* 12:33–53.

Dennis, M., & Whitaker, H. 1976. Language acquisition following hemidecortication: Linguistic superiority of the left over the right hemisphere. *Brain and Language,* 3:404–433.

Dennis, M., & Whitaker, H. 1977. Hemispheric equipotentiality and language acquisition. In S. Segalowitz & F. Gruber (Eds.), *Language Development and Neurological Theory* (pp. 93–106). New York: Academic Press.

DeRenzi, E., & Vignolo, L. 1962. The Token Test: A sensitive test to detect receptive disturbances in aphasics. *Brain,* 85:665–678.

de Saussure, F. 1916. *Cours de Linguistique Generale.* Paris: Payot.

Dewson, J., & Burlingame, A. 1975. Auditory discrimination and recall in monkeys. *Science,* 187:267–268.

Dewson, J., Cowley, A., & Weiskrantz, L. 1970. Disruptions of auditory sequence discrimination by unilateral and bilateral cortical ablations of superior temporal gyrus in the monkey. *Experimental Neurology,* 28:529–548.

Dickerson, L. 1975. Interlanguage as a system of variable rules. *TESOL Quarterly,* 9:401–407.

Dryden, J. 1968. *The Conquest of Granada.* New York: Gordian Press. (Original work published 1667).

Dubos, R. 1968. *So Human an Animal.* New York: Scribner's.

Dulay, H., Burt, M., & Krashen, S. 1982. *Language Two.* Oxford: Oxford University Press.

Eisenstein, M. 1982. A study of social variation in adult second language acquisition. *Language Learning,* 32:367–391.

Elkind, D. 1970. *Children and Adolescents: Interpretive Essays on Jean Piaget.* Oxford: Oxford University Press.

Elliot, A. 1981. *Child Language.* Cambridge: Cambridge University Press.

Ellis. 1985. *Understanding Second Language Acquisition.* Oxford: Oxford University Press.

Ervin, S., & Osgood, C. 1954. Second language learning and bilingualism. *Journal of Abnormal Social Psychology (Suppl.),* 49:139–146.

Esling, J., & Wong, R. 1982. Voice quality settings and teaching of pronunciation. *TESOL Quarterly,* 17:89–96.

Fathman, A. 1975. The relationship between age and second language productive ability. *Language Learning,* 25:245–253.

Felix, S. 1982. *Psycholinguistische Aspekte des Zweitspracherwerbs.* Tubingen, Germany: Narr.

Flege, J. 1980. Phonetic approximation in second language acquisition. *Language Learning,* 30:117–134.

Flege, J. 1981. The phonological basis of foreign accent: A hypothesis. *TESOL Quarterly,* 15:443–455.

Flege, J. 1986. The production of "new" and "similar" phones in a foreign language: Evidence for the effect of equivalence classification. *Journal of Phonetics,* 15:47–65.

Flege, J., & Eefting, W. (in press). Cross-language switching in stop consonant perception and production by Dutch speakers of English. *Speech Communication.*

Flege, J., & Hammond, R. 1982. Mimicry of non-distinctive phonetic differences between language varieties. *Studies in Second Language Acquisition,* 5:1–18.

Flege, J. & Hillenbrand, J. 1987. Limits on pronunciation accuracy in adult foreign language speech production. In G. Ioup & S. Weinberger (Eds.), *Interlanguage Phonology: The Acquisition of a Second Language Sound System* (pp. 176–203). Cambridge, MA: Newbury House.

Fraser, B. 1973. Some "unexpected" reactions to various American-English dialects. In R. Shuy & R. Fasold (Eds.), *Language Attitudes: Current Trends and Prospects* (pp. 28–35). Washington, DC: Georgetown University Press.

Fromkin, V., Krashen, S., Curtiss, S., Rigler, D., & Rigler, M. 1974. The development of language in Genie: A case of language acquisition beyond the "critical period." *Brain and Language,* 1:81–107.

Gardner, H. 1975. *The Shattered Mind*. New York: Knopf.

Gardner, R., & Gardner, B. 1971. Two-way communication with an infant chimpanzee. In A. Schrier & F. Stollnitz (Eds.), *Behavior of Non-Human Primates* (pp. 117–184). New York: Academic Press.

Gardner, R., & Lambert, W. 1972. *Attitudes and Motivation in Second Language Learning*. Rowley, MA: Newbury House.

Gaulin, S. 1978, December. Sociobiology and Hubbard's 19th century pseudoscience (Letter to the editor). *Pitt News*, p. 6.

Gazzaniga, M., Bogen, J., & Sperry, R. 1963. Laterality effects in somesthesis following cerebral commisurotomy in man. *Neuropsychologia*, 1:209–215.

Genesee, F. 1987. *Learning Through Two Languages*. Cambridge, MA: Newbury House.

Genesee, F. 1988. Neuropsychology and second language acquisition. In L. Beebe (Ed.), *Issues in Second Language Acquisition* (pp. 81–112). Cambridge, MA: Newbury House.

Gerard, J. 1967. *The Sea Dreamer*. Hamden, CT: Archon Books.

Geschwind, N. 1965. Disconnexion syndromes in animals and man. *Brain*, 88:237–294, 585–644.

Geschwind, N., & Behan, P. 1982. Left-handedness: Association with immune disease, migraine, and developmental learning disorder. *Proceedings of the National Academy of Sciences, USA*, 79:5097–5100.

Geschwind, N., & Levitsky, W. 1968. Human brain: Left-right asymmetries in temporal speech. *Science*, 161:186–187.

Glass, G., & Stanley, J. 1970. *Statistical Methods in Education and Psychology*. Englewood Cliffs, NJ: Prentice-Hall.

Gordon, H., & Bogen, J. 1974. Hemispheric lateralization of singing after sodium amylobarbitone. *Journal of Neurology, Neurosurgery, and Psychiatry*, 37:727–738.

Gott, P. 1973. Language after dominant hemispherectomy. *Journal of Neurology, Neurosurgery, and Psychiatry*, 36:1082–1088.

Gould, J., & Marler, P. 1987. Learning by instinct. *Scientific American*, January:74–85.

Gray, P. 1958. Theory and evidence of imprinting in human infants. *Journal of Psychology*, 46:155–166.

Gribbin, J., & Cherfas, J. 1982. *The Monkey Puzzle: Reshaping the Evolutionary Tree*. New York: Pantheon Books.

Griffin, D. 1976. *The Question of Animal Awareness: Evolutionary Continuity of Mental Experience*. New York: Rockefeller University Press.

Guiora, A., Beit-Hallami, B., Brannon, R., Dull, C., & Scovel, T. 1972. The effects of experimentally induced changes in ego states on pronunciation ability in a second language. *Comprehensive Psychiatry*, 13:421–428.

Hailman, J. 1969. How an instinct is learned. *Scientific American*, December:98–106.

Hakuta, K. 1986. *Mirror of Language*. New York: Basic Books.

Halloway, R. 1976. Paleoneurological evidence for language origins. In S. Harnad, H. Steklis, & J. Lancaster (Eds.), *Origins and Evolution of Language and Speech* (pp. 330–348). New York: New York Academy of Sciences.

Harley, B. 1986. *Age in Second Language Acquisition*. San Diego: College-Hill Press.

Harnad, S., Stecklis, H., & Lancaster, J. (Eds.). 1976. *Origins and Evolution of Language and Speech*. New York: New York Academy of Sciences.

Hasler, A. 1983. *Olfactory Imprinting and Homing in Salmon: Investigations into the Mechanism of the Imprinting Process*. New York: Springer-Verlag.

Hatch, E. 1983. *Psycholinguistics: A Second Language Perspective*. Rowley, MA: Newbury House.

Hayes, K. 1950. Vocalization and speech in chimpanzees. *American Psychologist*, 5:275–276.

Heinroth, O. 1910. Beitrage zur Biologie, namentlich Ethologie und Psychologie der Anatiden. *Verhandlungen des v. Internationalen Ornithologen-Kongresses*, Berlin.

Herman, L., & Herman, M. 1943. *Foreign Accents: A Manual for Actors, Directors and Writers*. New York: Theatre Art Books.

Hess, E. 1958. "Imprinting" in animals. *Scientific American*, March:81–90.

Hess, E. 1972. "Imprinting" in a natural laboratory. *Scientific American*, August:2–9.

Hewett, N. 1971. Reactions of prospective English teachers toward speakers of a non-standard dialect. *Language Learning*, 21:205–212.

Hill, J. 1970. Foreign accents, language acquisition, and cerebral dominance revisited. *Language Learning*, 20:237–248.

Hill, J. 1972. On the evolutionary foundations of language. *American Anthropologist*, 74:308–317.

Hockett, C. 1957. *A Course in Modern Linguistics*. New York: Macmillan.

Hoffman, H., Hendrik, E., Dennis, M., & Armstrong, D. 1979. Hemispherectomy for Sturge-Weber syndrome. *Child's Brain*, 5:233–248.

Holmstrand, L. 1982. *English in the Elementary School*. Uppsala Studies in Education (18). Uppsala, Sweden: Acta Universitatis Upsaliensis.

Horn, G. 1986. *Memory, Imprinting, and the Brain*. Oxford: Oxford University Press.

Ioup, G. 1984. Is there a structural foreign accent?: A comparison of syntactic and phonological errors in second language acquisition. *Language Learning*, 34:1–17.

Jansma, K. 1987, December. *English intonation: Do learners hear the pattern?* Paper presented at the annual meeting of the Linguistic Society of America, San Francisco.

Jaynes, J. 1977. Imprinting: The interaction of learned and innate behavior—II The critical period. In E. Hess & B. Slobodan (Eds.), *Imprinting*. Stroudsburg, PA: Dauden, Hutchinson and Ross.

Johansson, S. 1978. Learners' errors and communicative efficiency. In V. Kohonen & N. Enkvist (Eds.), *Text Linguistics, Cognitive Learning and Language Teaching*. Turku, Finland: Suomen Sovelletun Kielitieteen Yhdistyksen.

Johnson, J., & Newport, E. 1987. *Critical period effects in second language learning: The influence of maturational state on the acquisition of English as a second language*. Unpublished manuscript. University of Illinois. Department of Psychology.

Katchadourian, H. 1977. *The Biology of Adolescence*. San Francisco: W. H. Freeman.

Katz, J. 1976. A hypothesis about the uniqueness of natural language. In S. Harnad, H. Steklis, & J. Lancaster (Eds.), *Origins and Evolution of Language and Speech* (pp. 33–41). New York: New York Academy of Sciences.

Kent, R. & Rosenbek, J. 1982. Prosodic disturbance and neurologic lesion. *Brain and Language*, 15:259–291.

Kety, S. 1979. Disorders of the human brain. *Scientific American*, September:202–214.

Kimura, D. 1961. Cerebral dominance and the perception of verbal stimuli. *Canadian Journal of Psychology*, 15:156–165.

Kinsbourne, M. 1976. The ontogeny of cerebral dominance. In R. Rieber (Ed.), *The Neuropsychology of Language* (pp. 181–192). New York: Plenum.

Klaus, M., Jerauld, R., Kreger, N., McAlpine, W., Steffa, M., & Kennel, J. 1972. Maternal attachment: Importance of the first post-partum days. *New England Journal of Medicine*, 286:460–463.

Klein, W. 1986. *Second Language Acquisition*. Cambridge: Cambridge University Press.

Krashen, S. 1973. Lateralization, language learning, and the critical period: Some new evidence. *Language Learning*, 23:63–74.

Krashen, S. 1975a. The development of cerebral dominance and language learning: More new evidence. In D. Dato (Ed.), *Developmental Psycholinguistics: Theory and Applications* (Georgetown University Round Table on Languages and Linguistics, 1975). Washington, DC: Georgetown University Press.

Krashen, S. 1975b. The critical period for language acquisition and its possible bases. In D. Aaronson & R. Rieber (Eds.), *Developmental Psycholinguistics and Communication Disorders*. New York: New York Academy of Sciences.

191

Krashen, S. 1981. *Second Language Acquisition and Second Language Learning*. Oxford: Pergamon Press.

Krashen, S. 1985. *The Input Hypothesis*. New York: Longman.

Krashen, S., & Harshman, R. 1972. Lateralization and the critical period. *UCLA Working Papers in Phonetics,* 23:13–21.

Krashen, S., Long, M., & Scarcella, R. (Eds.). 1982. *Child-Adult Differences in Second Language Acquisition*. Rowley, MA: Newbury House.

Krashen, S., & Seliger, H. 1975. Maturational constraints on second dialect acquisition. *Language Sciences,* 38:28–29.

Krashen, S., & Terrell, T. 1983. *The Natural Approach: Language Acquisition in the Classroom*. Oxford: Pergamon Press.

Labov, W. 1966. *The Social Stratification of English in New York City*. Washington, DC: Center for Applied Linguistics.

Labov, W. 1970. The study of language in its social context. *Studium Generale,* 23:30–87.

Ladefoged, P. 1968. The nature of general phonetic theories. In R. O'Brien (Ed.), *Georgetown University Round Table Selected Papers on Linguistics, 1961–1968*. Washington, DC: Georgetown University Press.

Lambert, W., Hodgson, R., Gardner R., & Fillenbaum, S. 1960. Evaluational reactions to spoken languages. *Journal of Abnormal and Social Psychology,* 60:44–51.

Lane, H. 1976. *The Wild Boy of Aveyron*. Cambridge, MA: Harvard University Press.

Larew, L. 1961. The optimal age for beginning a foreign language. *Modern Language Journal,* 45:203–206.

Laughlin, C., & d'Aquili, E. 1974. *Biogenetic Structuralism*. New York: Columbia University Press.

Lebrun, Y., & Leleux, C. 1982. Agnosognosia et aphasie. *Schweizer Archiv für Neurologie, Neurochirurgie und Psychiatrie,* 130:25–38.

Lecours, A., & Lecours, J. 1980. Linguistic and other psychological aspects of paroxysmal aphasia. *Brain and Language,* 10:1–23.

Lenneberg, E. 1967. *Biological Foundations of Language*. New York: Wiley.

Lettvin, J., Maturana, H., McCullock, W., & Pitts, W. 1959. What the frog's eye tells the frog's brain. *Proceedings of the IRE,* 47:1940–1951.

Lieberman, P. 1982. Can chimpanzees swallow or talk?: A reply to Falk. *American Anthropologist,* 84:148–152.

Lieberman, P. 1984. *The Biology and Evolution of Language*. Cambridge, MA: Harvard University Press.

Lieberman, P., & Crelin, S. 1971. On the speech of Neanderthal man. *Linguistic Inquiry,* 2:203–222.

Linden, E. 1976. *Apes, Men, and Language*. New York: Penguin Books.

Long, M. 1987. *Maturational Constraints on Language Development*. Unpublished manuscript. University of Hawaii, Department of ESL.

Lorenz, K. 1935. Der kunpan in der Umwelt des Vogels: Die Atgenosse als auslosendes Moment sozialer Verhaltungsweisen [Companionship in bird life: Fellow members of the species as releasers of social behavior]. *Journal of Ornithology,* 83:137–213, 289–413.

Lorenz, K. 1952. *King Solomon's Ring*. London: Methuen.

Lorenz, K. 1966. *On Aggression*. London: Methuen.

Lorenz, K. 1979. *The Year of the Greylag Goose*. New York: Harcourt Brace Jovanovich.

MacKay, I. 1987. *Phonetics: The Science of Speech Production*. Boston: Little, Brown.

Maclean, C. 1979. *The Wolf Children: Fact or Fantasy?* Middlesex, England: Penguin Books.

Major, R. 1987. Phonological similarity, markedness, and rate of L2 acquisition. *Studies in Second Language Acquisition,* 9:63–82.

Malson, L. 1972. *Wolf Children and the Wild Boy of Aveyron*. London: New Left Books.

Marks, J. 1980. *Foreign Accent and the Interlanguage Hypothesis*. Unpublished master's thesis, University of Toronto.

Marshall, R. 1985, October. *Communication techniques: Classroom applications*. Paper presented at the 5th joint conference of the Washington Association of Foreign Language Teachers and the Oregon Foreign Language Teachers, Tacoma, WA.

Marshall, W., & Tanner, J. 1974. Puberty. In J. Douvis & J. Dobbing (Eds.), *Scientific Foundations of Pediatrics*. London: William Heinemann Medical Books.

McLaughlin, B. 1978. *Second-Language Acquisition in Children*. New York: Erlbaum.

McLaughlin, B. 1987. *Theories of Second-Language Learning*. London: Edward Arnold.

Mead, M. 1935. *Sex and Temperament in Three Primitive Societies*. New York: Morrow.

Menyuk, P. 1977. *Language and Maturation*. Cambridge, MA: M.I.T. Press.

Miller, G. 1981. *Language and Speech*. San Francisco: W. H. Freeman.

Molfese, D., Freeman, R., & Palermo, D. 1975. The ontogeny of brain lateralization for speech and nonspeech stimuli. *Brain and Language*, 2:356–368.

Monrad-Krohn, G. 1947. Dysprosody or altered "melody of language." *Brain*, 70:405–415.

Montgomery, C., & Eisenstein, M. 1986. Real reality revisited. *TESOL Quarterly*, 20:317–334.

Morris, B., & Gerstman, L. 1986. Age contrasts in the learning of language-relevant materials. *Language Learning*, 36:311–352.

Morris, D. 1967. *The Naked Ape*. New York: Dell.

Morse, P. 1972. The discrimination of speech and nonspeech stimuli in early infancy. *Journal of Experimental Child Psychology*, 14:477–492.

Morse, P. 1974. Infant speech perception: A preliminary model and review of the literature. In R. Schiefelbusch & L. Lloyd (Eds.), *Language Perspectives: Acquisition, Retardation, and Intervention*. Baltimore: University Park Press.

Morse, P. 1976. Speech perception in the human infant and Rhesus monkey. In S. Harnad, H. Steklis, & J. Lancaster (Eds.), *Origins and Evolution of Language and Speech* (pp. 694–707). New York: New York Academy of Sciences.

Myers, R. 1976. Comparative neurology of vocalization and speech: Proof of a dichotomy. In S. Harnad, H. Steklis, & J. Lancaster (Eds.), *Origins and Evolution of Language and Speech*. (pp. 745–757) New York: New York Academy of Sciences.

Neufeld, G. 1977. Language learning ability in adults: A study of the acquisition of prosodic and articulatory features. *Working Papers in Bilingualism*, Ontario Institute for Studies in Education, Toronto, 12:45–60.

Neufeld, G. 1978. A theoretical perspective on the nature of linguistic aptitude. *IRAL*, 15:15–25.

Neufeld, G. 1979. Towards a theory of language learning ability. *Language Learning*, 29:227–241.

Neufeld, G. 1980. On the adult's ability to acquire phonology. *TESOL Quarterly*, 3:285–298.

Neufeld, G. 1987. On the acquisition of prosodic and articulatory features in adult language learning. In G. Ioup & S. Weinberger (Eds.), *Interlanguage Phonology: The Acquisition of a Second Language Sound System* (pp. 321–332). Cambridge, MA: Newbury House.

Neufeld, G., & Schneiderman, E. 1980. Prosodic and articulatory features in adult language learning. In R. Scarcella & S. Krashen (Eds.), *Research in Second Language Acquisition*. Rowley, MA: Newbury House.

Newport, E. 1984. Constraints on learning: Studies in the acquisition of American Sign Language. *Papers and Reports on Child Language Development*, 23:1–22.

Nordeen, E., & Yahr, P. 1982. Hemispheric asymmetries in the behavioral and hormonal effects of sexually differentiating mammalian brain. *Science*, 218:391–394.

Nottobohm, F. 1970. Ontogeny of birdsong. *Science*, 167:950–956.

Novoa, L., & Obler, L. 1985. A neuropsychological approach to adult second language acquisition—A case study. In L. Obler & D. Fein (Eds.), *The Exceptional Brain: Neuropsychology of Talent and Special Abilities*. New York: Guilford Press.

Olsen, L. & Samuels, J. 1973. The relationship between age and accuracy of foreign language pronunciation. *Journal of Educational Research*, 66:263–268.

193

Oyama, S. 1976. A sensitive period for the acquisition of a nonnative phonological system. *Journal of Psycholinguistic Research*, 5:261–283.

Patkowski, M. 1980. The sensitive period for the acquisition of syntax in a second language. *Language Learning*, 30:449–472.

Payne, A. 1980. Factors controlling the acquisition of the Philadelphia dialect by out-of-state children. In W. Labov (Ed.), *Locating Language in Time and Space*. New York: Academic Press.

Penfield, W. 1963. *The Second Career*. Boston: Little, Brown.

Penfield, W., & Roberts, L. 1959. *Speech and Brain Mechanisms*. Princeton, NJ: Princeton University Press.

Pike, K. 1967. *Language in Relation to a Unified Theory of the Structure of Human Behavior*. The Hague: Mouton.

Pilbeam, D. 1970. *The Evolution of Man*. New York: Funk & Wagnalls.

Porter, R., & Berlin, C. 1975. On interpreting developmental changes in the dichotic right-ear advantage. *Brain and Language*, 2:186–200.

Premack, A., & Premack, D. 1972. Teaching language to an ape. *Scientific American*, October:92–99.

Ptacek, P., & Sander, E. 1966. Age recognition from voice. *Journal of Speech and Hearing Research*, 9:273–277.

Ramsey, C., & Wright, E. 1972. A group, English-language vocabulary test derived from the Ammons full-range picture vocabulary test. *Psychological Reports*, 31:103–109.

Ramsey, C., & Wright, E. 1974. Age and second language learning. *Journal of Social Psychology*, 94:115–121.

Redl, F. 1969. Adolescents—Just how do they react? In G. Caplan & S. Lebovici (Eds.), *Adolescence: Psychosocial Perspectives* (pp. 79–99). New York: Basic Books.

Reich, P. 1986. *Language Development*. Englewood Cliffs, NJ: Prentice-Hall.

Reynolds, E., & Wines, J. 1948. Individual differences in physical changes associated with adolescence in girls. *American Journal of Diseases of Children*, 75:329–350.

Reynolds, E., & Wines, J. 1951. Physical changes associated with adolescence in boys. *American Journal of Diseases of Children*, 82:529–547.

Riva, D. 1987, July. *Early hemispheric damage in children: Effects on intelligence, language, and spatial abilities*. Paper presented at the meeting of the 10th European Conference of the International Neuropsychology Society, Barcelona, Spain.

Rosansky, E. 1975. The critical period for the acquisition of language: Some cognitive developmental considerations. *Working Papers in Bilingualism*, Ontario Institute for Studies in Education, Toronto, 6:92–102.

Rumbaugh, D., & Gill, T. 1976. The mastery of language-type skills by the chimpanzee (Pan). In S. Harnad, H. Steklis, & J. Lancaster (Eds.), *Origins and Evolution of Language and Speech* (pp. 562–578). New York: New York Academy of Sciences.

Salk, L. 1962. Mother's heartbeat as an imprinting stimulus. *Transactions of the New York Academy of Sciences*, 24:753–763.

Satz, P. 1983. Lateralization of language in the child: Some recent evidence revisited. Review of *Lateralization of Language in the Child*. *Journal of Clinical and Experimental Neuropsychology*, 5:289–298.

Satz, P., Bakker, D., Tenunissen, J., Goebel, R. & Van der Vlugt, H. 1975. Developmental parallels of the ear asymmetry: A multivariate approach. *Brain and Language*, 2:171–185.

Satz P., & Soper, H. 1986. Left-handedness, dyslexia, and autoimmune disorder: A critique. *Journal of Clinical and Experimental Neuropsychology*, 8:453–458.

Schumann, J. 1978. The acculturation model for second language acquisition. In R. Gingras (Ed.), *Second Language Acquisition and Foreign Language Teaching*. Arlington, VA: Center for Applied Linguistics.

Schnitzer, M. 1978. Cerebral lateralization and plasticity: Their relevance to language acquisition. In M. Paradis (Ed.), *Aspects of Bilingualism*. Columbia, SC: Hornbeam Press.

Scovel, T. 1969. Foreign accents, language acquisition, and cerebral dominance. *Language Learning*, 19:245–253.

Scovel, T. 1978. The effect of affect on foreign language learning. *Language Learning*, 28:129–142.

Scovel, T. 1981. The recognition of foreign accents in English and its implications for psycholinguistic theories of language acquisition. *Proceedings of the 5th International Association of Applied Linguistics* (pp. 389–401). Montreal: Laval University Press.

Scovel, T. 1982. Questions concerning the application of neurolinguistic research to second language learning/teaching. *TESOL Quarterly*, 16:323–331.

Sebeok, T., & Rosenthal, R. (Eds.). 1981. *The Clever Hans Phenomenon: Communication with Horses, Whales, Apes, and People*. New York: New York Academy of Sciences.

Seeley, T. 1982. How honeybees find a home. *Scientific American*, October:158–168.

Segalowitz, S., & Gruber, F. (Eds.). 1977. *Language Development and Neurological Theory*. New York: Academic Press.

Seliger, H. 1981. Exceptions to critical period predictions: A sinister plot. In R. Anderson (Ed.), *New Dimensions in Second Language Acquisition Research*. Rowley, MA: Newbury House.

Seliger, H., Krashen, S. & Ladefoged, P. 1975. Maturational constraints in the acquisition of second language accent. *Language Sciences*, 36:20–22.

Selinker, L. 1972. Interlanguage. *IRAL*, 10:201–231.

Selinker, L. & Lamendella, J. 1979. The role of extrinsic feedback in interlanguage fossilization: A discussion of "rule fossilization: A tentative model." *Language Learning*, 29:363–375.

Seright, L. 1985. Age and aural comprehension achievement in Francophone adults learning English. *TESOL Quarterly*, 19:455–472.

Shattuck, R. 1980. *The Forbidden Experiment*. New York: Washington Square Press.

Shuy, R., & Fasold, R. (Eds.). 1973. *Language Attitudes: Current Trends and Prospects*. Washington, DC: Georgetown University Press.

Singh, J., & Zingg, R. 1942. *Wolf-Children and Feral Man*. London: Archon Books.

Skinner, B. 1957. *Verbal Behavior*. New York: Appleton-Century-Crofts.

Sladen, B. 1981. Major variation in language skills apparently under genetic influence (discussed from the viewpoint of human evolution). In K. Diller (Ed.), *Individual Differences and Universals in Language Learning Aptitude* (pp. 22–36). Rowley, MA: Newbury House.

Sluckin, W. 1964. Imprinting and early learning. *Studies in animal Behavior. Volume 1* (Robert Martin, Trans.). London: Methuen.

Sluckin, W. 1970. *Early Learning in Man and Animal*. London: Allen & Unwin.

Snow, C., & Hoefnagel-Hohle, M. 1978. The critical period for second language acquisition: Evidence from second language learning. *Child Development*, 49:1114–1128.

Sommer, B. 1978. *Puberty and Adolescence*. New York: Oxford University Press.

Sorensen, A. 1967. Multilingualism in the Northwest Amazon. *American Anthropologist*, 69:670–684.

Spitz, R. 1945. Hospitalism. *Psychoanalytic Study of the Child*, 1:53–74.

Springer, S., & Deutsch, G. 1981. *Left Brain, Right Brain*. San Francisco: W. H. Freeman.

Steinberg, D. 1982. *Psycholinguistics: Language, Mind, and World*. London: Longman.

Stern, H. 1976. Optimal age: Myth or reality? *Canadian Modern Language Review*, 32:283–294.

Stern, H. 1982. Issues in early core French: A selective and preliminary review of the literature 1975–1981. *Research Service Report #163*. Toronto: Board of Education.

Stevens, K. 1975. The potential role of property detectors in the perception of consonants. In

G. Fant & M. Tatham (Eds.), *Auditory Analysis and Perception of Speech* (pp. 303–330). New York: Academic Press.

Stillings, N., Feinstein, M., Garfield, J., Rissland, E., Rosenbaum, D., Weisler, S., & Baker-Ward, L. 1987. *Cognitive Science: An Introduction*. Cambridge, MA: M.I.T. Press.

Strange, W., & Jenkins, J. 1978. The role of linguistic experience in the perception of speech. In R. Walk & H. Pick (Eds.), *Perception and Experience* (pp. 125–169). New York: Plenum.

Streeter, L. 1976. Language perception in 2 month old infants shows effects of both innate mechanisms and experience. *Nature,* 259:39–41.

Sundet, K. 1986. Sex differences in cognitive impairment following unilateral brain damage. *Journal of Clinical and Experimental Neuropsychology,* 8:51–61.

Suter, R. 1976. Predictors of pronunciation accuracy in second language learning. *Language Learning,* 26:233–253.

Tahta, S., Wood, M., & Loewenthal, K. 1981. Foreign accents: Factors relating to transfer of accent from the first language to a second language. *Language and Speech,* 24:265–272.

Tanner, J. 1973. Growing up. *Scientific American,* September: 34–43.

Tartter, V. 1980. Happy talk: The perceptual and acoustic effects of smiling on speech. *Perception and Psychophysics,* 27:24–27.

Tartter, V. 1986. *Language Processes*. New York: Holt, Rinehart & Winston.

Tartter, V., & Eimas, P. 1975. The role of auditory feature detectors in the perception of speech. *Perception and Psychophysics,* 18:293–298.

Taylor, B. 1974. Toward a theory of language acquisition. *Language Learning,* 24:23–35.

Terrance, H. 1979. *Nim: A Chimpanzee Who Learned Sign Language*. New York: Washington Square Press.

Teyler, T. 1976. An introduction to the neurosciences. In M. Wittrock (Ed.), *The Human Brain*. Englewood Cliffs, NJ: Prentice-Hall.

Tinbergen, N. 1952. The curious behavior of the stickleback. *Scientific American,* December:22–26.

Titone, R. 1968. *Teaching Foreign Languages*. Washington, DC: Georgetown University Press.

Tomaszczyk, J. 1980. On accented speech: The Polish of Polish Americans. *Studia Anglica Posnaniensia,* 12:121–137.

Tsunoda, T. 1985. *The Japanese Brain: Uniqueness and Universality*. Tokyo: Taishukan.

van Els, T., Bongaerts, T., Extra, G., van Os, C., & Janssen-Dieten, A. 1984. *Applied Linguistics and the Learning and Teaching of Foreign Languages*. London: Edward Arnold.

VanLancker, D. 1975. *Heterogeneity in Language and Speech: Neurolinguistic Studies*. UCLA Working Papers in Phonetics, No. 29.

Von Frisch, K. 1950. *Bees: Their Vision, Chemical Senses, and Language*. Ithaca, NY: Cornell University Press.

Von Frisch, K. 1962. Dialects in the language of the bees. *Scientific American,* August: 2–6.

Walberg, H., Hase, K., & Rasher, S. 1978. English acquisition as a diminishing function of experience rather than age. *TESOL Quarterly,* 12:427–437.

Walsh, K. 1977. *Neuropsychology—A Clinical Approach*. Edinburgh: Churchill Livingstone.

Walsh, T., & Diller, K. 1981. Neurolinguistic considerations on the optimum age for second language learning. In K. Diller (Ed.), *Individual Differences and Universals in Language Learning Aptitude* (pp. 3–21). Rowley, MA: Newbury House.

Warren, J., & Nonneman, A. 1976. The search for cerebral dominance in monkeys. In S. Harnad, H. Steklis, & J. Lanacaster (Eds.), *Origins and Evolution of Language and Speech* (pp. 732–744) New York: New York Academy of Sciences.

Whitaker, H. 1976. A case of the isolation of the language function. In H. Whitaker & H. A. Whitaker (Eds.), *Studies in Neurolinguistics, 2* (pp. 1–58). New York: Academic Press.

Wilson, E. 1975. *Sociobiology: The New Synthesis*. Cambridge, MA: Harvard University Press.

Wind, J. 1970. *On the Phylogeny and the Ontogeny of the Human Larynx*. Groningen: Wolters-Noordhoff.

Witelson, S. 1977. Early hemisphere specialization and interhemispheric plasticity: An empirical and theoretical review. In S. Segalowitz & F. Gruber (Eds.), *Language Development and Neurologic Theory* (pp. 213–189). New York: Academic Press.

Zacharias, L., Rand, W., & Wurtman, R. 1976. A prospective study of sexual development and growth in American girls: The statistics of menarche. *Obstetrics and Gynecology Survey* (*Suppl.*), 31:325–337.

NAME INDEX

SUBJECT INDEX

Accultural/instructional factors, 5, 90–91
Acoustic detection. *See also* Neonatal
  speech detection
  of age, 78
  of sex, 78
  of smiling, 78
Acquisition/learning, 5, 96–98
Acting, 167
Adolescence, 48, 52–53
Advanced tongue root, 18
Affective filter, 95, 97
Age, 47, 86, 97–99, 109–111, 115–123, 127,
  132, 134, 137, 141–151, 167–168,
  170–174, 176, 184–185. *See also*
  Adolescence, Pubescence
Alcohol, 96
Amazon, 90–91
Anthropology, 6
Aphasia, 55–56, 58, 105, 111–113, 141,
  143–146, 178, 182–183
Apraxia of speech, 183
Arabic, 106, 113, 120, 171–174, 177
Autism, 181. *See also* Feral children
Automatic language, 89

Backsliding, 166
Bees
  dialects, 36, 38
  migration, 36
  round dance, 35
  wagging dance, 34–37
Bell-shaped curve, 179–180
Bengali, 136, 139
Bilingual education, 3, 54, 58, 64–65, 83,
  98–99
Biology, 6
Bird song. *See* White-crowned sparrows
Black and white English, 175
Bottom-up processing, 121
Boyer, 93

Brain. *See also* Aphasia, Hemispherectomy,
  Hominid evolution, Lateralization,
  Plasticity
  of cats, 23, 27
  changes during puberty, 51–53
  congenital absence of a hemisphere, 147
  corpus callosum, 148–149
  crenulation, 27
  cytoarchitecture, 27
  of dogs, 27
  endocasts, 24
  feature detectors, 77–78
  of fish, 27
  of frogs, 77
  frontal lobes, 28
  growth in size and weight, 151–152
  homunculus, 20–21
  myelinization, 151
  neurotransmitters, 151, 153
  proliferation of nerve pathways, 151
  of rats, 82
  of reptiles, 23
  of Rhesus monkeys, 27, 30
  right hemisphere imaging, 138
  sensory and motor interconnections, 26
  split brain patients, 28
  unequal size of hemispheres, 54, 146
Brazilians, 120–121. *See also* Portuguese
Breathing, 15

Cerebral dominance. *See* Lateralization
Chimpanzees, 11–13, 16, 21, 68–69, 131
Chinese, 106, 155–159, 173, 177
Communication strategy, 102
Competence, 14, 103, 170
Compound/coordinate bilingualism, 5
CPH, 86–87, 89. *See also* Critical period
Critical period. *See also* Foreign accents,
  Imprinting, Optimal period, Sensitive
  period

203